W9-BTP-410

Friends Forever

Friends Forever

How Girls and Women
Forge Lasting Relationships

Suzanne Degges-White
and Christine Borzumato-Gainey

ROWMAN & LITTLEFIELD PUBLISHERS, INC.
Lanham • Boulder • New York • Toronto • Plymouth, UK

Published by Rowman & Littlefield Publishers, Inc.
A wholly owned subsidiary of The Rowman & Littlefield Publishing Group, Inc.
4501 Forbes Boulevard, Suite 200, Lanham, Maryland 20706
http://www.rowmanlittlefield.com

Estover Road, Plymouth PL6 7PY, United Kingdom

British Library Cataloguing in Publication Information Available

Library of Congress Cataloging-in-Publication Data
Degges-White, Suzanne.
  Friends forever : how girls and women forge lasting relationships / Suzanne
Degges-White and Christine Borzumato-Gainey.
     p. cm.
  Includes bibliographical references.
  ISBN 978-1-4422-0200-9 (cloth : alk. paper) -- ISBN 978-1-4422-0202-3
(electronic)
  1. Female friendship. I. Borzumato-Gainey, Christine. II. Title.
  BF575.F66D44 2011
  158.2'5082--dc22
                         2010040894

∞™ The paper used in this publication meets the minimum requirements of
American National Standard for Information Sciences—Permanence of Paper for
Printed Library Materials, ANSI/NISO Z39.48-1992. Printed in the United States
of America

Contents

Acknowledgments

This book would never have been written without the many, many girls and women who were willing to openly and honestly share their stories when invited: "Tell us about your friendships." Our deepest gratitude goes out to all of the women who shared their challenges, successes, failures, and needs. Special thanks go to Beth McCabe, Barbara Long, Betty Mooring, Jennifer Dinell-Humpher, and Helen Jancich, who all went out of their way to bring us the stories of many diverse girls and women to enrich this project.

S.E.D. & C.J.B.

To my co-author—thanks for your patience and gifted critique. Sharing the journey of a life or a book is infinitely more rewarding when accompanied by a friend! I am indebted to my amazing family—my partner, Ellen, and our kids, Georgia, Andy, and David. I am also grateful to my "mom-in-law," Elsie, and to my sister-in-law, Vickie, for their support. My parents inspired in me the love of words and written expression and, as the years go by, I grow increasingly aware of what a valuable legacy this has been.

S.E.D.

Heaps of love and gratitude to my children, Brooke and Drew, for the hours of playing nicely so I could focus on writing. Hopefully the lessons I've learned about building friendships will assist you in your own pursuits of lifelong friends. And to Suzanne, the visionary and driver of this project, thank you for being such a phenomenal friend and inviting me on the journey.

C.J.B.

Friendship Basics:
An Introduction

Most of us count our friends among our most precious treasures. Depending on our needs at the moment, friends may be our sounding boards, our support groups, our partners in crime, or our gentle "I told you so" without any recrimination. So ingrained is the drive for social connection that we usually choose a "best friend" well before we learn to write our names. Some of us hold onto childhood friends well into adulthood; others cultivate shifting circles of friends. Unfortunately, the more our lives and circumstances change, the harder it can be to find and cement new friendships.

As one moves through life, identity and relationships often transform with each new stage or transition. Perhaps you are leaving a circle of single friends as you walk down the aisle or move in with a partner. Scheduling time with friends may become more complicated if you have recently added a new child to your family. Leaving a long-term relationship may require leaving behind some of your couplehood friends, as well. Relocating to a new town can make you feel as if the effort required to make new friends is too much on top of setting up a new household. Shyness, a lack of confidence, past betrayals, and an overly busy lifestyle are a few of the personal obstacles that may require attention. But there are times when we *need* to seek out new friends or nurture existing relationships.

The need for a heart-to-heart, friend-to-friend conversation or for a companion in your exploits can be the necessary motivation to set new relationships in motion. The goal of this book is to support you in this quest for healthy friendships. Its mission is threefold: (1) to share a celebration of female friendships that will ideally entertain you and

1

motivate you to invest in your own relationships; (2) to serve as a guide for learning more about the role you play in your friendships; and (3) to be a bountiful resource of ideas and suggestions to help you find new friends, revive existing friendships, and nurture the friendships that you want to keep.

There is a great deal of research acknowledging the benefits of maintaining healthy relationships—it not only *feels* good to have friends, it *is* good. Active involvement in close friendships is predictive of a healthier, longer, and more balanced life.[1] One of our interviewees noted that it is her interaction with friends that truly gives her life flavor—as she nears her 75th birthday! Superior health, both mental and physical, is related to healthy friendships. In fact, individuals who seek mental health care, regardless of age, are much *less* likely than the general population to be able to name more than a single friend in their support networks.[2] We need friends to keep us engaged in life and to allow us to feel that we matter to someone beyond ourselves.

Connecting to others is clearly an innate drive, but what draws us to the intimacy of close friendships? How are friendships different from other relationships, particularly kinships? These types of questions have been pondered by ancient Greek philosophers and modern-day researchers, but we are still grappling for answers. Defining the relationship and dimensions of friendship are challenging tasks, as noted by Beverly Fehr in a comprehensive review of friendship research.[3] Robert B. Hays has also acknowledged the difficulty in crafting an all-purpose definition of friendship. He did find that there are two elements of a possible definition on which researchers most agree: that friendships exist within the social/emotional realm and that friendships are hallmarked by *interdependence* and *voluntary* interactions.[4] With the lack of precision surrounding even a definition of friendship, perhaps it is no surprise that there are multiple theories describing how friendships are actually formed.

Two theories are considered to be the most likely explanations for friendship development: the Social Penetration Theory[5] and the Social Exchange Theory.[6] Altman and Taylor's well-researched Social Penetration Theory is used to explain both platonic and romantic relationships. Using the metaphor of an onion, Altman and Taylor observed that each of us has layers of personal defenses that get peeled away, one by one, as we let others get closer to us emotionally. As we get to know potential friends, we give them deeper access into our exterior and interior lives. As we grow into relationships, our defenses are peeled away—just as the layers of an onion might be.

This mutual melting away of defenses relies on the development of personal trust through mutual self-disclosure and honesty. Friendship development is seen to evolve in stages as self-disclosure deepens from chatting about superficial topics to revealing intimate feelings and experiences. Honest self-disclosure is necessary for authentic communication; Altman and Taylor believe the breadth (the variety of topics discussed) and depth (the personal significance of the topics discussed) of self-disclosure play a role in our level of relationship commitment. This theory was strongly flavored by another relationship theory, the Social Exchange Theory, which is all about maximizing the rewards and minimizing the costs in a relationship.

The foundation of the Social Exchange Theory is the assumption that we choose to pursue and maintain relationships based on two factors: (1) the rewards must continue to outweigh the costs; and (2) the relationship feels about as good as we believe that it could. Indeed, this theory relies on mathematical calculations to predict relationship behavior. We make deposits and withdraw benefits under the unspoken assumption that we will *receive* in proportion to what we *provide*. Friendships solidify into relationships of interdependence as a pair of friends provides and receives rewards from one another; unbalanced relationships may need realignment or termination.

These theories are among the most widely researched explanations that try to make logical sense of a subjective process. But regardless of whether the metaphorical peeling of an onion or a set of mathematical matrices best describes relationship development, it is clear that humankind has an interest in making sense of why we choose the companions we do. Long the object of philosophical contemplation, friendships are sought after from nursery school to high school and throughout adulthood. These close relationships offer us the opportunity to select our alliances, our confidantes, and, for many, our chosen family. After having invited hundreds of women to "tell us about your friends," the most consistent message conveyed is that women are passionate about their friendships.

The experiences of our interviewees illustrate the zeniths and the nadirs that female friendships reach and their stories personify and amplify the existing empirical studies. Organized into five sections, this book integrates research with the experiences recounted by the hundreds of girls and women interviewed for this project. Their ages spanned a nine-decade range! The first section is an exploration of the science behind the human drive for social connection. The second section provides a chronological exploration of the roles played by friends at different stages in life. The third and fourth sections include self-exploration exercises for assessing both your personal identity as a friend and your relationship needs. The final section offers insights and ideas for growing and strengthening your own friendship network, or *friendscape*, as we have termed it, to reflect the careful cultivation and nurturing that healthy social support systems require. As you make your way through each section, we hope that you are entertained and enlightened by the stories shared by these girls and women. We believe that their experiences and truths will support you as you seek, cement, and sustain lasting friendships of your own.

I

WHY WOMEN NEED FRIENDS

1

⟨❧⟩

The Biology of Friendship
To "Tend and Befriend"

Females seem to enter the world preprogrammed with a "friendship for-mation response." Most young girls pair up with their first "best friend" early in life as they enter the social world, whether on the playground, in a day care center, or at the schoolhouse. The membership of her troupe of friends may shift over time, but a woman's need for friends endures throughout her lifespan. Striking gender differences emerge early in the areas of social inter-est and social interaction that involve brain activity, sensory processing, and communication behavior. These differences play a contributing role in how females approach relationship formation.

No matter what age you are today, we bet you can remember your very first friend, your very first *best* friend, and, no doubt, you are definitely able to recall a time when you have been hurt by a friend. Friendships play a significant role throughout our lives. We may enter this world solo as vulnerable newborns, but we are primed and ready to form and navigate social connections from the start. It is as if we are driven to find a place of belonging and a sense of community from the moment we join the human race. Not only do women speak "in a differ-ent voice," as Carol Gilligan's book of the same name announced some decades ago,[1] but women also go about building relationships with strat-egies and intents different from those men choose to use. These gender differences in social predispositions and friendship configurations appear quite early in our development and are expressed in both our physiology and our behavior.

"It's like she was ready to be homecoming queen from the moment she was born!" was how Dana, an elementary school girl's mother, described her daughter Janey's social prowess. Dana had a son, Trevor, a couple of years older than her daughter, and Dana had been surprised at the difference in social skills and social interest displayed by her children. Dana felt that she and her son had "bonded" as well as any of the books she'd read on mothering had glowingly described the process, but Trevor had never been as intent as his sister on forming *relationships*—and Dana acknowledged that this word was a deliberate choice. Janey had been keenly aware of others' feelings since she was able to sit up in her bouncy chair and Dana had wondered whether this was a "girl thing" or just a temperament thing. After chatting with other mothers, Dana came to the conclusion that it must be a "girl thing," and she is definitely on target.

Yes, it's true. Girls and boys enter the social scene programmed with different *game plans*—not just different *equipment*—for connecting with others. Based on the findings of recent physiological and neuroscientific research, it is apparent that young girls are ready to build alliances and interact socially with others much more readily than their male counterparts are. A deeper and more complex connection to the social world continues for young girls throughout their lives in many different ways, including brain development, neurochemical activity, sensory experiences, and, of course, behavior.[2]

THE FRIENDSHIP-READY BRAIN

Gender differences in brain development become apparent well before birth. Every embryo begins as female, but at around the eighth week after conception, the child's encoded gender establishes the combination of hormones and brain chemicals that will soon begin to flow and continue to shape the child's development from that moment onward. While still in the womb, little girls are already building up the specific brain circuits that support a successful social life. Neuroscientists have dubbed the portion of the brain that oversees this area of activity the *social brain*, and striking differences between the genders are found here.[3]

Many of us believe the key differences between boys and girls are embedded in the visible differences in reproductive equipment and the presence of the sex-specific hormones, estrogen and testosterone. But the differences are deeper—there are visible and significant differences between the brains of females and males. And it is the chemicals, or neuropeptides, produced in the brain, not only the sex hormones from the gonads, which control much of the behavior differences between the genders.[4] We are all familiar with the blame game played with testosterone and estrogen, such as when PMS is blamed if a woman is moody or attributing a teenaged boy's risky behaviors to his being high on testosterone. Yet estrogen and testosterone are only co-players in the endocrine system's complex influence on behavior. In fact, it appears that two specific neuropeptides, oxytocin and vasopressin, are the true forces behind the gendered social behavior patterns that play out over a lifetime.[5]

These two peptides are produced in the hypothalmus and stored in the pituitary gland until they are released into the bloodstream or into the brain. Oxytocin is a "feel-good" peptide that works to minimize a woman's stress response. It encourages social bonding in a lot of different situations, from helping new moms bond with their babies to helping group cohesion in stressful circumstances.[6,7] It can also jump-start your memory in social situations. Research studies have shown that when oxytocin is released into your system, you have an easier time figuring out whether you've seen someone's face before.[8] Vasopressin plays a role in typically male-identified social behaviors, such as resorting to aggression in the face of challenges or protecting loved ones or possessions. Somewhat like oxytocin, it can help lower anxiety when someone is faced with a threatening situation. As for vasopressin's role in relationship formation, its presence in the system kicks up the appeal of monogamous behavior and pair bonding. Although the sex hormones, testosterone and estrogen, play a role in the regulation of vasopressin and oxytocin, it is these two peptides that govern our social behavior and that lead us into social alliance or enemy attack.[9] These peptides begin shaping our gendered social development just weeks after conception.

During development in the womb, girls' brains are already being prepared to handle the tasks of communication, reading emotions, understanding social nuances, and nurturing others. The sections of the brain responsible for supporting social behavior are primarily the temporal lobe and the amygdala. These areas of the brain allow us to recognize faces and to express our emotions, and—as many women probably presume—these structures mature more quickly in girls than boys.[10] In sharp contrast, the chemical changes that work on boys in the womb actually lead to a reduction in size of the brain areas responsible for communication, observation, and emotional expression and processing.[11] Girls enter this world better equipped to observe and remember emotional details. They are also able to comprehend the nonverbal components of communication, including vocal tone, facial expressions, and body language, and to assess meaning more successfully than males.[12,13] Girls are able to make good use of these skills when trying to negotiate social connections and resolve conflicts among their circles of friends. Their better memory for emotional details may likely be connected to their physical senses, including the sense of smell.

SCENTS AND SOCIABILITIES

We are all familiar with the strong emotional responses certain scents evoke—a richly detailed memory of a certain place, a certain event, or a certain person can come flooding back when we catch a whiff of a particular aroma. Researchers have found a relationship between the role our memories play in social learning and the influence of our hormones and peptides on this process.[14] Not only does our olfactory sense give us a lot of support in eliciting memories, but it is also a key component in social connection.[15] As infants, we use the sense of smell to identify the people who are most familiar to us and on whom we can rely to provide nurturing and caregiving. And, as you might guess, infant girls surpass infant boys in the development of a strong sense of smell, and this sensory superiority continues throughout the lifespan.[16]

Parents who have both daughters and sons probably know all too well that boys have a much higher tolerance for unpleasant odors than their sisters. Whereas a man might notice that a woman is wearing cologne, a woman is typically more likely to recognize the brand of the cologne. Our sense of smell alerts us to potential dangers—from a candle left burning to the smell of soured milk—and lets us know of the proximity of friends and family, too. Women use their sense of smell in associating certain scents with family members and close friends, thereby solidifying the relationship between olfactory processing and social connections. In addition to the unique function that the olfactory sense plays in social connections, the sense of sight is also an important factor in early relationship formation.

LOOKING FOR CONNECTION

Fairleigh had just given birth to her second child, a little girl named Amy, a week earlier. James, her 4-year-old son, always seemed to be rushing around the room wherever she and Amy settled in for feeding. Fairleigh said that she already knew that raising a daughter felt different than raising her son. "After nursing, Amy settles into my arms and just looks up at me so intently, as if she can see deep into my eyes and really knows, deep down, that I'm her mother. It probably sounds crazy, and James probably was doing the same thing, but with him being my first, I was anxious a lot of the time trying to make sure I didn't screw up. At least the second time around, I can hopefully focus on the baby more than the worries!" Actually, Fairleigh is probably noticing an actual difference between her children. Female infants are much more interested in extended eye contact than boys tend to be.

Newborn girls land in the hands of the waiting obstetricians ready to look them in the eyes and form their first face-to-face connections. In fact, girls are noticeably more likely to respond to social stimuli than same-age boys from virtually day one.[17,18,19] Human faces and the human voice are beacons of interest for the newborn girl, and she is much more interested in making and holding eye contact than an infant boy tends to be. In a longitudinal comparison of girls and boys, measured at age 5 days and then at 4 months, only the girls increased their gazing and eye contact behavior during this period.[20] Moreover, infant girls spend the first three months of life increasing their skills in holding eye contact and mutual gazing by more than 400 percent. For adults, women have been found to be most successful in negotiations when eye contact can be made with another; for men, however, successful negotiations are best reached in the absence of any face-to-face contact.[21] From the outset, girls appear to be focused on connecting to their communities through visual behavior well before they are able to connect verbally.

LIMITED VOCABULARY, BUT READY TO CHAT

Along with enhanced olfactory and vision development, infant girls are also expressing greater interest in mutual communication than boys do. Boys are slower to provide a consistent response to the spoken word. And infant girls, although not yet able to articulate intelligible words to express their opinions, are eager to be included in the conversations around them. Attention and inclusion are important to girls from the start. Compared to boys, young girls generally learn to talk sooner[22]; use longer phrases and sentences to get their points across; incorporate more accurate grammatical structure[23]; and employ a larger vocabulary.[24] This language precociousness is underscored by the fact that girls and women use both sides of the brain for language functions, but males generally use only the left.[25] Apparently the typical teenage girl's obsession with communication—whether cell phone, landline, texting, or IMing—is a natural phenomenon that her biological make-up pretty much prescribes.

WOMEN'S INTUITION—UNPLUGGED

One thirty-something mother shared the following story:

I was surprised and happy to get a real, old-fashioned letter in my mailbox a few weeks ago. I recognized the handwriting on the envelope—it was from one of my great aunts who lives a thousand miles away and is at least 80 years old, I guess. I was smiling as I maneuvered the twins' double stroller into the house and was looking forward to settling down on the couch to read the letter. I got the kids each a juice box and graham crackers and grabbed a water bottle for myself. Tabby sat down on the couch with me; she and Mikey are 2½. She must have caught my pleasure at the letter. Michael just wandered over to the corner of the room where the toys were kept. I giggled at Tabby, and told her I would read the letter out loud to her, which made her beam. I opened the letter, and was doing a quick read first to myself, when I read that my great aunt's husband had suffered a life-threatening stroke three weeks ago! Tabby seemed to know before I did that the tears were about to start, because she jumped from the couch, grabbed the tissues from the coffee table, and said, "Mommy, it gonna be okay, I promise." These were the words she heard me use when she or Mikey were sad or had taken a tumble. I couldn't believe she knew that I was sad as soon as I did!

Again, girls get a head start on boys in the skills needed to express empathy.

As infants, girls are already learning how to "read" others' emotions and feelings with surprising accuracy.[26] The babies who loudly offer their own "sympathy tears" when another infant is crying in a nursery are usually female. The ability to empathize with others develops much earlier and more effectively in girls than boys. During the preschool days, young girls lead the boys by far in their ability to recognize others' facial expressions and related emotions. Studies with adults offer support for the presence of a connection between empathy and specific neural pathways in the brain. It appears that the gender difference in empathy is hard-wired from birth.[27] This natural empathy is a skill that will serve girls well in all of the friendships they form and it is a gender difference that tends to last a lifetime.[28]

It makes sense that because females have an easier time reading others' feelings that they would also have an easier time understanding their own. Indeed, most girls are able to process and share their feelings with others relatively easily unless their emotional expression becomes blocked due to an outside influence or socialization parameters set up by caregivers. A young girl can usually openly express what makes her happy, what makes her sad, what gets her angry, and what frightens her. Girls' brains have a strong connection between the seat of emotion, the amygdala, and the cerebral cortex, which allows them to process and articulate their feelings. However, the brains of boys and men use a different physiological connection, and they have a much harder time processing their emotions or accessing emotional memories—except for those related to aggression.[29] They may know they feel sad, but they would have a difficult time verbalizing their emotions and the specific reasons behind their feelings.[30] This gives girls an advantage in being able to connect and relate to others on a personal and emotional level.

ENTERING THE WORLD OF SOCIAL CONNECTION

It's been asserted that the main job of the female brain is to develop connections within the community.[31] The neural wiring and sensory sensitivities combine in such a way that women work toward collaboration, consensus, and harmony. Women prefer to *include* rather than *exclude* others in social settings and also prefer to seek mutually beneficial decisions. This desire for fairness begins early. Young girls have been observed to take turns much more frequently than same-age boys in play activities.[32] Women, today, still organize many of their social activities in an inclusive manner and use symbolic names for their gatherings, such as "church circles," "sewing circles," and "quilting bees." The term "bee" was supposedly chosen in honor of the social nature of that particular insect. But within many of these inclusive groups, there may be power struggles simmering under the surface. Although women are less physically aggressive than men, there is still a strong drive in some women and girls to be seen as a group leader. Being seen by others as the leader of a group to which they belong can boost the self-esteem of many girls and women.[33]

Traditionally, girls and women assess their self-worth based on the external cues provided by the others in their worlds, whether family, peers, or community members. Boys and men use their own level of independence as a measure of their self-worth, whereas females gauge their self-worth on the strength of their close relationships.[34] This can produce an extremely potent need for approval in girls and women. This can lead to choices and compromises that benefit others, rather than themselves, in the pursuit of approval and acceptance. For many of us, the reward of being accepted in a clique or social group is worth yielding to others in certain circumstances. It turns out that being with friends and engaging in social behaviors— talking, gossiping, shopping, and so on—promotes the production of the "feel-good" neurochemicals.[35] Girls and women are neurochemically programmed to create social connections, seek out social acceptance, and to promote social harmony. It makes sense that a girl would be willing to endure a level of personal sacrifice in order to access the neurochemical reward that arises from social success. The biology of the female clearly is developed to encourage and support strong alliances.

BORN TO BEFRIEND?

Mikkie was a born negotiator, according to Tonya and Sal, her mom and dad. "And she has to be, for all of the trouble she gets into!" her dad laughed. Sal recounted that Mikkie had older brothers and that she had learned how to push the boundaries from watching the boys' exploits for 16 years. "However," continued Tonya, "rather than throwing baseballs in the house, Mikkie tries to bend rules about curfews, having friends over, and borrowing my clothes!" Sal chuckled and shared that what amazed him most about Mikkie's efforts to negotiate her way out of trouble was that her crazy stories usually worked with his wife. "Yep, Mikkie is late getting in one night and Tonya and I are sitting up in the living room waiting for her. When she shows up, and before we can even read her the riot act, she's 'confessing' to her mother that she knew she was late, but that she couldn't just drop her best friend, Megan, off at her house. Megan's parents were going to be ticked at Megan being late, so Mikkie says she had to go in with her and help explain that her car wouldn't crank at first and try to help Megan stay out of trouble." Mikkie's story helped her avoid trouble at home with her own parents, as she was able to successfully play on Tonya's instinctive desire to help others in need. Mikkie then pretty much clinched the deal when she reminded her parents that she had learned how to be a good friend and put others first from her mom, Tonya, and that she did what she thought her mom would have done for a friend.

For decades, we have heard about the "fight or flight" response, which supposedly worked as an evolutionary survival tool used in the face of danger or stress. Everyone just assumed that it was an equal opportunity reflex and that both men and women would respond to threats to safety in the same manner. However, as the twenty-first century dawned, a new perspective on the stress response of women was presented that has been termed the "tend and befriend" response.[36] This new concept is based on the recognition that stress produces unique and specific physiological reactions that are dictated by gender. Our endocrine systems spring into action when we are faced with a threatening situation, and although both men and women's bodies are quick to secrete the stress hormones (adrenaline and cortisol), women also secrete oxytocin, a peptide that instigates a variety of responses. As noted earlier, this particular chemical is a relaxation-inducing and anxiety-lowering peptide. Oxytocin also promotes trust when it is secreted,[37] and when a group is facing imminent danger, being able to strengthen your trust in the company you're with is likely to lead to quicker and more effective group cohesion and group action. Men, however, get a surge of testosterone when confronted with threatening situations, and this hormone propels men to respond with hostility and aggression. This difference may have developed as an evolutionary adaptation that matched size with task. While the stronger males were using physical force to confront the challenge, the women would be protecting the young and creating a strong female alliance to better overcome or outsmart the challenger, if necessary. The stressors and challenges we face today may be vastly different from those in centuries past, but social connection is still an exceptionally effective and satisfying method for handling stress.

Women have long been the target of stereotypic teasing—some gentle, some not—for their alleged tendency to talk too much, to spend too much time on the phone with friends, to expect men to talk about their own feelings, and to want men to notice their new hairstyle or fashion find. Many of these activities and desires are expressions of primal genetic coding that guide contemporary women's behavior. Women essentially get a "natural high" when they are in the company of their friends and are able to kick back, relax, and let their feelings and their words flow. Oxytocin pumps up the relaxation response and women revel in the deep, social bonding that is fostered during an evening spent with good friends. A woman's best friends will "dish the dirt" and tell you what they *really* think about the outfit, the lipstick, the haircut, the back stabbing co-worker, and the new lover. Women need best friends, weekend friends, work friends, neighborhood friends, potential friends, and lifelong friends. Friendships are a necessity and lasting friendships are the olive in the martini or the icing on the cake.

2

❧❧

Friendship in Context

Social Relationships in the Twenty-First Century

*In this chapter, we focus on ways in which the organization and function-
ing of society influence social relations. Taking a look at friendship from a
broad perspective, we examine the influence of collective cultural values on
the social behaviors of its people. For instance, if you are lonely, you are not
alone. People today report much higher levels of loneliness than in previous
generations; in this chapter, we share some of the reasons this may be so.*

Social scientists have found that our society, as a whole, encourages us
to make *less effort* to be civil to people unfamiliar to us than it once
did.[1] It's as if it requires more effort to engage in the once-basic social
niceties that might lead to lasting friendships in our world today. We are,
in fact, facing living conditions that are dramatically different than those
our parents faced:

*My grandmother tells the story of how her friends in the neighborhood
(a couple of city blocks in a predominantly Italian section of Brooklyn)
came together to help with my brother's physical therapy routine three
decades ago. He needed an intensive kind of therapy that required the
combined labor of three adults at five different times over the course of
each day. My mother was always one of the adults assisting Joey. Often,
my grandma was another of the helpers. But the third helper was always
one of my grandma's friends. After Joey completed the therapy session,
my grandma's friend would be "compensated" with cookies, coffee, and
a little neighborhood gossip. Twenty-five times each week my family
received instrumental help from a friend. No financial compensation was
ever expected. This shared, intensive effort lasted until our family moved*

to Long Island, where there was no built-in community of support, mak-
ing the therapy no longer possible.

Nowadays, most people would handle this same challenge quite differently. Parents of a child with special needs would find a way to manage
the therapy on their own or, if income allowed, hire additional home-
based help. Special day cares with subsidized therapists might provide
therapy sessions on weekdays, but on weekends, it is likely that parents
would depend solely on family members to help. To consider asking
friends for assistance would be a cause for trepidation for fear of asking
too much. How has the social exchange system changed so much, and
how do these changes affect the friendship formation process? Let's see if
we can find some answers.

It is from our culture that we develop expectations of what friends
should do for one another. For example, how close would you need to
be to a friend to spend a year's worth of Tuesday and Thursday mornings helping her provide physical therapy to her child? Pretty close, most
likely. You are probably from a different generation, a different community, and a different social network than the one my grandmother represented. What you would do for a friend is probably more typical of what
other women in your neighborhood would do. Friendships, like flowers,
are strongly influenced by the soil in which they grow. The growth of a
friendship is influenced by the cultural values in a given country (though
Western values are increasingly dominant in our shrinking world), the
area of the country, the general community, the neighborhood, and finally, a woman's personal social network.

CURRENT CULTURE: WHY IS THIS TYPE OF
PITCHING-IN TO HELP FRIENDS A RARITY TODAY?

A host of environmental factors influenced not only the ability, but also
the willingness of earlier generations to provide labor-intensive personal
assistance to friends. Societal factors interact to either promote or hinder
the development and maintenance of friendships. Generations ago, not
only did fewer middle-class women engage in paid, full-time work outside the home, but they also lived within walking distance of one another,
which fostered informal interaction. The structure of their daily routines
promoted more neighbor-to-neighbor communication. Neighborhood involvement enriched and deepened their social connections and relationships. Close friendships extended beyond a precious few and responsibility extended beyond the boundaries of the family unit and more broadly
into the community.

Due to major changes in structural aspects of life today, we are less embedded in community life and an extended social network. These changes
are attributed to shifts in cultural values and social behaviors as well as
massive transformations in contemporary personal habits. These changes
have been explored at length by Robert Putnam in his groundbreaking
book, *Bowling Alone*. Putnam investigated a host of obstacles that have
been identified as possible causes for the disintegration of American community life and social networks. Major causes were pinpointed as changes
in work, suburban sprawl, technology, and the nonreplicable events experienced by different generations, such as WWII.[2] There are additional,
unique factors that influence the ways in which women live and love.
Changing gender roles, the influence of living in a male-oriented context,
and the culturally expected and unpaid work world of nurturing others
must also be considered. The areas requiring the most scrutiny are work,
time, and values.

WORK: BRINGING HOME THE BACON

Due to various economic pressures and increased career opportunities,
women have entered the workforce at increasingly higher rates over the
past several decades. Today, roughly around three-quarters of all women
between 25 and 54 are hard at work in paid employment.[3] Unfortunately,
despite our natural inclinations to befriend, work-related constraints often
make the creation and maintenance of friendships a true challenge for us.

With the transformation of industry over the decades, we often move
away from our families-of-origin and lifelong friends to chase the American Dream. Or, perhaps more realistically, we uproot ourselves for job
opportunities in order to support our families. More than 40 million people relocate each year,[4] and it is increasingly rare to live your entire life in
the community in which you were born. This means that we may move
into new communities as virtual strangers, leaving behind any sense of
connectedness, family history, and family identity that would help others
know us. Each move requires us to start at square one with no familial
context and no ties to bind. Although this can allow us to gracefully start
anew with each acquaintance, our new friends will share a more limited
history with us.

As a military spouse, Amanda knows some of the pleasures and pitfalls
associated with uprooting:

*When we lived in Hawaii, our neighbors in military housing were is-
land-bound transients just like our little family. They needed friends just
like we did, so everyone got together several times a week and quickly*

became friends. But after that stint, we were moved to Key West, which sounded like more fun than it was. We were in off-base housing with a mix of neighbors who seemed to have enough friends already. I was only a six-hour drive from my parents, so that's where I went when Ryan was out to sea and I got lonely. In a year and a half, I still haven't made any friends here.

Massive migrations from the cities and farms to the suburbs have exponentially increased our dependence on personal automobiles. We spend a significant portion of our day commuting, with some estimates of an average commute at 100 minutes per day.[5] Living relatively far from work creates a chasm between our work life and home life. We may seldom socialize with our work colleagues. Perhaps most telling of all is that as we move up the professional ladders of success and status, we are increasingly inclined to give up hanging out on the front porch, a place where neighbors traditionally meet and greet, to lounging on our architecturally designed decks in our professionally landscaped and privacy-fenced backyards. Years ago, unrelated women cooked meals together and scolded each other's children. Now we seek privacy and the uninterrupted solace that provides comfort in exchange for casual social interaction. We sit at our computers or clean our homes solo, becoming functionally independent but isolated in our struggles. The increased income that may accompany geographic mobility, long commutes, and private spaces may bring a rather expensive white picket fence of loneliness.

Between the absence of personal history and the absence of personal connection to place, there is a resulting absence of a sense of community responsibility coupled with limited interaction with those with whom we live in close proximity. Our disconnect from our local community greatly influences the friendships we choose and how our free time is spent. For instance, in order to spend time with work friends, we must either stay later in the municipality of our workplace or "commute in" to have friend time. But the structural obstacles that persist even after the timecard has been punched out are even more noteworthy; when paid work is over for the day, women continue to work, work, work.

FRYING THE BACON

When we asked women what hurdles they had to overcome to develop and maintain friendships, one of the most frequent answers was the lack of time. Clearly, women are still the primary caretakers and schedule keepers in their homes and, at a certain age, become sandwiched between the needs of their children and their aging parents. Despite their prevalence in the workforce, women still shoulder the bulk of the housekeeping responsibilities, which requires them to work what is colloquially known as "the second shift." Women also provide much of a community's unpaid work and social collateral, such as church committee service; nonprofit, volunteer work; school-based organizational leadership (e.g., PTA committees); and neighborhood organizational tasks. Though some men and their partners assert that they share equally in household tasks, several studies confirm that women spend significantly more time devoted to housework and family-related tasks than their male peers.[6]

Go to lunch with a group of working mothers and you will hear tales of the struggle to balance work and family pressures that shapes life for modern women. Few women can discuss their friendships without addressing the practical elements pertaining to this struggle. Karen, a busy college administrator, proclaimed:

Between long work days, commuting to and from work, trying to sneak in a little exercise, shuffling my daughter to her events, and running errands, I'm too exhausted to even call friends in the evening. Saturday is family day and very important to my marriage. So my only day to catch up with anyone is Sunday. And since it is my day, and I need my friends to survive, I use it wisely. Sometimes it means I have to put my daughter's demands on the side burner. Though I feel kind of guilty about that, especially because I work as hard as I do, but I think it's better for her to see me as a role model taking care of myself than to see me constantly harried.

Karen's choice to place her own needs on par with the needs of other family members is counter to cultural expectations.

Making matters more complicated and burdensome is the growth in child-centeredness in the United States over the past 50 years. This new priority puts pressures on women—and, to a lesser degree, men—to have their children involved in as many activities as the family can manage with available resources of time and money. It is no surprise that the parent in charge of chauffeuring the children to school and other events spends an average of 104 minutes (even longer than the average commuter!) in the car each day.[7] Shuttling between practices, games, and home, soccer moms are busy women; the upside of this added time sink is the opportunity to find new friends via children's activities. At least while children are young enough to require the sustained presence of their parents, time spent with fellow soccer moms (or band moms, lacrosse moms, etc.) offers a foundation for gaining fellowship and instrumental and emotional support.

"FREE" TIME: BEYOND THE BACON

We, as a country, increasingly feel that we are overworked, perhaps based on our over-accessibility to work through such devices as pagers, cellphones, and emails. People feel pressured by work demands and, even when returning work emails takes ten minutes, there is a perception that we are constantly in work mode.[8] However, our leisure time does exist! Due to reduced housework from time-saving appliances, ready-made meals, and rearing fewer children, Putnam asserts that women have 4.5 more discretionary hours than they did in 1965; in a stark contrast, men apparently have 7.9 more hours.[9] Although many women acknowledged being tired at the end of the day, taking weekend hours into consideration, perhaps there are more clock hours available for friendship than perceived. So how do all those hours disappear? Putnam staunchly avows that our dependence on television entertainment is the *primary* predictor of our civic and social disengagement.[10] He notes that our virtually ritualized viewing patterns have claimed priority over virtually any social activity outside our homes. This particularly limits our time for social gatherings and casual, informal conversations with others. It seems that television may be the single largest thief of our discretionary time, encouraging lethargy, and fostering pseudopersonal connection, all of which leaves us lonely and dissatisfied.

Relating these findings to the opening description of "community physical therapy," it is significant to note that the women in that generation were much less likely to spend their discretionary time watching television than women in more recent generations. Today, according to the American Time Use Study (ATUS) , we spend more than 50 percent of our discretionary time in the company of the cast and characters of our favorite television programs and only about 13 percent in the company of our friends and neighbors. Marie, a 46-year-old bookkeeper, attests to the absorbing power of television:

TV watching has always been a part of our family life. Back when our daughter was a child, it was comedy sitcoms before bedtime. My husband and I started our family much younger than our neighbors and didn't seem to share many interests except for just being neighbors. I think this may be how our TV viewing grew. Today, with the creation of nighttime soaps and reality TV, it has become a "lockdown"! Just wouldn't dare miss an episode! For years, our evenings were spent watching TV, never socializing. In recent years, I've made efforts to spend time with friends and family so if an invitation crosses my path I no longer decline because of a TV show. However, if there's a good show on, I don't seek out people like I probably should. One other troubling part of our TV viewing habits is that it is very often the only

"quality time" spent with my husband. And it is not really "high quality."
Now, in a world of DVR, my hope is that the lockdown can be lifted, but then
again, there may be more shows recorded and calling my name to watch them
than there is available time.

Not only have high levels of television viewing been found to inter-
fere with the time normally spent socializing and communicating with
friends and family, it has also been connected to additional negative consequences. TV viewing has been found to cause and exacerbate physical
ailments such as obesity and headaches as well as chronic isolation and
depression.[11,12] Given our widespread tendency to watch hours of TV
daily and its negative ramifications for physical, mental, and friendship
health, it is worth suggesting that if you feel closer to television personalities than you do your own real-world associates, turning off the set and
joining a neighbor for a walk might be an excellent start to improving
your social connectedness.

Another thief of social time is the family computer. As personal computers become standard issue for families, new questions about its role in
our lives arise. Especially relevant is the impact of the Internet on social
connectedness and whether time spent on social networking sites is actually "social time." We may well wonder if time spent connected to the Internet is time spent disconnected from reality. This "web of connection" is
such an immense, hotly debated, and relatively new social influence that
we spend a chapter later in the book exploring the ways that communication technologies both divide and connect us.

WHAT WE VALUE

Although decades have passed since the height of the feminist movement,
women still function in a world that is predominantly run and governed
by men. How does the culturally embedded focus on men and male
dominance influence female friendships? Let's look at a couple examples
of how patriarchy may impact women's friendships:

I typically do better with male friends than female friends. I don't know why or
what it is about me, but I seem to have a harder time making friends with women.
Either women think I'm trying to "hit on" their guy or I feel I can't trust them
for some reason. It seems like I have always had better guy friends. —Mistie,
24-years-old

It doesn't feel much like sisterhood. The main interest of my sorority
sisters appears to be the fraternities. Which frat party to attend, which

fraternity you are a little sister for; the guys even get to decide which so-
rority membership is going to be the "hot" one on campus by inviting the
girls from that sorority to a social. Little did I realize being in the "hot"
sorority was not the right sisterhood for me. —Tina, 19-year-old college
sophomore, describing her disappointment with her sorority experience

I am one of those girls whose friends probably get really upset with—
whenever I get involved in a dating relationship, it seems like I lose touch
with my girl friends. I don't ever intend for this to happen, but it seems
like time gets away from me. I go to college full-time, work part-time, and
have very limited "social time." So, I end up spending a LOT more time
with a boyfriend than my other friends. And this has come back to hurt
me more than once. When I've had a guy to break up with me, sometimes
I have a hard time finding a shoulder to cry on, so to speak. —Merri, 20-
year-old college student

In a society in which women continue to earn only about 80 percent of
what men earn and in a culture that values heterosexual marriage over
any other form of relationship, especially singledom, women tend to focus on acquiring the best possible mate. Little girls enjoy "playing house"
with the boys in their preschool class, and the intense pursuit of this attachment becomes clearly visible in adolescent females. Once "caught,"
a male partner with desirable attributes (e.g., earning power, stability,
strength) may remain the object of actual and perceived competition
among women for some time. Even long-married women can feel threatened by women who they perceive to be "on the prowl." Competition
among women is not limited to mates, but also for the attributes men find
desirable in mates such as physical beauty, weight, stylishness of clothes,
and popularity. Our contemporary perspective on physical beauty requires that women strive to possess a youthful, wrinkle-free face, and
a body with a youthful waist-to-hip ratio.[13] In addition, and despite a
degree of sexual liberation since the 1970s, women must still maintain
an unblemished sexual reputation.[14] If you think the push to get a man
is avoidable until a girl is safely in her twenties, check out the images
and values being communicated to young women today. For instance, a
popular teen magazine, *Cosmo Girl*, offers an online survey where teen
girls can discover their perfect romantic match. Whether it is more a mirror of society or a motivator of social behavior, the media emphasizes and
possibly magnifies the drive to catch a man.

The lengths to which women go in their efforts to be appealing to men
spans the extremes from the relatively innocuous wearing of shiny lip
gloss to the frequently uncomfortable wearing of high heels to the potentially risky and definitely costly submission to cosmetic surgery. In

fewer than ten years, from 1998 to 2005, the number of breast augmenta-
tions doubled.[15] In 2007, for a variety of reasons, almost 400,000 breast
implant surgeries were performed in the United States.[16] More harmful
to friendships, however, are some of the other approaches women use
to "win" a man. The main approach women use to beat out the competition— beyond spicing up their looks—is to slander the reputations
of other women. Gossip and malicious rumors were often cited by the
women we interviewed as reasons they found some of their friendships
crumbling. In one study, competition for desirable men was shown to go
from verbal charges to physical attacks.[17] Sadly, more than one interviewee shared accounts of friendships ending when intimacy grew between
the interviewee's romantic interest and a friend. Although not all of us
will experience significant issues of competition with our friends, it definitely showed up as the death knell of friendship for a good number of
the women we interviewed. These incidents certainly provide support for
the negative influence interpersonal competition for desirable men can
have on female friendship.

Generational Values

The generation of American women who were in their middle years and
the most socially connected during the 1950s were far less individualistic and less materialistic than succeeding generations of Americans.[18] A
pervasive cultural belief about the road to personal success requires that
we buy into the spirit of individualism; we believe that each of us con-
trols our own destiny through independence, self-reliance, and agency.
Though we also pride ourselves on being "doers" and "joiners," attendance rates in social activities as diverse as church services and bowling leagues indicate we have stopped "joining" groups and, moreover,
stopped "attending" group activities.[19] As a nation, we have increasingly
and sadly removed ourselves from engaging with our neighbors, our
community, and even our friends.

A second major cultural value change that has affected our social
interactions is the ongoing increase in materialism that began with the
baby boomers.[20] Although there is debate over the issue, many social
scientists agree that Americans have grown overly concerned with the
accumulation of personal wealth and the ownership of material goods.
For instance, the life goal of vacation home ownership has dramatically increased over time, and the rate of those who wish to positively
impact the world has dropped. This hyperconsumption was strikingly
represented by a comment from former President G. W. Bush describing Americans as addicted to oil and the lifestyle it provides.[21] The Gulf
Coast oil disaster in 2010 underscores the damage that this addiction can

wreak. Perhaps even more troubling is Resnick and Wolff's proposal that the materialistic focus of the American way of life has led to significant and tragic results.[22] Specifically noted were physical ailments, including exhaustion, stress, and dependency on drugs. Social ailments included loneliness and disconnection from our civic roles. Also noted were the rises in dysfunctional families and endemic violence plaguing our lives. As spending levels have soared, so have levels of credit card debt. Unfortunately, as economic situations worsen, people become even more self- and family-focused, thus creating a downward spiral.[23] Plainly put, financial woes limit our social involvement and drive us indoors into a self-inflicted solitary confinement.

As we review the major influences on the social development of Americans, we are again brought back to the heavy-handed influence of the television. Not only does TV viewing absorb our time, but it is also believed that a large number of the generational social trait differences are due to television programming.[24] It is easy to see that too much time spent exposed to heavily researched and disturbingly effective commercials intent on making people desire a given product could shape our visions of happiness or success. Watching TV shows mislabeled "reality shows," seldom resembling any woman's real life, or addictively following "housewives" from what appear to be other galaxies have also influenced viewers' perceptions and values over the decades. Not only have perceptions of how to look, what to wear, and how to function in relationships been shaped by television programming, but we have also learned an important lesson. It is easier to stay at home and laugh at *Seinfeld* than it is to join a local club, attend meetings, risk rejection from potential friends, or even contemplate the potential time demands that a new friendship would require.

CONCLUSION

Our broader culture and our immediate subcultures influence the shape our friendships take, their salience in our lives, the extent to which we allow them to influence us, and the support they provide. Our current context and unique demographics influence our behavior on a very personal level. Hence, friendship behaviors will be affected by the year of our birth, the geographic locale in which we were raised, our family traditions, and our parents' circumstances. Race, color, and gender all interact to influence our opportunities for building and maintaining friendships. Though a structural transformation of our culture would be helpful, our "friendship fates" are not written in stone; we have choices within our realms of opportunity. Awareness of obstacles and advantages within our own social landscape will help us maximize our prospects. If we wish for friends who would be willing to help out when we need them, then we can make the choice to be that same kind of friend for others. More than four decades ago, my grandmother called for support from her network of friends and they all showed up. Through intention and commitment, we can still create a landscape of friends who will be there for us today, just as my grandmother's friends were there for her then.

3

⋘⋙

"Friendology"

The Science of Friendship

This chapter provides an overview of what could be called the "science of friendship." This includes what we know about our expectations and interactions with friends, including who we choose as friends, how friendships typically develop, the "rules of friendship," and whether there are differences in how women and men do friendship.

Although each of us may hold personal definitions of friendship, several common themes of what friendship entails were found among the women interviewed for this book. First, friendships were considered to exist when pleasure is taken in the company of another; when spending time with someone becomes a duty, rather than a preference, friendships often wane. Second, the construct of friendship implied reciprocity and give-and-take. An immediate "even exchange" economic model of behavior is not expected, but it is assumed that support will flow both ways as the need arises. Third, the level of friendship commitment varied over a lifetime, depending on the energy required by family or other commitments at the time. From what we learned from the research and our interviews, it appears that only "basic survival" and "survival of the species" are prioritized over friendship for most of us! However, many women believe that when crisis strikes, *true friends* can be counted on to offer support, regardless of any inconvenience or challenges they may face to do so. We engage in friendships on a voluntary basis and we recognize that friends also consciously make the choice to engage in the relationship. This strong mutual alliance was concisely summed up by one woman who shared, "I feel like my circle of friends are the family I *chose*."

WHO DO WE CHOOSE AS A FRIEND?

Models of friendship show that there are two main types of factors that influence our choice and pursuit of potential friends. These are individual/dyadic factors and contextual/environmental factors.[1,2,3] Individual and dyadic factors include such influences as approachability, social skills, self-disclosure, similarity, and closeness. Contextual and environmental factors include influences such as proximity, geography, activities, and life events.

Research shows that we prefer friends we believe are similar to us and who have personalities that we enjoy; this decreases the possibility for interpersonal conflict.[4] A potential friend's level of attractiveness is relevant in the initial stages of friendship.[5] Americans tend to be drawn toward beauty and we tend to believe that attractive people are more like us in their attitudes and values—regardless of where we actually rank ourselves in the world of beauty or style. This seemingly innate predilection for attractive people has been studied and some interesting things have turned up. For one, an attractive face will appear familiar to us, fostering a feeling that we have already interacted with the person before—even though we have not.[6] This feeling of recognition may partly explain why we are initially drawn to attractive people—they may help us feel comfortable in social situations. It is still unproven whether attractive women actually *have* more friends than less attractive women; in fact, research suggests that we pretty much choose friends that we rank at the same level of attractiveness that we rank ourselves.[7] We also want friends with strong social skills—this makes friendship development that much easier on both parts. Not only do healthy social skills facilitate a budding friendship, but also research also reveals that when someone shares positive words with us, a feeling of familiarity arises within us.[8] We are simply drawn to those people in whose presence we feel comfortable.

Most often, friendships ease forward following a path of increasing closeness. Occasionally, though, friendships can materialize out of nowhere. This almost instant recognition of a like soul could be termed the "click factor," and several interviewees described it as feeling as if they'd known someone for years even though they had just met. There are as many different personalities as there are individuals and friendships can develop between unlikely pairs. There are some friends with whom we "just click," and we recognize early on that our personalities are a good match. One adolescent we interviewed described the "click factor" when she related the story of how she met her best friend, Katie:

It was summer and my family had just moved into a house on Katie's street. We were both going into the fourth grade. When we first met, she was walking by while I was playing alone in my front yard. We decided on the spot that we were going to be best friends, just like that. Eight years later, we're still best friends, and we still don't know how it happened!

An older interviewee in her forties described meeting her current best friend at a community event:

We were sitting in the room, listening to everyone speak with self-importance and boring detail, and we just caught each other's eyes across the room. It was like we both had the same reaction to everyone's long-winded stories and we just clicked. We're still best friends over ten years later.

Opening Up in Early Friendship

Determining who would be a good fit as a friend requires that both members of a pair of potential friends engage in self-disclosure. This requires that we reveal authentic information about ourselves to which no one else is generally privy. The depth to which we disclose can vary greatly based on family customs, personal comfort, and apprehensions. As we begin to open up at increasingly deeper and more intimate levels, we expect potential friends to mirror this behavior and to reveal personal information about themselves at a pace and depth that matches our own. However, to borrow a term from popular culture, TMI, or "too much information," revealed too soon in an acquaintanceship can halt a potential friendship in its tracks.[9,10] Inappropriate sharing of personal information can cause discomfort for the listener—and for the speaker a day or so down the road. If potential friends move into a synchronous and interactive engagement with us, and unveil intimate information at a similar rate, feelings of like-mindedness and accord are generated. When someone self-discloses to us, in an appropriate and well-timed manner, our positive feelings about this person are enhanced. Mutual sharing and the breaking down of personal defenses will build trust, which is a requisite of friendship. For some of us, the process of opening ourselves up so completely to another can be difficult. Numerous fears can inhibit self-disclosure including the fear of rejection, the fear of abandonment, the fear of being ridiculed, and the fear of misplacing our trust. Learning to open up to another is a process that can be learned, practiced, and perfected, especially when weighed against the reward of new or deepened friendships.

Not only do we appreciate the self-disclosures of others,[11] we actually feel positive feelings and attraction to the people to whom we have self-disclosed.[12,13] As friends share personal and intimate knowledge, the friendship bond is deepened and cemented and feelings of attraction and liking between friends are increased.[14,15] Although we feel comfortable with balance shifts in levels of intimate self-disclosure in well-established friendships, reciprocity and matching are extremely important in the early stages of friendship. As we learn more about a potential friend and they learn more about us, we begin to discover similarities and the things we have in common. This helps us determine whether the person will be a good fit in our social landscape.

Recognizing Yourself in Your Friend

The level of similarity between two potential friends is directly proportional to the chance that a friendship will be launched.[16] Similarities might be related to demographic factors, such as gender, ethnicity, neighborhood, or to our attitudes, beliefs, and values. In fact, shared attitudes is one of the most dependable predictors of friendship development.[17] Most of us would rather spend time with people who feel the same way about life as we do. We also prefer the company of people who enjoy the same types of activities that we do—we want friends to be pleasant companions when we engage in our favorite pastimes.[18] It may be a surprise to some, but research has *not* shown any strong support for similar personality styles or personality traits as predictors of friendship development.[19] Although a pair of friends might include such opposite types as a extroverts and introverts or dreamers and doers, we definitely favor friends who mirror our philosophies, activities, and demographic variables—and these preferences can be strong.

Beverly Fehr has explored the three most highly regarded and potentially valid explanations for our preference for similar souls as friends.[20] There are three separate schools of thought, including (1) a somewhat commonsense type of explanation, (2) an existential explanation, and (3) an evolutionary explanation. In support of the more basic, commonsense explanation, Fehr cited research that described the positive validation we receive when someone agrees with us. In essence, we all like to be "right," and when friends affirm our views, it simply feels good.[21] In the same way, we enjoy spending time in our favorite activities with those who also enjoy these same pastimes, validating the "goodness" of the activity choice. The next explanation, the existential perspective, relies on the construct of "I-sharing," or joining with another person who possesses similar attitudes or perspectives.[22] It is based on the idea that we long to share ourselves with another to remedy the sense of isolation that existential philosophers believe to be endemic to the human condition. Thus, we look for friends who can understand and connect with us on a deeper level than mere acquaintances are able to do. The third explanation rests on the biologically based assumption that our innate drive to procreate and leave a lasting impact on the gene pool leads us to choose companions, friends, or mates who are most like us in order to ensure our genetic legacy.[23] The close bonds that we develop with our friends position them within our social/kin networks—and these are the people we would endeavor to protect. Their survival increases the chances of survival for their offspring; thus the choice of similar friends increases our chance of keeping our own genetic type alive and well for future generations in the gene pool. Each of these explanations has some level of empirical support, yet we may never determine whether one explanation is categorically more relevant than the others. Regardless, it has definitely been proven that birds of a feather flock together.

A Friendship of Equals?

Similarity can also be viewed as a criterion of equality, which is another condition relevant to the success of friendships. We choose our friends based on the belief that they are equal to us in their moral perspectives and their views of the world and research suggests that friendships fare better when friends view each other as equals. Although we may initially be drawn to friends who are significantly different from us,[24] in terms of beliefs, values, socioeconomic circumstances, or education, these differences can negatively influence the development of a friendship.[25] Perhaps the belief that our friends are equal to us—and capable of giving to the friendship at the level at which we are able to give—reinforces the belief that we can rely on our friends. This touches on the construct of reciprocity in friendships.

Give and Take and Give Again

Reciprocity must be in place for friendships to thrive[26,27]; we must feel confident in a friend's ability to return the favors that we provide for her if we are to stay invested in a friendship. Although lasting relationships are not built on a strict quid pro quo basis of even exchange, there is an expectation of a give-and-take interrelationship with our friends. This has been termed a *symmetrical reciprocity*[28] and is integral to any healthy relationship. Our expectation of reciprocity includes both communication behaviors and interactions. As noted before, reciprocal communications of a self-disclosing nature are mandatory in friendship development. In terms of interactions, when we take part in social activities with friends, we enjoy a higher level of engagement in the activity and a more mutual orientation than when involved in interactions with nonfriends.[29] Friendships involve a communal-centered focus rather than an exchange-centered focus. Within an authentic friendship, neither friend believes that any specific debts *must* be repaid, but an expectation of shared investment does exist.[30] Unfortunately, in some relationships, one friend may believe that she is always on the "giving" side and never the "receiving" side, and the equality of relationship may need to be reevaluated.

As a corollary to our belief that friends provide support without expecting repayment, an *unsolicited* offer of support can lead to the development of friendship.[31] One of the women we interviewed, Barb, a 57-year-old newly retired former teacher, shared a story of how a cherished friendship began some 20 years ago. Here is an example of how the provision of unasked-for support to potential friends can open the door to friendship:

My son wanted to play soccer, but there was a shortage of coaches that year. Not enough fathers to go'round. My husband volunteered to help out so that our son could play that season. It was a big commitment for my husband, but one that meant a lot to both of us, and we shifted our schedules to find the time for the team. Well, the parents of Jeremy, another boy on the team, Beth and Dan, stepped in to help out. They were just so dedicated and supportive of their own son and the whole team and did so much without being asked. Beth and I became friends that year and are still close friends today.

PATHWAYS TO FINDING FRIENDS

There are three ways by which we typically find new friends. The first is *propinquity*, or proximity, to potential friends, which is an environmental factor.[32,33] Empirically investigated more than 50 years ago, the proximity theory describes our tendency to become closer friends with individuals to whom we are more closely physically or functionally situated. In fact, for the most part, the greater the exposure we have to a person, the greater the positive feelings we have toward the person.[34,35] This means that you are most likely to become emotionally closer to people with whom you come into contact on a regular basis. This might be the women whose desks or cubicles are closest to yours, or the woman whose path you cross on your daily walk, or the person in the apartment right across the hall from your own. One woman provided the following example of "functional" proximity. Nadia, a 57-year-old environmental regulator for the state, shared that in the neighborhood in which she resided, she had found herself feeling closer to one next-door neighbor over the other and she wasn't sure why. Both neighboring houses held warm and thoughtful couples and both neighbors had children, although Nadia did not. She also denied that it was a personality match, as she really hadn't interacted at much depth with either family. Nadia believes that the only real reason she felt closer to one family over the other had to do with the side of the house her driveway was on. Nadia said that because she spent more time on the driveway side of her own home, going to work, getting her paper or the mail, that she "felt" closer to the neighbor on her "driveway side." Nadia laughed as she added that she'd noticed the same phenomenon at the first home she and her husband had lived in decades ago.

The second path to new friendships is through involvement in shared activities; this is considered a situational factor.[36] Women who were interviewed for this book gave a myriad of scenarios of friendship development that began via structured and casual activities. These include work settings, classroom settings, church settings, support groups, volunteer activities, and social clubs, among others. Not only do shared activities bring us into close proximity with others, they also include parallel or shared tasks or pursuits with potential friends. These might involve classroom or professional projects, social events (such as steering committees for community events, leadership roles in an organization, and so on). Several of one woman's closest friendships were initiated through her involvement in a 12-step program for family members of substance abusers. She noted the strongly positive tone these friendships could take even after the sharing of details of the abuse suffered at the hands of family members. She noted that she and her new friends were rebuilding their lives and building friendships concurrently. She also elaborated on the sense of belonging and intimacy she could allow herself with friends who had experienced similar childhoods; thus, they could enjoy a deeper level of self-disclosure with one another than they might with other friends.

Life events are the third path via which we find new friends.[37,38] These situationally located events may range from the kind that bring great happiness, such as meeting other moms-to-be in a natural childbirth class, or bring sobering changes to our lives, such as a support group for widows. Though we may be exposed to new people and new places that provide opportunities to find new friends, it is often life events that set the stage for these opportunities. New jobs, new schools, and new life phases such as marriage, childbirth, and divorce are all life events that may introduce us to new people who may become friends. Life events place us in positions in which social support is sought, and in finding this support, we are building our social networks. The life events that brought our interviewees into new friendships were as diverse as being left by their husbands, giving birth, adopting children, returning to school, moving into a new town, and coming out as a lesbian in mid-adulthood, among many others. Each of these events, and others like them, will move us further along the path to finding new friendships based on fresh aspects of ourselves that come into our awareness and bring influence on our lives.

As we grow into the "next stage," however we define this, we may lose some of our existing friendships and feel the push to forge new alliances. The changes we witness in ourselves and our networks may alter our social identity and our own perceptions of our core identity. If left unchecked, we may start to limit our social outlets and social networks to only those friends who share a particular facet of our identity. A regretted example of this was shared by a 62-year-old divorcee. After her divorce was finalized, she chose to socialize exclusively with other divorcees. Although this shared experience offered the women a unique sense of empathy for one another, our interviewee said that she eventually felt overwhelmed by her friends' negativity and entrenched unhappiness. She felt isolated from the social world she had once known, so she forced herself to seek out new friends with whom she had things in common that had nothing to do with marital status. Her divorced friends had been unable to resolve the residual pain and anger related to their marital breakups and this led to an unbalanced relationship among friends. Maintaining balanced perceptions of our identities allows us to maintain diverse social networks.

Each of these three pathways to expanded social circles—proximity, shared activities, and life events—provides unique opportunities to create new connections with potential friends. The actual development of new friendships relies on our interest and motivation for forging new bonds, yet whether new friends are found through serendipity or necessity, similar phases or stages are involved in the process of friendship formation.

From Acquaintance to BFF ("Best Friends Forever")

One recent model of friendship development has been used to describe contemporary adult women's friendship.[39] This model, developed by Sias and Cahill, supports a developmental paradigm that pinpoints three significant transitions in evolving friendships: (1) Acquaintance-to-Friend, (2) Friend-to-Close Friend, and (3) Close Friend-to-Best Friend. During the initial stage, as we begin to consider an acquaintance as a potential friend, we are recognizing that we share some similarities with this person, and it is theorized that while these commonalities are becoming apparent, we are also developing an appreciation and affinity for one another.

Next, as our friendship commitment grows and we begin to enjoy shared activities, we learn even more about each other through mutual interactions; this self-disclosure helps the relationship transform from acquaintanceship to friendship. One interviewee, Laura, a 33-year-old teacher, described this transition as she shared how she and a co-worker had grown to be friends. Laura and a fellow teacher had classrooms that were side by side at school. They would smile and engage in surface conversation in the morning and at the end of the day. They began to time their exits from the building to coincide and the walk to their cars at the end of the workday became a pleasant daily ritual. Their relationship deepened when the colleague mentioned to Laura that she was having some problems with her husband that were similar to those Laura had experienced in a previous relationship. This connection was the springboard that moved the pair from acquaintances to friends as their trust and their self-disclosure grew.

As communication becomes increasingly focused on personal matters and as it grows in frequency, openness, and breadth, mutual trust also increases and it becomes safe to allow the relationship to grow into a close friendship. In the final stage of the Sias and Cahill model, a deep and unique bond is understood to grow from a combination of the engagement in shared interactions and the social support provided by shared communication. Best friends share a relationship that is less reliant on the common predictors or indicators attributed to the earlier stages of relationship building and they enjoy a unique and stable relationship that grows with them as a unique entity within itself.

The "BFF" acronym and all it represents have become a cultural phenomenon in recent years. These three letters have been popularized through media commercials and appears in everything from jewelry to tattoos! Whether the term is being used by preadolescent girls or adult women, it represents a special category of friendship that embodies the qualities described by the third stage of Sias and Cahill's model. True best friendships are able to withstand significant challenges and poor behavior that would likely lead to the breakup of less close friendships. A 24-year-old woman described her best friend as her "soul mate," and laughingly shared that if only her best friend were a guy, she'd have found her true love. She also noted that even though she and her best friend had gone a year without speaking to each other when they were in high school, they were able to get past their "blown way out of proportion" argument and the relationship had continued to strengthen since then. Women feel passionate about their closest girlfriends and recognize the rewards these relationships provide. In fact, research shows that the emotional strength of women's closest friendships is no different in intensity than their relationships with their husbands and lovers.[40] One 68-year-old interviewee shared that her husband knew from their first meeting that her "soul sisters" were part of the package—she says that decades later, "the deal is still the same." This sense of connection and expectation of commitment to friendships also gives rise to the need for equity in the relationship. And, contrary to the sentiment expressed in the old adage that "all is fair in love and war," there are several unspoken rules for fair play in friendships.

PLAYING BY THE RULES OF FRIENDSHIP

Friendships serve a variety of functions that are relatively consistent across the life span. Argyle and Henderson explored the roles and functions of friendships and they uncovered the presence of unspoken rules of friendship and found that there are more than 40 rules at play.[41] These rules fell into four categories: exchange rules (trading favors and services), intimacy rules (mutual trust and confidence-keeping), third-party rules (accepting that friends engage in additional relationships), and coordination rules (honoring your friend's privacy).[42] Breaking these rules can put relationships at risk and 10 of these 40 rules are most frequently cited as reasons for friendships ending or suffering significant damage. These rules are:

- Do not be jealous or critical of your friend's other relationships.
  I had a good friend who I'd been friends with since we were 12 years old. We'd been through so much together, teenage stuff, high school, romance; you know how drama-filled those years are. Well, after graduation, I met my future husband that summer. He and I were crazy about each other, knew that it was serious, and started spending a LOT of time together. Yeah, and my best friend, who'd stood by me through so much, and now that I was in a "real" relationship—suddenly my friend was jealous. I didn't have as much time as I used to for friends, Randy and I were moving fast—he was in the service and we wanted to get married. Then the kids came, and my best friend was like "Why can't you spend the day with me?" Sometimes friends just don't get it. But, now, with the kids getting older, I do have more time for friends, and we're starting to reconnect. And I am really glad about that. Rene, 42-year-old retail customer service manager
- Never break your friend's confidences.
  I was a sophomore in college and dating a guy that my parents didn't approve of. They'd never met him, but they had heard me talking about him, how wild he'd been in high school, the way he bragged on himself. I gave a really bad impression of him because he seemed "dangerous" and I thought that was sexy. My parents called my dorm room during a major college basketball game because they knew I'd be watching. Well, I was watching it, but at my boyfriend's apartment and I'd asked my roommate not to let my parents know I was seeing him. When my parents called, my roommate told them where I was. My dad got that phone number so fast, then called me there, and blessed me out every way but Sunday! I was so angry at my roommate and that started the end of our friendship. No,

I shouldn't have expected her to lie for me, but I do feel that she shouldn't have just volunteered the information, either. Lissa, 46-year-old antiques dealer

- Volunteer help when a friend is in need.
  [When my husband left me for another woman, my friends] were just so supportive. They just cared so much for me, they felt bad for me and they knew how bad I was hurt. I mean, they'd come get me out of bed when I couldn't do it myself in the beginning. They would still invite me to do things. One couple, they took me out to dinner with them every Friday night for a year after Steve left me. They were always there for me. All of my friends, except for one, stuck by me. They knew what had happened, and they were so good to me. Lorraine, 68-year-old teacher's aide

- Be willing to trust and confide in your friends.
  I got diagnosed with a really embarrassing disease. It isn't fatal or anything, but it won't ever go away. I got it from, well, a one-night-stand when I was 21, and I was really ashamed. I felt like a "ho," or something, and that's NOT who I am. I was so stressed by this and I wanted to keep it secret. And my best friend was worried about me. Kept checking in, asking me what was up. Finally, after I made her promise not to judge me, I told her. Her reaction was so supportive — she didn't judge me or make me feel bad. Really, telling her made me feel so much better! It's weird, how keeping a secret to yourself makes it seem so much worse. Sharing it with my friend really put things back in perspective, and though I am still embarrassed, it's not as bad as it used to be before I opened up to my friend. Jennifer, 23-year-old bartender

- Do not criticize a friend in front of others.
  My friends and I were at this lake party, and most of us are still in high school, but there were a couple of guys who had graduated a while back. I was wearing a new two-piece and I thought I looked hot! Well, we're on the beach and I grab a handful of chips. Then a girl I thought was a friend yells out, "Be careful, Katie! That bikini doesn't look big enough to hold much more!" What the . . . ? I couldn't even answer her back; I was so [ticked off], in front of everyone. Well, that was the last time I showed up anywhere I thought she would be. End of story. Katie, 17-year-old high school student

- Show your friend positive regard and empathy.
  What do I value most about my friends? Unconditional love from my best friend is what I value most. No matter what one of us does or the other one does, we're going to be there for one another. Not all friends are like that. When I have problems with others, my best friends listen to me, respect my feelings, and let me know that they

are okay with whatever decision I feel is right for me. That really means the world to me! Amanda, 24-year-old stay-at-home mother

- Stand up for your friends when they are not present.

I lost a friend who was my best friend just recently. He lived down the road from me and we were always just hanging out together until something happened between him and his girlfriend. He treated her very badly and she was one of my closest friends. He didn't take responsibility for hurting her [when I tried to talk to him about it], so he's no longer a friend. I had to stand up for her because of what he did to her. Kim, 17-year-old high school student

- Understand that your friend has other friends and be accepting of these friends.

I have sets of friends. Some friends are on my tennis team, some are in the neighborhood, some are at the club, some are from work. I even have friends I've had since I was in my twenties! And there are times when I have conflicts, like one group plans something, another group plans something else. I'm lucky; they all seem to get that I can't just plan my life around one group. And when we have our annual July 4 extravaganza at our house, everyone is invited—adults, kids, it's a huge party—and everyone has a great time, gets to meet new people, it's fun. Vickie, 57-year-old human resources manager

- Show your friends emotional support.

[My best friend] is the most giving, loving person and treats people with such respect and dignity. She's very self-sacrificing. She's a teacher, but she's also a licensed massage therapist. The night my mother's husband, my stepdad, died, my friend came over and she gave us massages until midnight. She does things like that. I think she's a little more selfless than I am. Beth, 47-year-old teacher

- Don't nag your friends and do try to make them feel good.

A friend and I decided to join a weight-loss club together last spring. I needed to lose a lot more weight than she did, but she was "über eager" for us to help each other stay motivated. This worked fine until I got sidelined by some personal struggles, and rather than being empathic and accepting, my friend started nagging me about going to the meetings, exercising more, everything. Support I wanted, guilt-tripping I didn't need! Sindy, 38-year-old administrative assistant

The common threads that run through the research and our conversations with women and girls of all ages include the pleasures of shared experiences among friends and their commitment to one another. Friends allow us to be human, to need others and to be needed, and to feel accepted just as we are—no matter how imperfect or "in progress" we may be. Whether a friendship begins through small talk or you meet someone and a friendship arises almost organically without effort, we find that women and men typically experience friendship in two uniquely different paradigms.

GENDER DIFFERENCES IN HOW FRIENDSHIPS ARE DONE

The last quarter of the twentieth century opened up a new perspective on gender roles and gender enactment. As androgyny became more acceptable for both genders, men were invited to explore their feminine side concurrently with the birth of the "metrosexual" movement. Although many men may be uncomfortable with the idea, even mainstream, masculine consumer product marketing is flirting with inviting men to acknowledge their more emotional sides. A series of beer commercials used a tagline that became a part of media culture; the deep-voiced "I love you, man" admission still resonates on Internet video sites and apparel items. The portrayal of "regular guys" acknowledging their deeper feelings over campfires, ball games, or gas grills grew traction as it humorously supported the breach of an unspoken cultural taboo against the expression of affection for another man. "How-to" guides appeared online to help men share an acceptable "man hug." These took a humorous dig at the strong antipathy society communicates toward public displays of affection between heterosexual men. Regardless of the apparent easing of cultural constraints, evidence of a gender divide regarding social interaction with friends is not hard to find.

Compared to women, men are much less likely to participate in self-disclosure with their same-gender friends—including the discussion of feelings and fears.[43,44,45,46,47] Women also enjoy more emotional support exchanges with others outside their nuclear families than men do.[48] Men actually *do* experience distress when they talk about personal feelings and emotions.[49] They prefer to engage in less-intimate discussions with friends and stick to current or topical events and they prefer the conversation include more people than women might.[50] It has been suggested that these differences can be traced back to evolutionary patterns of survival instincts and behavior. Women were traditionally expected to leave their families and kin at marriage to join their husband's family household. Diplomacy and strong social skills were necessary for forging solid relational ties with the nonkin members of her new household. Because men continued to dwell among their kin and existing social networks, less-intimate disclosure and fewer one-on-one interactions were necessary, as relational ties would already be strong. Regardless of whether ancient social patterns determined our contemporary preferences, most men definitely prefer less self-disclosure and larger group settings than women.

Another persistent gender variation in friendship patterns involves just how "friendship is done." Men prefer "doing" activities with friends over just "being" with friends and women expect friendships to be more reciprocal than men do.[51] Women prefer friends who can serve a variety of functions in their lives—whether they opt for just one good friend or a large group of friends, women prefer that each of them be one with whom they can confide, shop, dine, walk, and so on.[52] Men, however, create social networks that include what have been termed "activity friends," "convenience friends," and "mentor friends."[53] These groups consist of friends such as poker buddies, carpoolers, and the neighbors from whom they borrow snowblowers, respectively. Whereas women's friendship patterns may be attributed to genetic programming for survival among nonkin groups, men's obstacles to closer friendships have traditionally been attributed to three factors.[54,55,56] First, competition between men may keep intimate friendships from forming, which may also be a genetically programmed response. In concern over scarce resources, including food, shelter, potential mates, and safety, men may perceive close friendships as threats to their control of resources. Second, traditional stereotypes support the image of males as the strong, silent, independent gender that does not need to rely on others for survival or success. Finally, especially for heterosexual men, there is a pervasive fear of homosexuality—either being perceived as gay or opening up to feelings of attraction to another man—and this limits men's interest in intimate friendships. However, recent shifts in our culture have allowed—or encouraged—a collection of "men's movements" to organize and become visible. Many of these groups strongly promote the involvement of men more fully in intimate relationships with their partners, their male friends, and their communities. Perhaps this century will see the men leave their "den" or "man cave" and more fully and authentically develop friendships with increased depth and openness.

Regardless of how a friendship plays out, whether it is deepened through mutual self-disclosure of thoughts, feelings, and core identity, or through companionship and engagement in shared activities, friendships protect us from loneliness, isolation, and compromised physical and mental health. Although women seek kindness and emotional support from their friends more so than men,[57] men do value their friends and also reap the benefits of stress reduction and decreased susceptibility to prolonged depression from their own style of friendship. Women tend to seek out a shoulder to cry on when things get tough; men rely on the "buddy system" and active engagement to help them de-stress.

II

FRIENDSHIP CHRONOLOGY

4

❧❧❧

Early Childhood
First Friends

This chapter will acquaint you with the role friendship plays for young children from birth through elementary school. It will highlight the importance of friendship for the earliest years of life, styles of attachment, and the implications for later friendship development. This chapter will describe how children make friendship decisions including how children behave with their friends when the behaviors are successful in friendship formation and maintenance and when they are not so successful.

Friendships are sought after and treasured from early childhood into old age. As adults, we tend to recognize friendship between two people as an outward commitment, the verbalization of intimate feelings, and the sharing of life experiences. However, young children are not talk-oriented but rather activity-focused. They live in the present and are too young to have shared years of experiences. Thus, adults can frequently miss the signs or undervalue the power of friendship between two youngsters.

As early as age 3, researchers have found that many children can name a best friend, and virtually all children can do so within a couple of years.[1] These friendships are not just temporary attractions or distractions. Given the opportunity, children maintain their early friendships for years.[2] Barbara, a mother and playschool director who was interviewed, stated that it is "amazing how early children choose friends." Children as young as 2 show strong friend preferences and, over the course of her 25 years as playschool director, she has heard from many young adults and teenagers who are still close with the friends they made at her playschool. She has also seen many very young children grieve the loss of a friend who withdraws from their class. Thanks to Barbara's knowledge and sensitivity to young children's perspectives, her own grown daughter was able to maintain a friendship with a playschool friend that began when they were 4 years old. The friend's family eventually moved away, but the mothers helped them maintain the friendship by arranging two regular contacts each year. Once they were a little older, the girls were able to maintain the friendship by letter writing and, nowadays, using email. More than 22 years later, one playschool friend was a bridesmaid in the other's wedding. Several of the women interviewed for this book continue to cherish friends dating back to diaper days. The intensity of young children's attachment to friends may become readily apparent once you have witnessed the sadness and tears when a play date comes to an end.

EVERYONE LIKES TO PLAY

Every child benefits from having at least a friend or two. Young children we interviewed expressed the desire to spend large amounts of time with friends, and if given the choice, they stated a preference for playing with friends over spending time with family. One little girl cleverly solved the family–friend dichotomy by stating that she'd like to play with her friends and family together. A few young girls said they'd like to have more friends; most children, however, expressed general satisfaction with the number of friends they had. It's interesting to note that the number of friends the young girls claimed was wide-ranging, from a close-knit set of 3 friends to 100 friends (perception is important!). All children desire and enjoy having friends, yet each child has a particular set of friendship needs that underlie her own friendship temperament.

Parents may worry when their child's preference for affiliation is not what they hoped it would be; however, early childhood experts recognize an innate variability in children's preference for sociability. The most notably sociable of children are also generally the strongest extroverts. Gaining emotional energy by interacting with others, they may have large friendship networks, spend many hours with friends, and hold the expectation that friends should be readily available at most times. These sociable children are less likely to spend time alone in social settings and more likely to move in packs. Introverted children can also be social but are more likely to have a smaller number of friendships than extroverted age mates. Introverts invest much time and energy into relationships and often find a strong sense of security with the higher level of intimacy provided by more intense relationships. Independent children often have a handful of friendly and satisfying relationships, but friendships that are not especially close or intimate. Overall, sociable children more often initiate collaboration; less sociable children exhibit more individualistic behavior.[3]

What Do Children Seek in Friends?

Children's earliest friendships are often dictated by their parents' choice of friends. The most frequent alliances between two toddlers stem from the regular and frequent interaction between their mothers. Whether it is mothers who meet weekly to share a cup of coffee or connect at events involving older children, this regular contact forms a bond between youngsters. As infants, they begin to smile at each other and, as they learn how to interact with one another, they grow increasingly comfortable in each other's presence. Sometimes these early friendships begin in playschool, church child care, or other community-based groups. Once children enter school, peer choice increasingly determines friends.

School-age children have a variety of children from which to choose their companions; these are the years when friendships and popularity grow in importance. There are significant differences between children who are popular and children who are easily able to make friends—being popular and having friends are not one and the same. One social schema for children places kids in one of six social groupings along the popularity continuum: very popular, accepted, average, neglected, controversial, and rejected.[4] The "very popular" grouping holds the class leaders, children with strong social skills and a good bit of social power. Unequivocally social creatures, the majority of children fall into the "accepted" category, meaning they are generally well-liked by their peers; these children could be considered somewhat popular. They are smart, friendly, not overly aggressive or disruptive in the classroom. Children in the "average" or "ambiguous" group may not be popular, but they do have friends. Though the remaining three categories are composed of much a smaller percentage of children, these kids experience more frequent painful social circumstances than others. Children who are "neglected" by their peers tend to be less sociable, quiet, nondisruptive, and perform fine academically, so their teachers do not fret about them either. "Controversial" children tend to be the clowns, rebels, cut-ups, and lightweight bullies. A few children fall into the most worrisome "rejected" grouping. These kids often experience high levels of peer rejection and may be unduly teased by their peers. They may respond by becoming either explosive or socially withdrawn and may become the "school bully" or the "outcast." With few or no friends and limited social skills, these children are at the highest risk for major behavioral and emotional problems.

Some children tend to be downright popular with their peers from their earliest years. Studies on young children's peer choices show that children choose to spend the bulk of their free time with the peers that provide the most positive social interactions and devote little time with the remaining kids in the class.[5] Popular children's peers see them as "safe to be around" and predictable in that they are generally well-behaved and not overly emotionally reactive.[6] Moreover, popular children tend to have that elusive quality of charisma that is often paired with a great sense of humor, making them fun to be around. Children with many friends tend to be more self-confident, cooperative, altruistic, and socially competent than children with few or no friends.[7] Considering the wide range of behaviors children display in social settings, it is easy to wonder what exactly *social competence* looks like for young children.

As soon as children become aware of each other, they begin to engage in parallel play—playing *alongside* each other, not with each other. But as children mature, they seek interaction and their play begins to require social skills such as cooperation and turn-taking. Barbara, the playschool director, explained that this is when skilled teachers and/or parents should encourage children to develop those crucial social skills. She explained that each child naturally likes to be in charge of play but must learn to "self-regulate the need to be boss," take turns, and be respectful of their friends' needs and wants.

According to the research and the young girls interviewed, children prefer to play with children who are "nice" to them. Young children typically experience this kindness through the sharing of toys. In fact, the single most important friendship-winning skill for a child is the ability to share.[8] Very young children expressed sharing in very concrete terms such as "she shares her dolls with me." Early on, children become aware of who does and does not share well. Andrea, a 4-year-old preschooler, began naming the "best sharers" and the "worst sharers" in her class. She said the best sharer "knows the rules" while the worst sharer frequently asserts, "That's mine!"

The Gift of Fitting In

Children enjoy socializing and most have at least a few friends they can count on to play with on the playground or sit with at lunch. While the average preschooler has one or two friends, the average school-age child has three to five "best friends."[9] Childhood friends tend to have similarities in a host of realms. These may be environmental factors as well as personal characteristics. Communities are often composed of families with similar education levels, incomes, and interests. The children often attend the same schools, the same religious institutions, and the same organizations that support the community. Homogenous, interacting communities of people tend to create a system of mutually reinforcing socialization. Therefore, children tend to reinforce each other's behaviors in ways that fit within a community's norms and expectations.

Children with differing cultural norms or personal interests may have difficulty breaking into a tightly bound group of kids. Even very young children put pressure on their friends to refrain from play with children who are not part of their "in group."[10] Cliques may become particularly intense starting around second or third grade. Amy, now a young woman, reflected that her earliest childhood friendship experiences were positive. However, when her family moved to a new town, the children were so different from her she felt out of place for a long time and painfully remembers the "feelings of being a misfit." Even within a homogenous community, some children feel out of place. A child may have an interest unique in her social circle that sets her apart from others. One young girl shared a sense of frustration in response to the teasing she received due to her love of playing the violin—quite a departure from the activities other young girls enjoyed in her community in the rural Deep South. Friendships can cross cultural lines and friends can certainly differ in interests. For example, one 8-year-old girl, Bea, loved to draw and paint; her best friend was more inclined toward sports. Friendship pairs often display forms of similarity not as readily apparent to untrained observers such as temperament, activity levels, degree of school success, and level of language acquisition.

Current research indicates that personality development is influenced by the interaction between inherited temperament and actual experiences with caregivers and peers.[11] One study of preschool children found that mutual friends were similar in the level of aggression, peer competence, and peer acceptance.[12] Brooke, a conscientious and agreeable 7-year-old who is well-liked in her class, described this affinity when she responded to the question "How do you choose who is going to be your friend?" She said, "I look at if they get in trouble or if they are friendly. If they get in trouble I'm not that good of friends with them." This makes sense, but leaves the more aggressive children left to befriend each other, for better or worse. Though some intervention programs encourage interaction between less socially skilled children and more skilled peers to promote competence, left to make their own choices, children who are high in social skills tend to befriend each other and form an "in crowd" early on.[13]

Children's school experiences clearly affect their social and emotional well-being. Beyond the clear benefits derived from learning to read or solve math equations, children who perform well academically are often at a social advantage. Teachers tend to rate strong performers higher on likeability scales.[14] Early on, children notice which peers earn the teacher's praise or reprimands. Because school-aged children universally seek attention and yearn for approval from adults, they will gravitate to the kids who receive her approval. Academic success reinforces social position and self-esteem for children and higher academic self-perceptions have been linked to leadership skills.[15] In turn, leaders generally have low social anxiety and exhibit a secure orientation to their peers. This suggests that being a strong student can lead to strong and successful social connections and friendship formations.

Language acquisition is essential to academic success, but it is also integral to social success. According to psychologist John Gottman, two children are able to become friends if they are able to: (1) exchange information successfully, (2) establish a common ground activity, and (3) manage conflicts.[16] Though these abilities typically manifest as physical behaviors for toddlers, the use of language to negotiate this terrain grows increasingly important with age. A child who is either too far ahead or too far behind her peers in language proficiency may suffer some degree of social disconnection. Although an advanced vocabulary may cause a child to sound more like an adult than an age mate and even intimidate or confuse potential friends, indistinct enunciation or a limited vocabulary may put off peers and limit potential friends to those younger than she is. The ability to use words and language effectively is crucial to successful communication. Even at an early age, the gift of gab is a girl's good friend.

As a child attempts to move from playing with a single new friend to playing with a group, the skills involved become even more challenging and complex. In a series of research studies on social exchange patterns between children, researchers found that a child's performance when trying to enter the play of a group of youngsters greatly influenced peer judgment and behavior toward the child.[17,18] A child who can assess the framework of a peer group and establish "common ground" or connected verbal exchanges has the highest likelihood of being accepted. The second most successful entrance to a peer group occurs when a child is able to move a formal connection to a friendly connection, such as chatting with a group of fellow students after class. Unsuccessful attempts to enter a group were marked by disruptive behaviors, self-focused comments, and disorganized behavior such as moving around a lot or incoherent talking such as mumbling. The exchanges that surround disagreements between children also influence a group's level of acceptance of a child. Children involved in disagreements, but still accepted by peers, usually provided a "rule" or reason that the ongoing activity should be done their way. Socially successful children have learned to accurately observe other children's behaviors and interests, to assertively vocalize their desire to join a group, to control their urge to dominate, as well to rationalize "rules" for play when they'd like to influence the play at hand. This is a sophisticated set of skills that must be mastered for children's friendships to succeed!

Venetian Girls and Martian Boys

Starting in preschool, children increasingly choose same-sex friends through the early years of puberty. The young girls we interviewed most often volunteered only other girls as "best friends." It was only when discussing their specific play activities or when the topic of boys was explicitly broached did they include boys in their list of close playmates. Most girls reported a preference for playing with girls rather than boys and for playing with their friends over playing with their families. However, preferences are often overruled when only brothers or neighborhood boys are available for play activities.

In a study examining group behavior of 10-year-old children, the girls preferred more intimate relationships and tended to join groups with fewer children; boys tended toward larger groups.[19] Even within groups, girls tended to focus more on individuals within the group rather than attending to the group as a whole. Generally, boys prefer larger groups with more active play. They also tended to be more competitive in groups or individually than the girls. Boys tend to be most competitive when in groups with unfamiliar children. Girls display the exact opposite tendency—they are more cooperative in groups with unfamiliar people than familiar people. Several mothers we interviewed also mentioned the tendency for their daughters to enjoy one-on-one relationships more than large-group interactions. And the need for relationship balance among young girls was supported by the many mothers who affirmed that a trio of girls trying to play together usually leads to hurt feelings, as it seems that one girl always ends up feeling left out. The "third wheel" syndrome is felt by even the youngest school girl.

Conflicts Are Inevitable

When children enter into conflicts with their playmates, their general lack of inhibition and limited self-control often makes it quite noticeable. Toddlers are notorious for their tantrums and for giving their friends a solid bite or hair pull. As children gain verbal skills, self-control, and social skills, conflicts become less frequent and less physical. In a "successful" disagreement, a child will practice calming herself down, increasing her tolerance for frustration, and, hopefully, offering a potential compromise or solution to the disagreement. When a child performs these tasks on her own, she is actively learning conflict management skills that can last a lifetime. Tensions, though, arise at every age and stage, even among close friends. One mother described her daughter Lucy's friendship with the next-door neighbor as "three hours of play and fifteen minutes of fight—every day." This pair of 6-year old girls typifies the joy and drama of little-girl friendship. They enjoy a variety of play activities from very active running, jumping, and dancing to quieter doll tea time. Their playtime, however, is interspersed with heated pushing, yelling, and sporadic tattling. These arguments are particularly frequent and heated on the days when a third little girl joins the duo. And though each girl's feelings get hurt in the process, their sustained friendships demonstrate how amazingly resilient *and* forgiving children can be.

Bullying is a different sort of conflict that involves a persistent pattern of one child trying to take away the power of another. It may start as early as preschool, where a child regularly targets another by physically hurting her or continually taking her toys. Though many people envision the classical image of a large boy physically picking on a smaller boy, bullying takes many forms—some of which girls are notorious for mastering. Bullying can appear as a classmate writing a mean note about another girl in class, calling her names at lunch, making fun of her clothes, or consistently and purposely leaving her out of group play. In later childhood, around 10 years old, "stealing" friends and gossiping are typical, but malevolent, forms of female bullying.

A bullied child often loses confidence and feels threatened, intimidated, and even physically ill. Children who bully have often been bullied by older children and may feel jealous or insecure. They may use bullying behavior to seek attention through a highly inappropriate and hurtful way. They may believe their behavior makes them appear smarter or stronger to their peers. Although most schools have implemented a zero-tolerance policy for bullying, it still occurs in more covert forms. Bullying is a very serious and cruel relationship for anyone to experience; its ramifications may be carried by both the bully and the victim for years. If your child is either bullying or being bullied, please schedule a visit with his or her school counselor. There are also books available in your public library that may help you help your child understand and put an end to the painful interactions.

FAMILY

Family greatly influences an individual's friendship network in a wide variety of ways—parents shape our formative attachments, model social skills, and possibly provide siblings as playmates. In addition, they often shape our play activities from our earliest years through the gifts of gender-specific toys such as large Tonka trucks and footballs for rougher play to boys and tea sets and dolls for nurturing to girls. Fathers are more likely to give their baby boys a little toss in the air than their little girls. Girls are taught to be modest, gentle, and willing to compromise. Yet, as children, women may learn even more foundational relationship behaviors from interactions with their parents.

Attachment Theory

The concept of attachment and its role in interpersonal relationships has been well researched over the years. Each of us has our own individual attachment style that is presumed to be formed during the first two years of life and that reflects our relationship with our primary caregivers, usually our parents. According to attachment theory, if a parent is warm, consistent, and responsive to an infant's needs, the child develops a secure attachment to the parent. A secure child feels confident that her parent is available when needed and is more willing to explore her surroundings. A serious deficit in parenting leads to one of three types of insecure attachment styles: anxious–avoidant, ambivalent or resistant, or disorganized. With unresponsive or inconsistent care giving, children experience higher levels of fear and anxiety in their worlds. They lack the comfort of knowing their caregivers will be there to support them and they are less likely to bravely explore their environments. In the long term, these children have either a tenuous relationship or an adversarial one with their primary caregivers.[20]

Many theorists believe that our mental and emotional foundation, our "internal working model," for future relationships is developed during these early years. This means that healthy relationships with parents set the stage for healthy relationships with peers and, in later life, romantic partners. Securely attached children tend to be outgoing, independent, and able to initiate successful social encounters with peers. These qualities generally remain stable over childhood years. A secure attachment orientation, a positive internal model of self, a positive model of others, and low social anxiety were found to be related to peer leadership qualities in fourth and fifth graders.[21] This overall disposition can be termed *pro-social*.

For a variety of reasons, not everyone's parents are physically and emotionally available during the early years. This often results in less secure attachment styles for their children. According to Sroufe, who has studied the behavioral implications of attachment styles of children, anxious–avoidant children tend to be active play participants but are liable to be hostile, negative, and distant.[22] They tend to elicit bullying behaviors from those around them and sometimes become bullies themselves. Bullies are often the product of rejecting, emotionally distant parenting; their victims tend to have over-involved parents. Anxious–resistant children tend to have poor peer relationship skills and to display helplessness, overly dependent behavior, and a tendency to become visibly distressed. They may be dominant in some social situations, but they tend to rank low in peer status.[23]

Best friend relationships are influenced by the attachment histories of both children. In a study of 4-year-old best friend pairs, when both children had secure parental attachments, their play was more harmonious, less controlling, more responsive, and happier than among pairs where one member was insecurely attached.[24] Although we may assume that "birds of a feather flock together," it is important to point out a major contrasting view on attachment styles. Not all researchers, and definitely not all women, believe that attachment style is set in concrete during childhood. Some interviewees reported that a friend later in childhood, the teen years, or even a life partner changed their outlook on relationships in general. It is entirely possible to progress from general insecurity in relationships to a more secure way of interacting and believing in one's self and the goodness and dependability of one's friends at any age.

Parents as Role Models

The child–parent relationship influences our level of security in relationships in general, but in addition, parents model friendship behaviors as well as social skills. We may learn to value friendships from observing our parents. Several of the women we interviewed who were particularly skilled in friendship building shared that they recalled that as children they saw their own mothers model the formation and maintenance of healthy and treasured friendships. Although women across the spectrum engaged in "girls' night out" and valued their friends, women whose mothers had overtly modeled healthy friendship behaviors were more likely to make time with friends an absolute priority. As a counterpoint, some women had seen how lonely their mothers had been without good friends and this fostered a determination to cultivate friends—requiring that they learn through trial and error how to befriend.

Siblings

Sibling rivalry may be a sore spot for children and parents alike, but the presence of siblings improves our social skills. Though not every study has shown a clear difference between only children and children with siblings,[25] in a study of more than 20,000 kindergarteners, teachers rated children with at least one sibling as significantly higher in interpersonal skills and self-control and lower in behavior problems than only children.[26] In fact, children with either brothers or sisters—sibling gender didn't matter—were rated higher in (1) forming and maintaining friendships; (2) getting along with people who are different; (3) providing comfort or help to other children; (4) expressing feelings, ideas, and opinions in a positive way; and (5) showing sensitivity to the feelings of others. Because siblings have similar levels of power, children have the opportunity to learn conflict negotiation skills and sharing with peer-level others. With the high number of opportunities available for disagreements among siblings, it seems evident that when it comes to learning how to get along with others, siblings provide almost nonstop opportunities for practice, practice, and more practice.

Violence in the Home

When children are sexually, physically, or emotionally abused, they carry this pain with them into the world of childhood friendships and later adult relationships. Witnessing adult domestic violence is similarly detrimental to children's well-being. If children experience violence at a young age, they may demonstrate insecure foundations for relationship formation. When life's early experiences cause a child to fear the reoccurrence of abuse, she may find it difficult to learn how to trust others.

Individuals react to trauma differently and children's responses will vary according to age, gender, and the intensity of the violence. Some common reactions are feelings of guilt, shame, self-blame, and feelings of hopelessness and helplessness. These feelings hinder our ability to learn necessary social skills and may ultimately inhibit our ability to form healthy, assertive, egalitarian relationships with friends. Children in violent homes may be particularly passive in their friendships or, conversely, have very stormy relationships. When we have lived with people who physically assault or belittle others, using demeaning remarks, name-calling, or other psychological bullying, we do not learn to discriminate appropriate types of relationship behaviors. These children may experience isolation from friends, lack an escape from their grim family circumstances, and suffer from the absence of a shoulder to lean on. Continued isolation can worsen the problem for children over the years as they grow up without a sense of being loved or supported and without the opportunity to learn or practice healthy relationship behaviors. People who experience violence in the home as children are more likely to enter abusive relationships in adulthood than those who experienced a safe, stable home environment.[27]

Experiencing violence in the home does not have to be a life sentence of remembered trauma. Healing can occur through engagement in healthy relationships filled with support, warmth, and acceptance. Counseling is available in most communities through domestic violence nonprofit organizations, community or private counseling services, or employee assistance programs. If you feel unable to seek help from a professional for any reason, there are many books are available to help women heal from childhood violence and abuse. It is important to note that if any form of child abuse is currently taking place or the victim is still a child (not an adult), all professionals are legally mandated to involve social services for the safety of the child. If you know of a child experiencing abuse, it is vital that you seek help for her or him.

NEIGHBORHOOD

Neighborhoods vary across the country, the state, and even the town. Many neighborhood characteristics drastically influence a child's formation and maintenance of friendships. For instance, consider the density of potential friends in a city compared to the suburbs or the countryside. In addition to the availability of young people, the safety of a given neighborhood can determine whether children enjoy ready access to each other's homes or yards. Some children are fortunate enough to live in safe neighborhoods dense with potential friends and some children enjoy easy access to natural parks and playgrounds. When they live close to each other and in safe environments, children begin visiting each other's homes starting around age 4. Slightly older children find open areas in the neighborhood to play sports, build forts, and seek out other private spaces considered free of adult supervision.

Sadly, there is growing concern about child molestation and kidnapping; understandably, parents are limiting their children's outdoor activities. In the well-researched book *Last Child in the Woods*, Louv argued that not only is this restriction unnecessary (or at least ineffective), because most molestations and abductions occur by perpetrators known to the family, but also this movement indoors negatively affects children psychologically, socially, and physically. He has suggested that children who are kept indoors and forbidden unencumbered access to friends, nature, and free play exhibit higher incidences of depression, ADHD, isolation, reduced creativity, and obesity. Nearly all the children we interviewed reported that playing outside or some form of outdoor play such as riding bikes was the favorite play activity with friends. Even in reference to school friends, children mentioned playing on the playground together as a favorite pastime. Children love to play outside with their friends and safe outdoor areas and time with friends are important for the healthy development of children.[28]

HAPPINESS AND HEALTH FOR A LIFETIME

Having good friends when young has been related to enjoying friends, happiness, and well-being over the life span. Friendships buffer us from stress and equip us to face new and challenging situations at every age and stage in life. Even when we are very young, friendships help us develop our physical abilities through active play; our cognitive abilities through imaginative play; and, most of all, our social skills through all kinds of interactive play. Having confidence to thrive in social situations is a major benefit for success in school and on the playground. If a young child does not learn to communicate well and share with peers, her school days and her efforts at making friends will become increasingly difficult. In adolescence, our friends help us prepare to know ourselves better and to move to the next level of social challenges, such as coupling in early adulthood. In each instance, successful friendships enrich our daily life and help us to achieve developmental milestones.[29] Positive experiences with supportive reciprocal friendships increase self-worth and well-being, laying the groundwork for future well-being and strong coping skills. The benefits of healthy friendships commence in early childhood and continue to accrue throughout the years. Whether it was playing kickball, playing hide-and-seek, digging for worms, or bringing Barbie dolls to the park, experiencing joy and laughter with our early friends provides us with positive "play memories" that stay with us throughout our lives.

5

⤞⤝

Adolescent Friendships
Seeking Ourselves in Our Friends

This chapter explores the passionate role friendship plays in the lives of adolescents. We look at identity development in terms of an adolescent's search for self and how this search is influenced by the presence or absence of good friends. Cliques, school and activity involvement, mood disorders, and family issues are also viewed through a lens of their influence on friendship development.

Whether they are good times or bad, the teen years are a period of self-exploration, powerful emotions, and tumultuous peer relations. Even brand names and hairstyles can weigh heavily on an adolescent girl's level of social and self-acceptance, and friends are particularly crucial to a young woman's successful navigation of this life stage. And what adolescent friendships lack in stability, they make up in intensity. Ashton, 16, shared this story:

On a scale from 1 to 10 for being a close friend, Morgan is a 10. I love her because she is loyal, supportive, and wants what is best for me. She tells me everything about her life. I can tell her anything too. We've gone through a lot together. She comes to the beach with me and my family each year. We were at a restaurant together when her grandfather died. We both came from a really small town elementary school. We started middle school together and whenever she met someone I became friends with that person. When I'd meet someone, she'd become friends with them too. It was nice to always have each other to rely on when meeting other kids. We do a ton of fun things together like go to games, tailgate, and hang out at our friends' houses. But one of my favorite things about Morgan is that I can be crazy around her. Sometimes I'm shy but not with her. We "dance" in the car driving around the mall parking lot. We rolled and spooned a friend's house. That was fun. We dressed in black with paint on our faces. We snuck around by rolling under bushes like secret agents. The guys tried to roll our house in return but we caught them—they had tried to roll it at 9:30 at night!

Christine, 41 years old, reflects on her best friend from adolescence:

I was crazy about a new friend I met when I was 10 years old. She was my new next-door neighbor, Veronica. I was a quiet tomboy, spending most of my time reading and daydreaming and she was outrageous and funny. I just adored her and she laughed at things I said and did too. As I entered adolescence, she introduced me to the amusement of having Barbie and Ken dolls do rather mature things with each other. We ate ice cream off the kitchen table, no bowls, no spoons. Starting in middle school, we used a hanger to pull up the zipper on our too-tight jeans. We became cheerleaders; we chased boys and reveled in them chasing us; and we pushed the limits relating to what was and was not exactly legal for minors to imbibe. Most of the time, we were inseparable; once in a while, she would "dump" me for either her older cousin who she worshipped or for a guy with a car. But in my opinion, I never, ever put her second.

After getting into a good bit of trouble together, her parents sent her to a boarding school for high school and my family moved away. A year later when her mother was killed in a car accident, I immediately hitch-hiked the 360 miles to be with her. Though I was only 14 years old, there was nothing I would not have done for her. In retrospect, I know the dumping part wasn't considerate and I know we got in a LOT of trouble together, but we had fun, we were committed to each other, and to this day, even though we live states apart and are even more dissimilar as adults, I still love, trust, and feel a connection to Veronica in a way that could never be replicated by another adult friend.

Our Bodies, Our Selves

The most difficult challenges of adolescence are usually considered to be the physical changes that it brings. And due to the visibility of these changes, they influence friendships at a level atypical of other developmental periods. For boys, height and muscularity are key components in peer acceptance as well as personal self-esteem. Boys are generally more popular if they are on the taller side and at least somewhat muscular. These characteristics tend to offer an athletic advantage that plays a further part increasing self-confidence, for some, and peer acceptance for the majority. But the relationship between physical development and social acceptance for girls is much more complicated. In many instances, it can be painful.[1]

Girls who physically develop earlier than peers gain the attention of boys and girls alike, but that attention may come with an unpleasant cost. Early breast development, in particular, places a girl under the peer microscope. One tall, physically well-developed sixth grader we interviewed shared that remarks about her body make her feel self-conscious and are especially painful when they come from girls who she considered as friends. In a side interview, her mother added that even longtime friends of hers have made unkind comments about her daughter's physique. A mother of an eighth grader shared that her own daughter faced social challenges in second grade when her daughter's breasts began developing; she was made fun of by the other girls for wearing a bra so young. The reactions of others place early maturing girls into a social context different from their age-mates. This often leads to negative consequences including higher involvement with older boys, increased conflict with adults, higher levels of delinquent behavior, and increased psychological distress, particularly depression.[2]

In some cases, and under certain conditions, girl may enjoy the extra attention generated by their early development, but the enjoyment is often double-edged. One adult interviewee disclosed that her looks helped her socially when she was a teen. But due to several factors, especially shyness, she was not popular as an adolescent. Yet because she was considered "pretty," she was not "shut out" of social life completely. On the flip side, she was tacitly expected to tolerate inappropriate behavior from males—including visits to her afterschool workplace from the assistant principal of her high school. Though his behavior and comments were clearly unethical, it is sadly not uncommon to find that males, even authority figures, give inappropriate, sexualizing attention to physically developed teen girls. This can catapult these adolescent girls into a very different and surprising social world.

Still young and ill-equipped to handle males' sexual innuendo clearly leaves some teens feeling degraded. Relationships with their peers and sometimes with adults may become awkward. The ongoing attention paid to a young woman's physical development may come at a cost of self-respect; she may view herself as an object or a body to be displayed— perhaps appreciated, perhaps just coarsely critiqued. Another hazard the physically mature teen might face is whether she is perceived as "easy" or promiscuous. Even with little trouble finding a date for Friday night, she may suffer the risk of being accepted by males only for her appearance or being rejected by females for appearing overly sexy. Physically mature girls may unintentionally intimidate less-developed peers, thus risking increased and unexpected rejection. Life experiences associated with earlier maturation may bear upon a woman forever; studies have found associations between early maturation and lower life satisfaction, smaller social networks, and poorer relationship quality into early adulthood.[3]

Being a "late bloomer" is no picnic either. As girls gain interest in boys, girls who are found attractive by boys gain social clout. Girls often want to hang out with the girls who have this social power, hoping the clout will "rub off" on the less powerful girls by association. Conversely, adolescent girls typically avoid those with lower social power to avoid the risk of compromising their own status. Thus, a less physically developed teen may be disregarded by her peers.

These forces create a somewhat narrow place for "acceptable" physical development. Teen interviewees consistently mentioned the issues of appearance at length. In adolescence, girls critique themselves and others on every aspect of appearance. One 13-year-old admitted that she spends hours looking at herself in the mirror trying to figure out how to improve her looks so *everyone* will "like her." Adolescence is a time when appearance is conflated with acceptance. The following is just a sampling of teen girl concerns: location and density of freckles; eye color; nose width and length; skin color; teeth whiteness; and hair color, density, and texture (especially for African American girls); and the even more pernicious trait of weight. Despite parental or programmatic efforts to educate teens about realistic body image expectations and to increase internal motivation and improve girl self-esteem, teens still judge themselves and peers against rigid and often unattainable standards of beauty. This emphasis on appearance is a major contributor in the occurrence of eating disorders. An estimated 7 million American females suffer from an eating disorder, and the average age of onset is 11 to 13 years of age.[4] Many adolescent girls with a poor body image and low self-esteem, however, do not develop full-blown eating disorders but frequently engage in moderately poor or restrictive eating habits. This strong emphasis on appearance often leaves girls stranded, lonely, and suffering emotionally. But good, true friends are often able to help a young woman counter this looks-based attack with support and unconditional love regardless of bra size or body fat. A friend's acceptance of a girl's appearance was a frequently reported bonding factor by several interviewees, particularly in early adolescence. Rachel, a middle school interviewee quipped, "If you don't wear makeup and UGG boots, some girls won't hang out with you. I don't have this problem with the girls I hang out with now. They are not concerned with appearances; they care about personalities."

Cliques

In middle school, early adolescents tend to become associated with a certain crowd or clique. This effort at "group formation" and labeling of each group represent the teens' attempts to make sense out of their daily social interactions and to define their social reality.[5] Not yet able to understand multiple levels of identity and complexity, teens tend to view each other in stereotypical ways; thus, they stereotype others. For instance, a group of girls who tend to dress more fashionably and to behave somewhat "prim and proper" may be labeled as "preps" by their peers. The same is true of the athletic students in many schools; these teens are usually labeled "jocks." Based on the identities that are more valued in a particular school, fashion or sports, the power awarded to individual cliques will vary. The same valuing process occurs with the groups made up of youth whose behavior is more deviant or aberrant such as the "druggies" or "heads." In some communities, teens who use large amounts of drugs or participate in other illegal behaviors may hold the most power. Group membership imposes the group's social ranking on the individual members. Thus, teens who gain membership in the popular crowd experience gains in their own social capital.[6]

Despite what individual adolescent girls may be doing behind closed doors, every member in a particular group is assumed to deviate little from the group behavior and appearance norms. This expectation may be especially rigid from other members *within* the particular group. One 18-year-old senior interviewee reflected, "During high school, it took me some time to find the right groups of friends to hang out with. The first group of girls seemed fun for awhile but then they started going out with older guys. They were doing stuff I didn't really want to be a part of but I had nothing to do if I didn't tag along. They kinda lost interest in me when I didn't want to cut class or was afraid to smoke inside the school bathroom. Then I met Stacey in my junior year English class and it's been fine ever since."

Middle schoolers often experience such intense levels of peer pressure to conform to rigid expectations, many look forward to high school. Even girls in the most popular groups often express a desire for less pressure to conform. Emily, an eighth grader attending a small private school, expressed a strong desire to attend the large local public school where she feels she "can be who I want to be." In high school, with a larger student body and an increased sense of identity, there is usually less rigidity in expectations and a greater variety of cliques than in middle school.[7]

The "In" Crowd

Social ranking is based on what is most valued and most visible in the student community. Typically, athletes of highly visible sports, such as football, and the team-associated cheerleaders tend to be most recognized and prized, but good looks and fashion sense often pull girls into the limelight. However, some teens are popular because they have particularly positive social skills, and these teens are well-liked in addition to being popular.[8]

During adolescence, perhaps more than any other time of life, popularity is more focused on the possession of social power than social skills. Some cliques are quite powerful within a student body and some girls within a clique are leaders holding more power than other girls in the same clique.[9] Being popular does not always mean being well-liked; popularity is simply a measure of how much others want to associate with you. The popular kids can often engage in activities that would be ordinarily frowned upon by others, but the glow of popularity allows them to maintain social acceptance and even gain the admiration or respect of their peers.[10] In fact, aggressive, destructive, and norm-breaking behaviors have been found to have a fairly high likelihood of occurrence with popular teens.[11] Although interviewees often referred to the most powerful groups of girls in their schools with derogatory descriptors such as "bitches," these popular girls continue to maintain power over other students. They also frequently set the standards for behavior, fashion, and decisions regarding who is invited to the best parties or the "cool" tables in the lunchroom.

Unfortunately for some, but fortunately for others, popular today does not mean popular tomorrow; neither the clout nor the membership of a given clique is stationary. As girls seek power in their worlds, they often experience or create social and personal drama. Virtually every adolescent girl interviewed believed that they were either a part of, or affected by, some amount of drama on a regular and, for many, a daily basis. Whether they were active creators of drama or the passive recipient, none expressed a fondness for it. An interviewee who is very pleased with her friendships felt stuck in the middle of two good friends as she described, "[They] get along great sometimes then they fight for months. Right now Vicky is mad at Haylee because she started dating her boyfriend the day after they broke up." Yet most teens have at least one group of close, relatively stable, supportive friends. Our more satisfied interviewees reported being able to minimize their involvement in the combative and competitive interactions often attributed to teens at large. Dana, a high school junior, shared, "I don't have very many friends at school. A couple years ago there were some girls I *thought* were my friends but then they were saying lots of trash about me. Since then I've been spending most of my time with either my boyfriend or the two girls I *know* are my friends."

Teens with Similar Feathers

Certainly the adage "birds of a feather flock together" applies to teenagers. The adolescent years are frequently associated with peer pressure and parents often express concern about the behavior of their children's friends. Peer pressure exerts influence across the spectrum of teens from troubled to well-adjusted and from low-performing to high-achieving. Though teenage interviewees claimed that their friends accepted them unconditionally, many studies have found that adolescents tend to be similar to their friends, especially in terms of school and achievement-related values and behaviors.[12]

Friendship groups often form based on school performance or level of interest in school-related and/or extracurricular activities. Bea, an enrollee of the gifted program at her school, opened our interview with the following explanation of teen friendship selection:

It depends on if you're smart or not. If you're smart, you have different friends. The popular people are not smart. The AIG people (gifted students) care a lot about their homework and their GPA. The "kooky" people are less mature, but have more connections and depend on other things like their looks. . . . [S]mart students fall into two general categories: the regular brainiacs and the extreme brainiacs. Extreme brainiacs have more social problems because they only befriend each other and are teased by the rest of the students.

Being a "brainiac," however, does not mean social inhibition or friendlessness. Again, friendship reigns supreme. By analyzing the daily time use of 700 ninth graders, one researcher found that despite spending more hours studying than lower-achieving teens, high achievers spent just as much time with friends.[13] Because the high achievers study more (especially on weekdays), but still deeply value friends, it seems they satisfy their yearning for contact with their friends through phone calls during the week and hanging out together on the weekend. Interviewees in the high-performing group often mentioned that they spend a lot of time with their peers talking about class content and reviewing homework.

Adolescents may be given the title of "nerd" or "dweeb" for reasons typically different from the mere exhibition of superior intelligence. Contributing factors include social issues that include any form of social awkwardness, such as not participating in the social events of their peers; pursuits or interests perceived as bizarre; and, of course, the habitual and highly visible fashion faux pas. Beyond simply being labeled a nerd, these students are often ignored or ostracized by peers and possibly the victims of gross mistreatment. They may face verbal, physical, and emotional bullying by their peers. When a teen strongly desires to be part of the popular group, but is unable to make that break, the social awkwardness intensifies, as does the emotional distress experienced in adolescence.[14] Some teens who identify as nerds, however, may have fundamental confidence in their individuality. Rebecca, a 15-year-old sophomore, stated:

I know I'm different than lots of kids I go to school with. I love taking care of animals with my friend, Josie. Some days we take neighborhood dogs on walks for spending money—plus, it's fun. Sometimes we hang out with the younger kids in the neighborhood because they're more creative than kids our own age. I really like to sit on my back porch and write short stories. Even though the kids at school think we're nerdy, we think we're okay.

Perhaps you or a teen you know falls into the "outrageous" appearance category. Interestingly enough, in a study of 1,200 youth, these teens were found to be shyer than the average teen and used the off-putting appearance as a form of self-protection to cope with their social anxieties and fears of peer interaction.[15] It also seems that striking appearances pull some of the attention away from the trendy popular crowd and, in a sense, helps teens gain some visibility and social clout.[16] Ultimately, though, if a teen's appearance turns off her peers, these teens do not gain the social interaction so badly needed during the teen years and often suffer from low self-esteem and depression.[17]

However daunting or uncomfortable it may be to have been a youth who was "on the edge," it may be worse to have gone unnoticed. In one study, the least liked and actually rejected teens were hostile youth who became increasingly unpopular and hostile over their middle and high school years if they (1) did not make supportive friends thus becoming increasingly isolated and (2) *viewed themselves* as not fitting in.[18] A teen may start out unpopular, but with the building of friendships, their world can shift dramatically. Like building blocks, adolescents must make their way through the social challenges of the teenage years, adding to the social skills they began learning as a child, in order to develop adequate skills for navigating the adult social world.

Problems in Teen Friendships

Searching to know and understand yourself is no easy task. And women best search as well as find best results when they do their searching while in healthy relationships. Given the challenge of intensifying this discovery process during a time when she is literally surrounded by yet-to-be-known-fellow-seekers, it is no wonder that the adolescence years are as exciting as they are difficult.

It would be impossible to detail the litany of problems teens face in their peer relationships. Like younger children, teens with poor language skills have difficulty in social situations.[19] However, two general behaviors often send a girl's world into deep turmoil. These are taking teasing seriously and, even more problematic, being one party in a breach of trust. In their interviews, teens often described the peers who experienced the most social difficulty as the ones who "overreact" or "get all upset over nothing." Girls reported being teased about the clothes they wore, their bra size, their hairstyle; for not having a cell phone, for not wearing makeup, for having braces or glasses; for how they stood, what they said, and how they said it, and on and on. Disparaging, critical, even rude comments are apparently part of the teen world and, point blank, the teens who have difficulty rolling with the punches either get pushed down by others or just emotionally worn down.

More sensitive and less resilient to issues of trust than young children, teens tend to react strongly to any perceived breach in trust from a friend. Backstabbing or talking behind a friend's back is at the heart of teen girl drama. Girls in middle school were especially susceptible to not knowing who their friends were due to breaches in confidence or just plain malicious statements by girls claiming to be friends. The hurtful statements reported were similar to the teasing topics but were more hurtful because they were voiced by presumed friends. The most toxic breach of trust is when one girl shares statements of another girl shared in confidence about a third party to either that third party or, even worse, to the entire gang. One teen described how this type of conflict had left her feeling depressed and friendless for several weeks after a friend broadcast things she had said about a common friend that she assumed would be kept confidential.

It may be safe to say that we all have been one of these players at some point during adolescence, whether you were the one who first said the pain-inducing statement, shared the statement with the subject of the statement, or were the subject of discussion. Furthermore, considering the interviews of women across the lifespan, it appears that many of the women who decide to avoid female friendships may do so after experiences with backstabbing during adolescence. But there are other ways females manage adolescent drama.

Surviving Adolescence

In a study investigating how teens can move from nerdy to normal as they move from middle school to high school, two paths were found to be most noteworthy.[20] On the first route, many young people find acceptance by embracing the standards of their peers or engaging in activities valued by the popular youth, such as student government or sports. These former "nerds" support mainstream teen culture and develop relationships with conventional peers. In fact, a key element to maintaining self-esteem is involvement in extracurricular activities that require students to belong to a group outside the classroom. One father emphasized his pleasure that his daughter enjoyed multiple groups of friends because when things are going badly with her school clique, she has other groups to choose from. Book clubs, dance classes, service organizations, and youth groups were a sprinkling of the avenues via which interviewees found and maintained healthy friendships. The most frequently mentioned venue outside of school was a sports club such as soccer, volleyball, or cheerleading. Teens with multiple friendships groups tend to have higher self-evaluations that may stem, in part, from having friends who see them in a variety of environments, thus reflecting back to the teen a more engaging, multifaceted view of themselves.[21]

The second route to normalcy happens as the teen makes large gains in independence, becoming emancipated in both thought and action. These teens, often rejecting the attitudes of their peers, learn to see themselves and others through their own valuations and life experiences. They tend to enhance "their self-perceptions through friendships that do not center around school activities nor connect them to the mainstream of the school."[22] Boys are more likely to take the first path; girls are more likely to take the path of independence and authenticity through intimate relationships. Numerous interviewees mentioned this second path as the way they escaped their struggles with the social culture of their adolescent years. It may, in fact, be part of the social fabric passed from older generations to young girls as a healthy means of coping with peer pressures.

An important survival tactic that teens (and their mothers) regularly mentioned was to avoid the drama by staying clear of or putting in perspective the cruel comments of mean or trouble-starting girls and by focusing on their true friends. Several interviewees purported that the mean comments were insecurity-based, as they believed that the mean girls were trying to feel better about themselves by hurting others. The concept of stepping on one person to gain footing on the social ladder and increase one's sense of worth is supported in Wiseman's best-selling book *Queen Bees & Wannabes*. While avoiding the dirt-slinging of their mean peers, girls described their own friends as "cool," fun, "down-to-earth," and "not snooty like other girls." (So many girls seemed to see themselves and their friends as more friendly and "down-to-earth" than other girls that it left us wondering where the snobs actually are!) Differentiating between friends who were disloyal and true friends, many affirmed that true friends did not judge their clothing or hairstyles. True friends do not talk behind their backs, do not try to steal friends from each other, and offer support when they were down or, as one girl aptly named her emotional roller coaster, "freaking out."

Concerns about peer acceptance and clique membership may actually be overridden by perception. In an examination of adolescent social functioning, researchers found that actually rating high on a popularity scale in order to feel well-liked was far less important than having a social niche, in or out of school, in which one *feels* accepted and valued.[23] How a girl *believes herself to be accepted* by others affects all aspects of her social functioning, including the view she has of herself, which becomes increasingly stable through these adolescent years. Her self-perception also has an impact on how she approaches others in relation to her expectations about attachment, her biases, and how sensitive she is to rejection.[24] An adolescent's sense of her social self begins to solidify into a self-fulfilling prophecy. Teens who expect social difficulties due to a history of rejection are more likely to either withdraw from social situations or attempt interaction in an unskilled fashion; teens who feel socially confident and comfortable with their peers tend to adjust well socially. As is true at any age, if we believe we are good at making friends, we are more likely to successfully make more friends.

Family

Teens with happy home lives are usually more successful at making friends than peers in homes with higher than average family conflict.[25] Strong relationships between children and their parents positively affect adolescents and the benefits carry into peer relationships. Despite common stereotypes about conflict-ridden relationships between adolescents and parents, many teens reported their parents as a source of support during their friendship struggles. One study found that teens whose mothers acted as peer conflict consultants had fewer behavioral problems and higher GPAs than the adolescents with less consultative mothers. Not surprisingly, high levels of conflict between mothers and teens about the teen's friends were related to higher levels of delinquent behavior.[26] Parents who view their teen positively essentially reflect back a positive image for the teen to see. In addition, happy parents are more likely to have friends and to be a positive relationship role model. Conversely, in a study of adolescent activity involvement, teens with depressed mothers participated less in extracurricular programs than teens with nondepressed mothers.[27] When parents are engaged and involved, their teens are usually more involved in extracurricular activities and enjoy higher levels of well-being.

When teens have problems at home, they often seek support from peers. Family relationships can be wrought with conflict. Between emotional and physical abuse, high rates of parental divorce, or plain old poor communication, home life can be hell for a teen (and *with* a teen). For adolescents with extremely poor home lives, their peers are often the only ones on whom they can rely on for support in the face of life's challenges.[28] Though friends can definitely be a lifeline, these same teens engage in more high risk behaviors and have lower self-esteem than peers from more stable and nurturing homes. Despite social support, these teens are still at risk for high levels of depression. Just as for the young child, family dynamics remain a potent ingredient in the well-being of the adolescent.

Mood Disorders: Beyond Moodiness

The teen years are a very hard time psychologically and interpersonally; even adolescents at the top of the social ladder grapple with peer issues that threaten their sense of self. In a 2005 study, approximately 30 percent of adolescents reported moderate to severe depressive symptoms. The teen years are a time of strong emotions coupled with rash decisions. Further complicating this stage is the fact that young people have not learned many of the coping skills that come with years of life experience.

A host of factors are related to teen depression; they span the personal and social worlds. High levels of family conflict and distant relationships between parents and teens are strongly related to low self-esteem and high levels of depression.[29] Under these conditions, teens are less likely to reveal their desperate thoughts to their parents, which makes it difficult for the youth to get help. Another important indicator of depression is a lack of friends. Small social networks that offer low levels of support are also related to depression as well as anxiety.[30] When a teen feels rejected by peers, she may believe that she has no one to care about her and no one to talk to about her feelings; this can leave her feeling intensely isolated. Feeling disconnected at school, sitting alone in the lunchroom, and walking through the halls feeling friendless, ashamed, or invisible are all detrimental to her mental health. Adolescents' social self-perceptions are crucial to their emotional wellness. Without the sense of belonging so necessary for adolescents, they can flounder. The various methods of treating teen depression are beyond the scope of this book; however, it is worth noting that early intervention is highly effective. Helping families resolve family conflict and helping teens improve friendship quality are two reliable routes to enhancing adolescent well-being.

Love, Connection, and Lots of Chatter

Teenage girls generally feel an all-consuming love for their friends. When interviewed teens spoke of their "true" friends, they smiled and laughed. They reported spending lots of time talking about everything from inconsequential things such as what show was on the TV to the big issues of what they wanted to do with their lives. They talked about everyone from movie stars to math teachers. Rachel, the middle schooler, had a very specific two hours of phone time built into her schedule—every evening after dinner with her family and between homework and sleep. Another teen reported sending more than 1,000 text messages every month, in addition to uncounted hours of online chatting, emailing, and talking on the phone. Emily, the eighth grader, discussed how she has certain friends with whom she discusses specific topics; her long-term friend was best for discussing family problems and she turned to less-competitive friends to discuss other friendship matters.

With their true friends, teen girls engage in supportive communication and hold a deep understanding of each other. They share common experiences and they help each other make meaning of these experiences. In general, friends help teens feel more confident in the world. With positive reciprocal relationships, it is easier to assign positive meaning to yourself. What our interviewees revealed clearly supported the research that adolescents who have accepting, supportive good friends perform better in school, have lower levels of depressed moods, have higher self-esteem, and experience greater health and happiness. Starting in adolescence, girls can articulate that friends morph from merely a playmate to someone who knows you well and enjoys time spent talking about the present *and* the future.

6

❧❧

Emerging Adulthood
Decisions, Decisions

In youth, the friendship journey is shaped by ritual and routine. School schedules, lunch periods, homeroom, and extracurricular activities all allow for regular, virtually daily interaction among friends. As high school graduation looms near, however, every girl faces a turning point. She must leave behind the familiar world she has known, make decisions about who she is and who she wants to be, and choose the path she hopes will get her there. The chosen path shapes every facet of her life journey, including the friendship choices made. In this chapter, we look at the interaction between this major life transition and friendship development.

One young woman, Ashley, 24 years old, shared her perspectives on the role of friendship in her life:

As far as friendships during college . . . I will tell you a couple things. It's the people you meet in college, not high school, that become lifelong friends. I personally only talk to about two people from high school and that's very rarely. My best friends who will be in my wedding are the ones I met in college. Most of the time, they are your roommates or a part of the same group you are in, whether you play a sport or join a fraternity/sorority. College is a time where you learn more and more about yourself; you figure out what kind of person you want to be and what kind of people you do and don't like. College is about partying too much, staying up late, procrastinating, and going out on dates; the people you call "friends" will see you go through so many emotions and situations. They are the ones that stick by your side, give advice, comfort you when you need it—because there's no way you could tell your parents what you did or have been doing. As time goes by, you realize they KNOW you better than anyone else. These are the people that after graduating, you can meet for lunch and reminisce about all the crazy times you had in college. The two girls who I lived with and played college softball with can take one look at me and know how I'm feeling, what I'm thinking, and what I need—they know my favorite places to eat and shop and vice versa. Many people will come in and out of your life during those four years, but there will be a couple people that will stay in your life forever and nobody will be able to replace them and those years you shared. Truth is, many people find their husband in college; I did not but it happens to more than not. College might not be for everyone, but I highly recommend it to anyone who is considering it. College made me stronger, wiser, more responsible. It prepares you for the real world. It's a time to make mistakes and then learn from them. I can honestly say it was the BEST four years of my life.

LEAVING THE NEST

At the high school graduation juncture, emerging adults find themselves straddling multiple developmental terrains. Simultaneously, they are seeking the answer to the archetypal question of "Who am I?" with enduring intensity; venturing into increasingly intimate relationships; and making major life decisions—all within a new context of independence and responsibility. With all this interpersonal *and* intrapersonal exploration, there are aspects of identity and interests that diminish as other aspects expand.

Even if a young woman is reluctant, changes in her own life and changes in her friends are inevitable. Friendship circles may be broken as women head to different colleges or different jobs; even long-term best friends may no longer hold a shared friendship reality. In a study of 137 college students, 97 percent of freshmen reported that they had a new "closest" friend one month into their college life and almost half said their high school best friendships had deteriorated to casual relationships or close friends by the end of their first year of college.[1] In cases in which high school best friends lived in close proximity to each other, their relationships were further strained by the conflict between staying involved with old friends and enjoying new friends.[2]

Allowing changes in your social network is not always easy. Some emerging adults fear the changes experienced in themselves and their friends. When young people are having a particularly hard time with the letting go process, they may have difficulty transitioning to their new environment. As Katherine, an 18-year-old college freshman, revealed:

I tried to go out with my roommate but I didn't feel comfortable with her friends. I'd much rather go home for the weekend if it weren't so far away. I spend most nights on the phone with my mom or my friends from home. We text each other all day long and it helps get me through the day. I really miss everyone. I hate it here [at the university] and hope my parents will let me go to school at the college near my home where some of my friends are going.

For women who gracefully navigate the initial transition to an adult lifestyle, forming new friendships and still cherishing the old friends, future holiday breaks may be turning points in the old friendships. Holly, age 19, college sophomore, shared:

I was stunned at how much my friends had changed in one year. I thought summer vacation would feel like the old days and sure enough, some of my friends were still into the same old thing. One friend was still talking about the same guy she liked during high school. I used to really like to tan by the pool, paint my nails, and talk about guys, but nowadays, I find I want to experience more. I'm planning on going to graduate school, so I need to spend my summers in meaningful internship positions—not talking about the same people doing the same old things. But then there is a part of me that would be so sad to not hang out with my old friends anymore.

Relationships with old best friends do sometimes thrive during emerging adulthood. Almost all interviewees counted a couple of friends from their adolescence years among their friendship network, if not a "close" friend. The most important protective factor in sustaining a friendship is frequent, positive communication.[3] In addition to frequent texting or social networking, several interviewees shared stories of fun-filled visits from their old friends. Ithica, a 19-year-old college freshman, elaborated:

My best friend came to visit me for the weekend. I took her for a tour of the campus and she met lots of my new friends. We went for a really long bike ride and talked endlessly. It was so cool. She knows where I come from; she really understands me.

These friendships help emerging adults deal with the stress of adjusting to new life circumstances and reduce the loneliness typically reported by first-year college students.[4]

Heightened Exploration and Identity Development

For most young women, emerging adulthood is a time to explore many possibilities—in work, love, and worldviews.[5] The majority of college students change their majors at least once[6] and emerging adults are more likely than any other age group to change residences.[7] This exploration stage is more accepted now than in previous generations and it sometimes lasts into the late twenties. The exploration process varies by individual; some young people explore life's options more fully than their peers. James Marcia developed a framework of four stages to describe the search for personal identity.[8] These identity stages, *identity diffusion, identity foreclosure, identity moratorium*, and *identity achievement*, exist on a continuum of exploration and commitment and occur at different ages for different people. The identity search process is motivated by a crisis or critical juncture in which a person is compelled to reexamine their beliefs formerly shaped by authority figures, parents, or cultural expectations. *Identity diffusion* describes individuals who have yet to reach a crisis or juncture and are therefore neither exploring nor committed to an identity. This stage can last well into adulthood. On occasion, commitment to roles, values, or goals for the future occurs before first exploring any options and is termed *identity foreclosure*. People in this stage tend to conform to the expectations of others regarding their future, such as following a parent's footsteps to determine a career choice. If an adolescent has faced a juncture, but is still in the midst of exploration, they are considered to be in the *identity moratorium* phase. After navigating this critical cross-roads through the investment of substantial energy into self-examination, a person will ultimately commit to an articulated identity and the status of *identity achievement* is reached.

Friends are important influences during the identity discovery process. It is possible that support from friends increases our willingness to try on or imagine possible selves. One study indicated that emerging adults in the *moratorium* or *identity achievement* stages had greater social sup-port than their *identity foreclosure* or *identity diffused* peers.[9] Openness to possibility and discovery shapes the friendship choices of this age group. One interviewee described the diversity of friends she enjoys as an emerging adult:

> *Now I've got friends who are different ethnicities, from different coun-tries; some are a lot older than me and some already have families. But they understand me and who I am now. I don't have to be just like my friends for acceptance. My friends now are also more reliable than high school friends. In high school, girls focused on themselves more, but now it seems like we all focus more on a friendship and thinking about being there for each other.*

In emerging adulthood, friends continue to serve as mirrors in young women's self-exploration by reflecting strengths and weaknesses, potential goals, and acceptable roles. When the reflection is positive and resonates with our experiences, we are better able to "see" ourselves and articulate who we are. As a young woman gains a stable identity, she develops the ability to be a steadfast friend in the face of disagreements inevitable between even the best of friends. However, if a young woman continues to struggle with her identity, she may foreclose or develop identity diffusion. Having an unexamined or shaky sense of self may leave a young woman feeling more easily threatened and exhibiting either rigid fanaticism or a lack of consistency. Without confidence in her identity, she may offer potential friends an image of who she *thinks* she *should* be. Yet by refusing to reveal our scars and flaws, we miss out on true intimacy in relationships and may remain lonely at heart.

FRIENDS AND LOVERS

Traditional psychology holds that identity development must be established prior to true intimacy.[10] Understandably, you need to know yourself well to possess an authentic self to meaningfully share. Yet emerging adults typically venture into the next developmental challenge of intimacy versus isolation before they stabilize their own personal identities. This process of self-discovery and identity crystallization *through* relationships with others may be quite appropriate for young women, as noted by Carol Gilligan almost 30 years ago.[11]

Beginning in adolescence and increasing throughout emerging adulthood, cross-sex relationships grow more important. Several emerging adult interviewees reported having males for best friends. One young woman described her male friend: "Our friendship moved from acquaintance to friend to best friend gradually through time and now we're pretty much family. His family thinks of me as a daughter/sister and I think of them as my own family. I love him like a brother." Though young women may become interested in befriending and growing these relationships, friendships with other women were reported as being more intimate, involving more relaxed and more frequent interactions, and exhibiting more commitment than friendships with males.[12] Additionally, women with clearer personal identities tended to have closer, more committed same-sex friendships than women with weaker personal identities.[13]

As the search for committed partner gains traction, relationships with romantic partners may overshadow friendships for emerging adults. In a study comparing the impact of multiple close relationships on the level of happiness reported by emerging adults, high-quality romantic partnerships were more influential on happiness than family or best friend relationships.[14] For the young women not involved in high-quality committed relationships, best friend relationships held the keys to happiness and the mother–daughter relationship took second place. It may, however, be vital to maintain friendships as romantic relationships develop. When love affairs turn sour, interviewees shared that supportive friends helped them through the heartache. In the words of Georgia, a 22-year-old college senior:

When you have a boyfriend, you really do focus all of your energy on THAT relationship. It's true. I've been on both sides—I've been the one to focus totally on a boyfriend to the extent that he was pretty much my only social outlet. It always seemed like a natural thing—to spend all my time with him. But the downside is breaking up—and realizing that you've possibly lost your girlfriends in the process. Last time I broke up, I really hoped that I'd still be accepted back by my friends. In fact, that's one reason I'm spending a lot more time with Chelsea—she was there for me when I broke up with my most recent boyfriend. She is really into a guy herself right now—she keeps breaking up and getting back together with him. And he's really all she wants to talk about when we're together—whether they're working things out or broken up. But I listen and let her talk because she was there for me a few months ago when I needed to reconnect with my girlfriends. This weekend I'm planning to do something with another friend who just broke up with her boyfriend a week ago. I know how hard it is to try and reconnect. It's really scary. You don't know if your friends will be willing to take a chance on you again. For me, I have to really force myself to make those overtures because you can end up really lonely if you've cut yourself off from everyone.

Not only do friends provide companionship when romances falter, but there is also reason to believe the influence of romantic relationships on happiness and well-being may actually flip-flop with that of friendships in subsequent life stages.[15]

LIFE AT THE CROSSROADS

Emerging adulthood is a time of identity exploration in which life decisions take on new significance. Jobs become steps along a career path, casual dates may lead to permanent relationships, and beliefs are embraced or discarded according to "personal fit" rather than family tradition. Arnett noted that this is not just a period of abundant decision making, but also that ramifications of these choices may be particularly significant and enduring.[16] Complicating the decision-making process, young adults are moving from a state of dependence on parents to independent decision making. Dr. Richard Kadison, chief of Harvard University's Mental Health Services, noted that this "shift can be too sudden and too drastic, leaving [emerging adults] stuck between two worlds in a state of uncertainty, bewilderment, and acute anxiety."[17] Kadison encourages young adults to establish vibrant and supportive social networks to provide stability as they make their trek to independence—without which many young adults eventually "break down." Quality friendships serve as a nurturing buffer from stress and other transition-related issues.

Choosing career and life paths is one of the primary decisions of emerging adulthood. Faced with this life-defining task, the emerging adult often relies upon friends to aid in the decision-making process. One interviewee, hired by a company at the same time as her best friend, reported that her friend was "especially good at listening and providing career-related advice." But all young women discussed lifestyle choices they were facing with their friends—whether it was prioritizing values of independence to income or choosing majors. High school graduation and the years that immediately follow this milestone present young women with a multipronged crossroads. Continued education, work, and establishing a family are its major arteries. The path followed will circumscribe and, in great part, determine who she meets, whom she might befriend, and the activities and interests they share.

College-Bound

Most emerging adults choose college as the path to continued education and expanded career opportunities. Exposed to a new group of diverse people, college students often learn about themselves and others at lightning speed. With various school events, group-based class projects, social and other types of extracurricular groups, it may be a busy time but will provide golden opportunities for making friends.

The need to belong and fit in with others is strong for college students. For instance, emerging adults with high social goals may spend large amounts of time socializing while neglecting their academic responsibilities.[18] No longer under the watchful eyes of parents, they must decide how to spend their days, whether to study or relax, where to go, if and what they will drink and eat, and when to come home. With fewer responsibilities and less supervision, many college students engage in heavy substance use and other risky behaviors.[19] Several interviewees described their earliest college friends as people they "partied with." In fact, it is well documented that friends often engage in compatible degrees of drinking.[20] Drinking tends to decrease with age and years in school and friends seem to change based on activities and personality preferences. These changes in risk-taking behavior and friendship formation are often intertwined with the identity search. Anna, a 22-year-old college senior, described her friendship journey in college as a three-part process:

First I spent all my time with other freshmen going to parties and for general companionship. It was fun, but now when I see those people we just say "hi" to each other in passing around campus. Then I met people through my involvement in a few campus organizations. We really shared interests beyond the next fraternity party. I still run into these people at organizational meetings and stuff. Those tend to be pretty structured events. Now the friends I hang out with most are people who drop by just to see me and talk about what's happening in each other's lives. We enjoy each other and it's a real stress relief to spend time together.

Roommates and suitemates were the most common sources of friendship for our college interviewees. Sometimes roommates were randomly assigned by the university, but after the initial year, living arrangements were intentionally chosen by the roomies. Resa, 21-year-old junior, reported:

As freshmen, my best friend and I were just randomly assigned the same room. I feel so lucky that we hit it off so well. I've seen some people actually leave school because they can't get along with their roommates. Megan and I like the same music, we're the about the same degree of neat, and we respect each other's privacy. So the following year, we chose to be together along with four other close friends. Sometimes it's a challenge for all of us to share a suite but for the most part, we get along really well. At the end of a big day I'm glad I can go home to her and tell her all about it. Our talks are real casual too. The fact that we touch base almost every day has helped us remain friends.

Despite its conduciveness to connection formation, college is fraught with academic, extracurricular, parental, and roommate pressures that may inhibit friendship maintenance. For instance, when a young woman has yet to narrow her interests or clarify personal goals, busyness coupled with over-commitment is a major hurdle to friendship maintenance. Competition between potential friends in highly competitive academic programs may hinder relationships. Most notably, intense interest in romantic relationships often promotes friendship neglect. On top of these hurdles, some emerging adults juggle part- or full-time employment with their academic responsibilities. College social activities may not hold the same allure for this group as they do for less time-crunched students.

Hearing a Different Drummer

Some emerging adults continue their life journey on a path that does not run through the middle of a college campus. Young women may pursue career ambitions or a traditional family route, starting sometimes with the child, sometimes with the life-partner. Along each of these paths, the opportunities for friendship differ.

For the work-bound emerging adult, the workplace may become the central location for friendship creation, as it is for working women of any age. However, the workplace may present both benefits and pitfalls to friendships specific to this age group. In many employment settings, the emerging adult may be the youngest employee in their work settings. One such emerging adult expressed that she feels isolated at work and especially dreads unstructured social engagements:

I don't really talk about my personal life at work and there's only so much I can say when my co-workers are talking about their own lives. I feel uncomfortable when we're not focused on our jobs. Like I just can't stand the employee picnic. Last year, I went to it alone. I don't have kids or a mortgage. I didn't have anything to talk about. Thank goodness this year I have a boyfriend to bring. Since he is more outgoing and good at talking sports, he'll be able to close the gap between me and my co-workers.

Yet when two or more emerging adults are on the beginning steps on the career ladder together, this dynamic may actually foster a friendship. As one young woman shared:

My best friend and I were both hired at the same time. The only other friendships that I have built outside of my core group of friends from my elementary years are those I have met through work. I have built a couple great friendships with my peers. The commonalities have been sports and how closely we live to each other.

Some young women engage in both work and college. Often their college of choice may be an online program, a community college, or technical college. Though opportunities to meet people may multiply, these women are particularly busy trying to meet college requirements while working to finance college or other life expenses. While modeling perseverance and "doing what must be done," these young women may miss some of the opportunities afforded by full-time college living. Many report not feeling fully "at home" in either world. Lindsey, a 25-year-old attending a community college, confided:

Sure, I see lots of people at school, but when class is over I don't have the option to grab something to eat with my classmate. I don't go to their parties, I don't join clubs. I have other responsibilities. I need friends who have to be responsible, too, though the main people I hang out with are my old friends from high school. Some of them work; some have small kids. Even these friends I rarely see.

MARRIAGE AND PARENTHOOD

The current cultural norm for women in the United States is to marry and give birth in their late twenties. As more young women enter college and envision opportunities beyond the roles of wife and mother, marriage and parenthood are often postponed. However, some young women do take on these roles and face many personal and structural changes. Parenting, in particular, seems to increase the likelihood that young women perceive themselves as full adults (versus the "in-between" place most emerging adults experience). Along with growing commitments and responsibilities, identity exploration becomes restricted.[21] Because their subjective sense of identity tends toward adulthood, despite their young age, their friendship journeys may resemble the friendships of women presented in Chapters 7 and 8.

HEADIN' ON DOWN THE ROAD OF ADULTHOOD

Some young adults do not fit neatly into any of the previous categories, as they vacillate between multiple worlds seeking their niche. Some aspects of emerging adulthood are consistent across each group, such as the continued search for identity, but the parameters of this search will vary. Just as we each must discover who we are meant to be, we must also discover the company we are meant to keep. Depending on the path chosen, the means to accomplish these ends may dramatically differ.

To establish healthy friendships, emerging adults have three general tasks in their friendship journeys. These tasks may happen sequentially, but given the challenges inherent in resolving multiple developmental crises, they are more likely to occur concurrently and interactively. First, each young woman must allow spontaneous change to occur in her existing network of friends. Second, she must engage in the developmental challenge of knowing herself more authentically. Emerging adults are finally at the place where they have more freedom to discover and explore their own interests and to choose how their time is spent. These developments teach the value of well-defined boundaries—both personal and interpersonal. Third, she must find and retain friends who cherish the person she discovers herself to be. As the pool of potential friends expands during emerging adulthood, it can be an exciting time, as young women are exposed to different personalities and cultures—far broader than previously experienced. It is vital for a young woman to ask herself, "Given the kind of person I know myself to be, with whom do I want to share myself and with whom am I most comfortable?"

7

❧ ❧

Coupled Up, But No Kids Yet

Entering a significant romantic relationship is often accompanied by significant shifts in existing friendships. Women face the challenges of finding time for girlfriends and determining the role their partner's feelings play in their own pursuit of "friend time." This chapter explores the role that female friendships play once a woman has chosen a partner/significant other, including the ways in which the presence of a partner supports or hinders their friendships.

There's an old song that laments the loss of friendships as wedding bells toll; and to hear our interviewees tell it, there is a fair amount of truth to that conclusion. Choosing a partner implies engaging in "exclusive behavior" that often includes both romantic and platonic exclusiveness, to a degree. As a woman pairs up with a partner and leaves a social circle of single women friends, in her wake she may leave behind women dealing with a sense of loss, confusion, and, in some cases, betrayal. If we are unhappy with our own single status, we may harbor a bit of resentment and envy toward our friends who have been able to find "the one." Others of us may celebrate the good fortune of our newly coupled friend, but grow increasingly disappointed when socializing with her becomes less frequent. When we are newly coupled, whether this means engaged, living together, partnered, or married, we must reprioritize and realign our schedules to mesh with those of our significant others. Making time for romantic partners takes precedence over spending time with existing networks of friends. We may also find ourselves thrust into the process of making friends as couples. It turns out that approximately 85 percent of women between the ages of 25 and 40 have problems keeping friendships strong and vibrant, often due to the new priorities that primary romantic relationships entail.[1]

WHAT WE KNOW ABOUT FRIENDSHIP AND THE NEWLY ATTACHED

The ages and stages of life have been divided up, defined, and described in multiple models by theoreticians, behavioral scientists, and sages, but the structure outlined by Erik Erikson still endures as one of the most applicable. Erikson described the years between ages 18 and 29 as the stage in which we wrestle with intimacy versus isolation. After using our adolescent years to figure out who we are, we move into this new stage ready to share ourselves with important others—including romantic partners and close friends. The drive to find a life partner often supersedes the desire to be a loyal friend, as described in earlier chapters. Learning to balance newly deepening romantic relationships with longstanding friendships can be a challenge for women—and for their unattached friends.

In a surprising twist, during the early married years and the new parent years, men typically have a larger network of friends than women.[2] This is most likely due to a woman's tendency to focus her energy on building the new life partnership during its early stages and on the rearing of her children during their younger years. A woman's romantic attachments are a primary focus during young adulthood and continued attention must be directed to sustaining other social connections, as well.[3] A significant change often occurs within platonic relationships as a woman attempts to integrate her new significant other into these other important relationships. As the literature states and our interviewees attest, the choice of a partner can bring reactions from others that range from joy and celebration to envy, disappointment, or even broken relationships. The reactions of our family and dearest friends to our romantic partner may actually seal the fate of a newly developing relationship.[4]

Getting Serious

The reactions, and the related provision or absence of support, from our friends and family can play a key role in how a romantic relationship plays out.[5] Most of us can recall the experience of beginning a new romance and being eager to introduce our new love interest into our existing landscape of friendships. Receiving approval of our partner is important and we definitely crave our friends' support. According to the research, our friends are right behind our romantic partners as the people we rely on for companionship and intimate sharing—and they usually place ahead of our families.[6] However, depending on the closeness of the friendship, if a friend has a hard time with our partner choice, this conflict may lead to an unexpected—and unwelcome—termination of the friendship. As one 27-year-old woman affirmed:

When one of my work friends refused to respect my choice and wouldn't give my fiancé a chance, it was the friendship that had to end, not the engagement. I don't know if she was jealous that I was spending so much time with him or jealous that I'd found such a great guy. It didn't really matter, though. The friendship wasn't going to survive.

There are times when friends may become aware of potential hazards a new romantic relationship might be bringing with it. These warnings can be strong enough to convince us to end a "bad news" relationship, but sometimes the excitement of new love can leave us blind to a partner's faults or incompatibility. One interviewee wished she had listened sooner to her friends' warnings about a partner. Laura, now 32, shared that when she was in her early twenties, she was not as wise about men as she would have liked:

I had grown up in an abusive household. My father thought nothing of using force to get his way—with my mother and my brothers and sisters and myself. On some level, I think I really believed that it was okay to live like that. But when I met Miguel, I was so ready to move out and become in charge of my own life, my own future, my own home. And everything seemed so good in the beginning—until my friends started sharing gossip they'd heard about Miguel. They'd tell me the things you never want to hear about someone you love—fighting, drinking, whatever. I didn't listen; being with him was better than living at home. Within a few months, Miguel and I were married. I was so proud of our little apartment, but it seemed like we were working like dogs to keep the rent paid and the bills up. Well, my friends continued to pass along what they'd heard from their boyfriends or brothers. They kept trying to warn me, but I was sick of their stories. I quit having them over after awhile, I quit listening. Then Miguel stopped paying the bills. And I asked him about the calls for money—the gas, the phone. These should have been paid. He got ugly and denied any problems. Turned out he gambled at the boats and in bars, lost our money, and then, of course, he turned his anger on me. My friends, my friends, I had sent them away, told them not to tell lies. But they had never told lies—they'd been trying to protect me. When I was able to get out of the marriage, I couldn't go home. But a dear friend was still willing to open her home to me. I should have listened earlier, but they were good friends, they were still there for me when I needed them most.

Although this story may be an extreme example of how conflicts can arise between romantic relationships and same-sex friendships, unfortunately it is not unique. Physical and verbal abuse from a partner are often preceded by "red flags" or warning signs that others may see before the victim realizes the danger she is facing. Learning to manage the interrelationships between your friends, your family, your life partner, and yourself is a critical step in successfully managing the "intimacy versus isolation" task inherent to this stage of life.

Officially a Couple

As women become engaged or make the decision to move in with their partners, friends usually expect them to withdraw a little from same-sex friendships. Newly married/partnered couples typically want to spend the majority of their free time together. Whether fixing up their homes, creating new routines, or just enjoying the connubial bliss that arises from simply having found one another, new couples may be highly exclusive in their socializing. In an amusing side note, one interviewee, Melissa, who was in her mid-twenties when she was planning her wedding, shared that she and her mother had been best friends for as long as she could remember. One of Melissa's favorite "single life" pastimes was to sit with her mom on the porch of her childhood home and talk about her life, her joys, her sorrows, her hopes, and the world around them long into the night. Melissa revealed, "As my wedding day approached, I got totally sad when I realized that I would have to actually leave my family's home and move into a new home with my husband." Melissa affirmed that she didn't doubt her love for her new husband, but she just knew that her priorities and social life would need to shift with her marriage and that she felt disappointed that she would lose the easy comfort and daily talks with her mother, her best friend.

Research has shown that coupled-up women withdraw more from the women who populate the outer edges of their friendship landscape while remaining more strongly connected to their more intimate friends.[7] Michelle, 24, in a committed relationship, described her dismay at the changes she was experiencing in her social circle. She and her partner had been members of what she felt to be a relatively stable network of other young couples with whom they'd connected through school and work. Yet friends' weddings, out-of-the-area home buying, and even a friend's job relocation were distressing for Michelle, as she confessed, "We're losing our friends, and we really need to bring more friends in. But it seems like every year, someone else goes away."

These years of new coupledom can bring shifts in our social landscape and in our sense of belonging. Expectations of how our friendship networks should look can be drastically upset when we, or our friends, step forward more fully into significant relationships and a new life together with our partners. Michelle went on to note that there were a couple of women that she'd met through graduate school that she'd like to bring in closer as friends. She quickly added the categorically essential requirement for a successful friendship, noting that "one is married; the other has a long-term boyfriend." With friends in similar stages in their own romantic relationships, there is a better chance of lasting friendships so Michelle hopes, as she ended, "I feel like we're not living the life that we'd like to be or having the social life we'd like."

For single friends, there may be greater challenges in maintaining the sense of connection they once felt for friends once they have entered significant relationships. One single woman, Candy, 26, described her feelings about her newly married friend:

Janica married one of our friends from high school. We all knew and loved him. Our circle of friends was so pleased to see them go from high school sweethearts to college sweethearts and then marriage. I was maid-of-honor in the wedding and it was like a fairy tale event—being part of the planning and standing up for her on the big day. And then it was like Janica and Rob were the only ones who got to see the "happily ever after." We knew the honeymoon period would last for awhile, but then it was over three months since I'd heard from Janica. I really felt left out and it was like us single girls had served our purpose and she didn't need us anymore.

Candy shared that things eventually "loosened up" and she began to see a little more of her friend. She noted, though, that once she began dating more exclusively the man who was now her husband, the four of them enjoyed getting together and hanging out. As you move from being a single woman to half of a couple, it takes a much more dedicated effort to keep precommitment friendships going strong.[8] We must believe that an existing friendship will fit well with our new role identity and that it will be worth the required energy investment before we try to adapt our new lives around the reentry of our single-life friends.

Some partnered women may feel the need to avoid single friends to prevent any opportunities for unpleasant feelings to arise on the part of their friends, such as a friend feeling like a "third wheel" when alone with the couple. A friend's negative reaction or less than enthusiastic company can motivate partnered couples to try to "fix up" single friends with potential romantic interests or to curtail socializing with some friends for a period. One married woman affirmed, "Most of my friends are couples. I think we all like to have an even number when we do things together. We don't like to have an odd number; it just doesn't seem right." One single woman we interviewed described her partnered friends as being "on a mission to fix me, as if being single meant there was something was really wrong with me." One interviewee shamefacedly shared that she was so delighted in her role as a new bride that she assumed *everyone* should know how fulfilling a committed relationship could be. She enthusiastically and repetitively "shared her story" until a friend helped her see that she was alienating some friends. She had to learn how to back off a little when she was with her friends who were as yet unpartnered and uninterested.

Settled into a Shared Life

Women may identify their partners as their most supportive tie, but they still count on their same-sex friends for a good deal of emotional support. As noted in the research, they rely on these friends especially in relation to their problems in their primary romantic relationships.[9] Because married women tend to have married friends,[10] they may look to members of their social circles as experts on couples-related issues. One 24-year-old interviewee confirmed that she considered her partner to be her closest friend, but noted that she had good female friends, as well. When asked if she shared things with her friends that she might not share with Troy, her husband, she laughed and responded, "Well, I actually run things *about* Troy by my friends." As we learn to manage committed relationships, we tend to seek advice from those friends who are a little further along the path than we are. Whenever we enter a new life stage, we look to our friends for guidance according to both the research and our interviewees. Lindsay, a 23-year-old who recently moved in with her partner, shared that she often asks her "long-married friends and married sister" how to manage changes her new living situation is bringing into her social and domestic life. Lindsay shared, "It's not just getting used to living with a guy, it's getting used to living as a couple. I need all the advice I can get from my friends!"

Judy, 26, is a busy woman—she works long hours as a news writer and has been married for two years to a videographer. Being in the business of bringing people the news translates into long and often unpredictable hours for both partners. Judy, though, is a very gregarious person and is the kind of woman who has never met a stranger—just friends she hasn't made yet. She described her friendships:

> [Friendships are] are like pieces of pie. I have my good friends at work who I love dearly. We often work together under stressful conditions—news stories that come in just before deadlines, too many news stories that need to be

cut, too little news which requires creative fixes. We all sometimes compare ourselves to "combat friends" because we get close really quickly and rely on each another for moral—and professional—support. These work friends are the ones that I laugh with, eat lunch with, chase news stories with, and treasure. That's a BIG piece of pie. Another piece of pie contains my friends in our apartment complex. It's an adults-only complex, as much as they can be now, and so none of us are parents yet and a lot of us are around the same age. Every weekend in summer we take turns bringing the margaritas and the chips to the pool. I love those women—and I wouldn't trade their friendship for a million dollars. Then, my husband and I have our "couples friends." There are three couples that we get together with usually at least once a week. Every Friday we try a new place and meet for drinks and appetizers. We un-wind, tell our horror stories from the week, and the guys do guy-talk and the women gossip or plan shopping trips or get-togethers at each other's homes for the whole group. This piece of pie, it's the yummiest—because Nick and I get to spend time together as a couple and so no one feels left out.

Judy's need to segregate her social connections isn't uncommon for this demographic. The desire to bond and spend time with one's partner is natural and some friends from the single days may still harbor twinges of competition or envy for the friend's success in the romantic relation-ship arena. Although much more likely to happen in years past, too many women are still willing to let go of friendships that their husbands feel aren't suitable or desired,[11] but men do not typically show this same level of dyadic commitment.[12] Women can be eager to see a new romantic re-lationship succeed, and although we like to believe in equality between the sexes, some women still feel comfortable yielding to partners' wishes when it comes to friendships. As one young wife described it, "Our pastor strongly believes that wives should defer to their husbands, and when I think about choosing to spend two hours with certain friends versus the lifetime I've promised to my husband, there really is no choice, in my opinion." Another woman sounded a bit baffled as she revealed, "Most of our friends are ones *he* brought into the relationship. I'm not really sure how that happened."

Other women may choose to actively maintain friendships with women their partners find objectionable, which requires balance and commit-ment.[13] Some women shared that they had "rules" about which friends they would refuse to give up for a partner. One 29-year-old woman, Patty, described these as "the friends who knew me before I knew myself," re-ferring to friends she has known since she was an adolescent. Patty is a self-described Midwest version of the *Real Housewives of New York City*, but "much tamer." She went on to share that was raised very differently from the way of life she now enjoys. Born and raised in a steel town in

Indiana, she shared that her mother had yet to set foot in Chicago—even though they lived just 30 minutes from the city. Patty's best friends had grown up in the same neighborhood as she had:

My husband, God love him, likes to forget where we came from, but I can't forget the friends who dreamed the same dreams I did about becoming "Someone." They don't resent our success and I can't ignore them now. I'm no Oprah, but I love it when we get together for dinner in the city and it's my treat. I have new friends, "husband-approved friends," but I'm not ready to give up my dearest and oldest friends. Life's too short to let go of the people who love you—when you're up or when you're down.

Another woman noted that the most important quality in her relationship is honesty, so she knows that when she chooses to spend time with friends with whom her husband doesn't get along, she must be up front and open about it with him. Many women expressed regret at having to loosen the bonds they once had with earlier friends, but acknowledged that a committed relationship brought new priorities. However, one young woman stated that if her current partner had complained early in their relationship or had trouble with any of her closest friends, she would have rethought her relationship with him long before she rethought her relationships with her good friends. Several of our interviewees communicated, in a variety of ways, that "you are the company you keep." They were referring to a belief that their friends were reflections of themselves. Christie, 24, believes that this is a fact, as well as a warning; she added that she is more careful of whom she chooses as a friend now that she is also in a committed relationship that she greatly values. She strongly believes that it's wise to avoid friends who might reflect poorly on her.

Best Friends—of the Opposite Sex?

A few years ago, a research study explored the role of best friends in the lives of married couples. Among the 654 married participants, none claimed an opposite-sex best friend.[14] In our interviews with married or partnered women, however, there were numerous acknowledgements of male best friends who were neither their partners or spouses. As one young woman, Amanda, 24, shared, "I've always been better friends with guys than girls. Even in high school. I have a male best friend now and he and I have been friends for years." And Jael, 29, shared, "My best friend is actually a man, and we met my freshman year at college . . . I look at him more like family than just a friend and I know he feels the same." When encouraged to discuss how these relationships might be different from those with a close female friend, one interviewee noted that there is "much less drama" with male friends. This was a common theme and many of the women who noted the preference for a male friend could also pinpoint a high-drama moment with a female friend that had left them bitter or hurt.

Another common theme within female–male best friendship was the longevity of the relationship between the friends. For most of the young, partnered women, the friendships had been formed during high school or early college years and were solidly in place prior to the start of their current romantic relationships. This is an important point for many of the women. More than a few women noted that there are still some concerns about the "propriety" of an opposite-gender friendship once a woman is in a committed relationship. Our interviewee recounted how the issue of a male best friend had been addressed early in her relationship with her husband:

My husband, he was really jealous. He had a bad time because of his ex-wife and other guys; she had cheated on him. So he didn't like me being friends with this particular guy, even though he knew that we were only friends. Well, once we got married, he changed—he was like, "Go ahead, invite him over." But earlier, at the time we were first getting serious, he wasn't cool with the situation after all he'd been through with his first wife.

Christie, 24, also felt that her closeness to a man might create problems for her by giving others food for gossip. She learned to be proactive:

My closest friend is a guy and he's also gay. But I don't think if he wasn't gay that I would spend as much time with him. My male friends, I felt I had to put them by the wayside with my fiancé. It wasn't so much him, but I would be feeling guilty hanging out with my guy friends and worrying what other people would be thinking.

Overall, it was somewhat surprising to discover the proportion of women in committed relationships who claimed men as best friends. They noted the lack of drama, the lack of competition in the friendship, and an ease in sharing and companionship as the advantages over friendships with other women. An even greater proportion of young, committed women noted that their best friend was their partner. A chapter in the final section of this book will explore this phenomenon and provide ideas for enhancing this noteworthy friendship.

Noah's Ark

Several of the young partnered women we interviewed were eager to talk about the tendency to socialize with other couples, like the woman mentioned earlier who likes to socialize in "even numbers." She had described various activities she enjoyed with other couples, including dinners, movies, and concerts—none of which really require an even number, but the preference for balance is strong. No longer competing for a life partner, there may be a sense of protecting the investment they have in the relationship, although women did not typically verbalize this notion, except for one notable exception.

The desire to protect one's romantic relationship was eventually put into words by Jill, 28. When invited to talk about her friendships and their interplay in her committed relationship, she laughed and said that she felt her social life resembled that of her grandparents, rather than her own parents. Living in a neighborhood designed for returning GIs from World War II who were hoping for upward mobility, the homes were all well-kept, artfully rehabbed and remodeled as needed, and still home to young, upwardly mobile professionals—both the husbands *and* the wives in this generation. Jill described a life of country club tennis, Junior League volunteering, and garden club meetings. She also described a life of part-time lawyering. Jill said that her closest friends all lived in her neighborhood—many were women with whom she'd attended high school and college. She said her professional life was just that, her *professional* time; her social life was centered on her home and social activities. Jill and her friends organize much of their social lives around *couples' activities*, so that they can spend more time together as a group. They enjoyed themed progressive dinners, cocktail parties, bridge nights, and tailgating during football season at an alma mater that over half of her crowd shared. Apparently feeling a need to justify her revelry with her friends, Jill affirmed:

> We all know how easy it is to see a marriage crumble—many of us saw it firsthand growing up. We also know that once we add a baby to the marriage, all relationships will have to shift. Taking time to make marriage—and friendships—full of fun and vitality is almost like a vaccine against future problems. And, yes, I know I sound more like my grandmother than my mother. Hopefully, I've learned some lessons about priorities and good friendships.

One young woman, a full-time employee and part-time graduate student, acknowledged the importance of doing things with friends as a couple, rather than independently. Feeling that she was already too crunched for time as it was, she felt the easiest way to guarantee time for socializing was to include her partner and to organize things close to home. Liz, 29, noted that her neighborhood was rife with young couples, so she and her partner inaugurated "full-on neighborhood cook-outs" the first year they lived there. The turn-out had grown each season and she felt that she and her partner had helped create a warm community within their subdivision. Other women shared the importance of a place of worship as a center of spiritual and social activity. Belonging to a couples' religion class was noted as a wonderful way to build and support the primary relationship as well as to introduce themselves to like-minded friends. Having a strong sense of your own values allows for easier clarification of the kinds of friends that would best fit into a shared life.

Noah's Ark, Plus One?

There were distinct groupings formed around the procreation issue among the women who were somewhere along the continuum of "coupled up, but no kids yet." One group included the women who looked at their current relationship as the stepping stone to the next phase of life which they believed would begin as soon as the first child arrived. One woman shared:

We're looking for friendships that will serve us as a family down the road. We both grew up in close-knit families, but since we're hundreds of miles away from our parents, we know that we will need to find friends who will be willing to stand in as family as our own family grows.

This certainty of the type of friends she would need over the coming years guided her choices in socializing and friendship pursuits today.

Another group had no plans whatsoever to add to their families and felt fulfilled by their romantic relationships as they were. Some of these women enjoyed the role of "surrogate aunt" for their friends' children, whereas others allowed new parent friends to slip out of their social orbit. As one woman described, "One of our couple friends had a baby, and it's like they evaporated into thin air. It's almost impossible to connect with them; their schedule just poses too many constraints. It's like they entered a black hole in the sky." She had tried unsuccessfully to connect, but now believes the friendship is on a necessary hiatus for now.

The third group of women included those who were unsure of their own plans for starting a family, but enjoyed including friends of any maternal status in their lives. One interviewee, Robin, provided a rich example of how inclusive and supportive these women can be. She recounted a shared vacation in which she and her partner had rented a vacation home together with another couple. The friends were childless, but were delighted to include Robin, her husband, and their 11-month-old son in their vacation activities. One morning, just a couple of days into the vacation week, there was something of a disconnect between the friends' plans for a day hike and what was doable and realistic for the young family. Robin laughed and said it took some work to convince her friends that hiking up a mountain with an 11-month-old in a backpack was a different journey than hiking up a mountain unencumbered. Robin laughed as she recalled that her friend phoned her shortly after giving birth to her own first child and marveled at how naïve she and her husband had been on that trip and she acknowledged how much more difficult navigating outings actually can be with a baby in tow!

CONCLUSION

When you enter into a significant relationship, you may also be significantly restructuring your identity and social network. As you redefine the roles you play in life, you must balance personal needs with partnership needs. Seeking out other couples as friends who are good matches for both yourself and your partner can be a difficult charge, but the shared friendships can create a solid and durable network of support. Another challenge may be the successful integration of friends from your single days into your newly coupled life. It may require finesse and compromise as the activities shared with single friends can be categorically different from the activities partnered women might choose. Compromise in many aspects of your relationships will be a necessity as you grow more comfortable and confident in the new role of partner. These years might be frenetically busy as you continue to define your personal identity while creating a professional identity and a newly formed partner identity. By understanding who you are, what you need from friends, and your role in your new romantic relationship, you will have a firm foundation for creating the landscape of friends that will serve you best.

8

⤙❧⤚

Motherhood
Kids on Board

*W*e asked women how their friendships had changed when they had their first child and we quickly found out about the extensive impact motherhood had on friendships! In the words of one interviewee, "How have children not changed my friendships?!" Indeed, children change us, our values, our goals, our activities, and almost every moment of our day. Children are work that does not end at 5:00 p.m. and they encompass much of our "free time" previously available to friends. Clearly these major shifts in so much of our lives—and our identities—strongly affect whom we choose for friends, how we make our friends, and what we do with our friends.

CHOOSING DIFFERENT FRIENDS

Women in this life stage *frequently* reported that many friendships were developed or ended according to whether the other women in their lives had entered this life stage as well. Traci, a 35-year-old physical therapist and mother of two girls, directly and frequently mentioned the term "stage of life" in our interview:

I like talking with someone who understands and can identify with what I'm saying. Not all my college friends are in the same stage of life, even though a couple are older than me. In the five years since Emma was born I haven't been very close to my best friend from college. It wasn't until a few months ago when she had a child that I have begun to feel like we've had anything in common. Instead, I have made some very good friends through the Sunday school class my husband and I joined that is specifically for parents of young children. The people in that group range from their mid-twenties well into their forties but we all connect on the central aspect of our lives, our children.

One major explanation for this constraint was the tendency to perceive other mothers as more likely than child-free women to understand the issues that permeate motherhood. Celine, a 31-year-old mother and book-keeper, shared:

I used to look at crying children and judge their mothers as incompetent or unloving. But now I know how hard parenting really is. It makes me so uncomfortable when my own child misbehaves around my friends who don't have children because I worry they may be thinking I'm not a good mother. Yet with my friends who are moms, we're always sharing our parenting frustrations and embarrassing stories of our children's misbehavior—and our own wrongdoings!

After a short while in the mothering role, most women grow to understand parenting to be complex and consuming and not necessarily the idyllic experience portrayed in the media. They also realize that women continue to have needs of their own beyond the rearing of children.

Women usually learn these powerful lessons being around other mothers who are honest and willing to share the hardships of their own experiences. This type of empathic exchange may in fact be crucial to the well-being of new mothers. Hormonal changes that accompany childbirth often impose the "baby blues," which generally dissipate with time and perhaps the camaraderie and assistance of family and friends. For greater than 1 in 10 women, childbirth and its surrounding life events inflict postpartum depression.[1] In O'Hara and Swain's meta-analysis of more than 12,000 women with postpartum depression, they found the more extended and profound women's isolation and perceived lack of social support from friends, family, and the baby's father during these infancy care-giving months, the more likely women were to suffer from severe depressive symptoms. Marty, a mother of two revealed:

It wasn't until I joined a mother's group that I found out I wasn't crazy. Thanks to a few particularly outspoken women in my group, I discovered I wasn't the only mother who feels like she got the shaft. You know, my husband would sleep all night, go to work during the day, and basically continue his life as usual. And oh, I had been feeling so guilty about getting angry at my 10-month-old baby. But it felt so good to hear other people say "it's okay to feel angry." And you know what? Hearing that helped me feel less angry.

Children as Bridges to Friendship

Not only do children inspire us to seek friends who understand us in our new role, but the arrival of a child in a woman's life also encourages the formation of bridges to other women for the remainder of her friendship journey. Not only do mothers feel compelled to seek out other mothers, but our *means* of creating friendships often change. While attending school, we primarily meet friends through classes and extracurricular activities; working women often make friends at work. But when baby's naptime is paramount and personal time is so limited, mothers seeking fellow moms must take different initiatives to finding friends. Though some women may be more naturally inclined toward one-on-one relationships, there appears to be a surge in group formation during the preschool years. Perhaps women are intuitively attempting to create the "village" necessary to help them raise their children.

Several organizations are dedicated to helping new mothers make connections with the intention of building a sense of community, helping families, and reducing maternal isolation and depression. Some mothers' groups are formal nonprofit organizations such as the Mommies Network, which has spread to more than 100 communities across 32 states since it was established in 1995.[2] This organization offers women family-friendly social events as well as child-free social opportunities to befriend other mothers. In addition, it maintains an online presence so women can access support and camaraderie 24 hours a day. There are several religious-based programs to support mothers seeking connections with each other such as Mothers of Preschoolers, International (MOPS). With church backing, these groups are sometimes able to provide childcare while the mothers enjoy some fellowship time. Most common were reports of informal groups of women who decide to connect on a regular basis. Some of these women's groups center around the interactions of the children, such as frequent visits to the park; other groups encourage the children to play while the mothers engage in a more structured activity such as scrapbooking.

Jessica, a 37-year-old mother of two elementary-aged children, met her motherhood compatriots at a breastfeeding luncheon offered by a hospital. She described the development of their friendship:

Though we were all so different from each other, the six of us liked each other and wanted to be with other mothers of newborns. We didn't want to pay a club where people attended functions sporadically and

*might be less committed. In the beginning, we would get together at each
other's homes once a week to have lunch together. We talked about our
children most of the time. We actually bonded over our children. As the
babies grew, we'd take turns creating fun activities for the kids and share
ideas with each other. We joined Kindermusik and other child-oriented
programs on top of our home visits. We picked up some other mothers
along the way but after the children started preschool, our group met
less and less frequently. Some of the moms were good at forming relationships beyond the children. But I rarely do anything without my kids
plus I couldn't afford to do the same things they would do. Since we live
in different parts of the city and we're all so busy shuffling our children
to their activities, I rarely see them anymore with the exception of Lisa,
who became my best friend. I miss having a relationship with everybody,
knowing what's going on with them and their kids.*

Children are a means to initiate communication, make acquaintances,
and build friendships. Even when their children are not in view, few
mothers can resist an inquiry about their children; they are knowledge-
able and able to converse about their children's interests, the children's
schooling, the parents' activities with the children, and so on. Women
who are willing to listen to mothers talk about their children have a
ready-made topic of conversation. Thus, our children offer us a conversational security blanket when other topics fall flat. Moreover, because
women value their children and their children's interests, children create a bridge to other women who have common child-related interests.
Some interests that help women befriend one another are obvious, such
as mothers of children on the same sports teams caring about the team's
performance, being active together in the school's PTA, or sharing the
lowdown on the latest sales at Gap Kids. Though chauffeuring children
to practices and competitions is time-consuming, expressing common delight at the children's events offers a meaningful point of connection and
a common passion to rally.

Sometimes interviewees befriended others through interests that
stemmed from being a mother but extended beyond their children's immediate activities, such as lobbying for safe streets and joining community-
wide efforts to improve education. The benefits to women who invested in
these child-inspired friendships multiplied when they found shared non-
child-related interests. According to interviewee reports, this broadening of
interests was vital to deepening and extending the friendship. Moreover,
children provide ample opportunities for us to reach out to others.

Finally, because of the nonstop demands of motherhood, children encourage us to exchange instrumental help with other busy mothers. Della,
a 42-year-old mother of four boys, shared:

During tax season my children just about live at my best friend's house. Liz is like a second mother to them; she treats them like she treats her own children. She feeds them dinner, looks over their homework, and since our children are in the same activities, she drives them to baseball practices. In my off-season, I try to return the favor though I'm not sure I ever provide her with as much help as she does me.

Allison, 40-year-old telecomm sales manager and mother of triplets, described a similar relationship:

One day when I had an important work meeting but my daughter was too ill to go to school, Judy brought her to the doctor for me. Now that is a friend I couldn't live without.

From trading hours of childcare to the joys of hand-me-downs, women's numerous reports of practical assistance received from friends clearly instilled a sense of appreciation for this type of friendship.

Children Build Tall Brick Walls

Women sometimes experience children as a blockade between themselves and their friends. Some obstacles were structural, such as a lack of time or the challenge of paying for caretakers in order to have a girls' night out. Sometimes women's friendships dissolved in response to friendship dissolution between the children; when children who had been close entered different social groups, mothers' friendships effectively disbanded. Other blocks were internal, such as feelings of guilt when spending discretionary time without the kids. And, unfortunately, judgments about parenting styles occasionally formed a wedge between two women who might otherwise have been closer friends.

The most prevalent obstacle to the creation and maintenance of friendships reported by women in this demographic was the time demands of parenting. Rachel, a preschool teacher and 36-year-old mother of twins, shared:

When there's not enough time to floss your teeth how do you go for coffee? Forget dinner and a feature-length movie! I haven't gone with friends to a non-Disney flick in the movie theater since the kids were born.

Time does not seem to reappear as children age. Melanie, a 42-year-old mother of two teenagers expressed her frustrations:

The demands themselves changed but the time it takes to perform them only grows. Obviously there are no more diaper changes but we used to be able to

bring the children to friends' houses or get a sitter if we wanted to go out to-
gether. Now that the kids are older we're pulling teeth to get them to come along,
they're more committed to their own activities that require even more practices,
we have to drive them to and from more places, and we can't just leave them at
home unsupervised all evening.

Even when time allowed and other childcare providers such as fathers and grandparents were willing and able to watch the kids, an intrapersonal form of roadblock to friendship occurs. Several women repeatedly expressed that they felt guilty spending discretionary time with friends instead of being there for their children around the clock. For example, despite the joy she feels going dancing with her good friend and how good it feels to be expanding her concept of herself, Traci stated:

I made a friend at the gym who is so vivacious and social. I feel like
the "anti-me" when I'm with her. She sets a boundary between being a
mom all the time and being able to go out and have fun on her own. We
love to go dancing. Yet I feel bad about enjoying going dancing. I feel torn
between enjoying myself out with others and being a mother.

Whether guilt is a self-imposed constraint or due to a narrow conceptualization of the "good mother," it plagued several of our interviewees and frequently kept them from pursuing or maintaining friendships. This was not, however, always the case. Many women, including Libby, a 39-year-old nurse, are champions of time with friends. Libby sets her "girlfriend time" as a top priority and engages in as many fun weekly activities with friends her energy and multiple roles can handle.

The barriers for women engaged in full-time paid employment could be imagined as a doubly high wall. These women are intensely busy, stressed, and reported far less time with friends, especially friends outside of work. Even women who seemed to be gracefully managing multiple demands shared a sense of being overwhelmed and "missing out," and friends seem to be the part of their lives that most often lost out—right after "me" time. This coincided with an examination of how women make sense of the work–family balancing act. The researchers reported that working mothers expressed an increased sense of self-worth and personal satisfaction, but also reported feeling a great deal of loneliness—when they were not too busy being overwhelmed.[3] Allison, the mother of triplets, used to be a social "powerhouse," but since she returned to full-time work, she has experienced a huge drop in the time spends with friends:

Juggling full-time work and family demands is exhausting. As much as
I love my friends, I just don't have time or energy to go out at night. My

work is too busy to take lunches. It is all I can do to spend an hour of TV time with the kids before I fall asleep exhausted on Friday night.

All mothers of young children tend to be busy. Full-time working women experience an even higher degree of busy-ness, titled "crazy mode" by one interviewee. These women *especially* need their friends to understand this dilemma. They also are in a time predicament that forces them to choose their friends prudently. Ethiel, stated frankly:

If you need me and call me, I am cool with that. I can't have friends who are needy. If you call me and say I haven't talked to you, do you still like me anymore? Well, I can't take that. Whatever purpose that friend served, the bus ride is over. If my true friends call me and say, "Are you okay?" That's okay because we haven't talked in a while, not because we're disconnected. I want friends who help me escape life's duties and responsibilities, not add to them.

Not only is judgment damaging to friendship at every age and stage, it is the exact opposite of the type of understanding that mothers explicitly stated they need most from friends. In a society that attributes a child's behavior to the mother's parenting practices, there are limitless opportunities for women to be victim to others' judgments and women often perceive disapproval of their children as a personal insult. Quite often, the criticism of friends, family, and professionals contribute to a mother's self-doubt and can create disharmony and fracture within social circles.[4] Yet why do women who are mothers not recognize this problem and, instead, continue to critique other mothers? One study has shown that a woman is more likely to disapprove of other women the larger her sense of personal inadequacy.[5] Thus insecurity and fear may encourage some women to repudiate another woman's parenting style in order to justify her own. Or sometimes women put their own child on a pedestal while disapproving of a friend's child's behavior, particularly when they perceive it as having an impact on their own child. One interviewee stated, "Once my daughter got old enough to learn from other children, I could no longer hang out with Donna and her kids. I was too worried my daughter would learn some pretty bad behaviors." Another interviewee shared several stories about the challenges in one of her mom's groups:

I feel like one of our members doesn't recognize her own children's shortcomings and it really limits our friendship. Whenever our children get into a mishap, she is so quick to blame anyone else's kids. It's crazy stuff too, like the time her son wouldn't let the other children have a turn with the Wii. She said, "Oh, he's just keeping the younger kids from messing with it—his father doesn't want the kids to play with it unsupervised." To me, it looked like her child just wanted to hog the toy like children often do. In fact, I know of two other moms in our group who get annoyed by the same thing. It's kinda' sad really because if it weren't for these silly competitions and blind spots about our kids, we might be much better friends.

Women varied in their response to the barriers that having children engendered. One mother stated that even though she missed spending time with friends, she was "okay with giving the children all my time since they're young for such a short period of time." Yet far more frequently women expressed a degree of sorrow and frustration, longing for more time to share with friends—without their children. Amanda, a 28-year-old mother of two and self-described "homebody," said:

Now that I have children I want to go out more *frequently in order to get breaks from the kids. I really love to go out with girlfriends to get pedicures, go shopping, and eat at restaurants. Most of my friends with older kids don't do that much with them besides watch their kids' sports. Our husbands watch the young kids while we go out. I want friends for my kids but I want to have friends too.*

In fact, in two separate interviews, women proclaimed that "getting out more with friends" was a New Year's resolution. In the few studies that examine the motherhood years, it is clear friendships play a crucial role in women's health and well-being, as it does at every stage of life.[6] Without a doubt, women must hold time sacred for friends.

Mothers at Play

Though not ruled out entirely, nightclubs, smoke-filled bars, and quiet movie theaters are not common leisure-time choices women in this life stage. Much more frequently, women visited more child-friendly locations along with other mothers and their children. When children are early elementary age or younger, friends most commonly engage in activities that include their young children such as home-based play dates or sharing coffee adjacent to a McDonald's play area. They venture out to parks, swimming pools, zoos, and children's museums.

Multifamily gatherings are wonderful opportunities through which women can build and maintain friends while their partners and children are doing the same. Alyse, a business owner and 34-year-old mother of one son shared:

I'm a believer in barbeques. You can invite as many or as few people as you wish. If they bring a dish, you do relatively little cooking and not too much cleaning either. The men can gather around the grill and talk sports. The women can sit and relax. Most of our time is spent just telling stories, sipping cool drinks, and enjoying the company while the kids jump on the trampoline.

Some interviewees have further commingled two or more families by vacationing together. In fact, one woman expressed that "if another family is interested in sharing their precious vacation time with my family— that's a really good sign."

Women develop a number of creative tactics in order to fit friendships into motherhood. They may meet in large groups in order to catch up "en masse." They may connect social time with exercise or have a sleepover "party." This generation of mothers utilizes email and social networking websites such as Facebook. One of the most illustrative examples of women's playtime was shared in an interview with a working mom. Shannon, a 32-year-old retirement center activities director and mother of two, joyfully laughed about the fun she had going grocery shopping with her good friend. "Our husbands had the kids for a couple hours on a Saturday afternoon. We went roaming around Costco gathering groceries. It felt so good to not have any kids with us; we had a lot of time to catch up and just be silly." Running errands was an often mentioned "fun" friendship activity. Another pair of young mothers enjoyed a standing biannual date—once in fall and once in spring—during which they would drop their toddlers off at the preschool they both attended and they would head out together to the nearby outlet mall to shop for the new season for the kids and themselves. Women may no longer communally tend a garden, but they enjoy tending to their families together.

"Aging-out"

The arrival and caring for our children changes so much about who we are as individuals and who we are in relationships. Although some of us are able to hold on to our old friendships through thick and thin and through singlehood, marriage, and parenthood, others see our social worlds reshaping with each new life stage. During the childrearing years, we learn more about where we stand on most every issue, and this new knowledge may lead us into conflicts or solidarity-producing discussions with other mothers. Indeed, we learn which other mothers in our community can appreciate that ten minutes past the hour is not late and which mothers comprehend that despite our yelling we still have an all-encompassing love for our children. These women offer us knowledge about practical considerations like assessing the contents of a diaper, understanding the dynamics of managing fussy babies, and handling tweens and teens with attitudes. But to limit our understanding of women to their mothering role ignores that we continue to have other needs to be met and often love nonmotherhood friends. One does not have to rearrange her own schedule to include child naps or extracurricular activities to have compassion for her friend's constraints. It is wise for women to cherish lifelong friends as well as new friends who can honor them beyond their mothering role and responsibilities. It may, in fact, be crucial for us to build friendships on more solid ground than carpool-sharing and soccer snack duty partnering. When the children we are raising move independently into a social world of their own making, we will still long for friends to love and understand us as we grow into our next new identity.

9

❧ ❧

The Midlife Years

Reconnecting with Ourselves and Seeking Companions

This stage of life often leads to even more questions about identity. However, as women become more assured about who they are, their friendship needs often shift as a result. This chapter shares the stories of women who have reevaluated their lives and found ways to make beneficial shifts in their social support networks.

Until very recently, reaching the fortieth or fiftieth anniversary of your birth was an event that could be considered a "ceremony of shame" for women. Age has long been viewed as an enemy of a woman's worth. Men were "allowed" a midlife crisis and excused for the fallout; women were consigned to suffer through "the change" and mourn the empty nest. No more! The years between 40 and early older adulthood are now considered to be the prime of life and boundaries and barriers once associated with aging have been pushed wide open by the Baby Boom generation. Expectations about how life after 40 should look differ markedly between this generation and that of their parents.

Women entering their forties and beyond are a powerful force in every sphere of society; the personal, the social, and the professional arenas provide women with the opportunity to freely self-explore and self-develop. With this renewed focus, we often begin to recognize the value of our time, energy, and relationships. This development is accompanied by two time-related phenomena that influence how we perceive our life paths: the internal clock and a shift in our time perspective.

Several decades ago, Bernice Neugarten described the internal clock we carry inside ourselves that we use as a measure of how well we are keeping our lives on track.[1] This clock is "numbered" by the significant milestones that mark a life (e.g., graduations, engagements, marriages, childbearing, retirements). For instance, generations past assumed that marriage would occur by one's twentieth birthday and babies would begin arriving by the first anniversary. The "gold watch" of retirement would be earned in one's mid-sixties. However, as average longevity lengthens, we have become more fluid in our expectations of the timing of milestone events. This is coupled with a relatively universal shift in time perspective that typically occurs around the time we are entering our forties. Somewhere around early midlife, we shift from thinking about our lives in terms of the period from our early years to the present to thinking about our lives in terms of the period from the present to the time we have left. Women who have devoted years to maintaining a family, a marriage, or a home often begin to examine their lives through a lens of personal identity rather than primarily in relation to children or a significant other. Women begin paring down nonessential activities, superficial relationships, and drains on their emotional and psychological well-being.

Often accompanying the realignment of identity and lifestyle that typically occurs during this period is a realignment of relationships and social support networks. After decades of being attentive to the needs and expectations of the others in her life, including children, partners, parents, extended family, employers, and so on, women are apparently ready to let go of obligations that no longer offer benefits or potential rewards. Research has shown that the number of friends in a woman's life decreases with age. Women in their midlife years have fewer friends than younger counterparts.[2] Women are now able to establish friendships based on their own interests and emotional needs, unlike in earlier years when instrumental friendships were integral to their successful functioning in multiple roles as parent, co-worker, carpool driver, or soccer mom. Even for a woman who has prided herself on being the perfect "corporate wife," realignment and renvisioning of her identity can occur, as shared in the words of Rochelle, whose marriage ended after 23 years:

Year 23 my son left the nest, [my husband] was a career man and I no longer had a role. At this point, he was thinking up ways to occupy my existence. As if I couldn't think for myself. . . . And I couldn't. Not yet. I had always been part of something. But never part of me. I was unhappy. I was mortally unhappy. That is what happened in year 23. I became aware that I was unhappy . . . I was unhappy. Today that is all I would need to know. Then, I needed to almost die before I could dare release myself. To stop asking others for permission to stop being unhappy . . . I think you have yet to just let go.

You are afraid if you do and you are afraid if you don't. There comes a day when we just have to say [to those who try to stop you], "You get to have your feelings and reactions, But I can't afford to keep my life on hold for one more minute to try to please the unpleasable."

I guess that is why the word "authentic" means so much to me. It's not about being right or wrong. Not me. Not them. It's only about being real. So I could stop constantly looking behind my back and over my head waiting for the big shoe to hit me. The threat was worse and longer lasting than the reality.

These middle years can be a time of significant transition for women and each of these transitions offers an opportunity—or the necessity—for new friendships to form and existing relationships to shift.[3] For too many centuries to count, positive emotional support has been shown to be vital to overall well-being and it can be absolutely essential during times of transition and personal upheaval. It is the nature of this support that typically undergoes scrutiny during the midlife years. Friendships may need to shift, to alter, or even end as we evaluate and reprioritize our roles in friendships and social support networks.

WHAT WE KNOW ABOUT MIDLIFE FRIENDSHIPS

Unfortunately, the midlife friendships of women have not been explored as fully as those at the polar ends of the life course; especially lacking is knowledge regarding friendship maintenance and friendship endings among this group.[4] Apparently friendship formation strategies and trajectories are not much different than those of other age groups—just the settings may shift. One researcher described the goals of friendship to be threefold: information seeking, self-concept expression, and emotional regulation, with younger adults being motivated by the first goal and older adults by the latter goal; for midlife women, there is a balance among these goals in their pursuit of friendships.[5] It has also been noted that friendships at this time of life are either "communal," which implies that the relationship is built on reciprocal emotional support, or "agentic," suggesting that the relationship is more activity-oriented and outwardly expressed.[6] As we move through the adult years, we depend less on spending time with our friends as a means to keeping a friendship going[7] and the qualities we look for in friends are no longer so tied to perceived similarity, the power we gain in a relationship, or unquestioned acceptance of who we are and what we do.[8]

In a review of the role of friendships over the life course, Hartup and Stevens[9] noted that adult friends experience conflict as frequently as children do,[10] which suggests that adults may be less concerned about the possibility of significant negative consequences from disagreements than adolescents and young adults tend to be. This finding is also in alignment with the tendency of midlife adults to feel more strongly about their personal identities and how they present themselves to others. The conflicts experienced by midlife friends are typically emotional disagreements, which focus on beliefs, values, and social partners; also included are criticisms, which are aimed at lifestyles, habits, and personal issues. These are definitely not inconsequential areas for many of us, as we feel that our beliefs and our lifestyles represent, in essence, our identities.

We also know that women in midlife greatly value their friendships.[11] As described earlier, we typically find our friends based on proximity to potential friends, through shared activities, or through life events[12,13,14] and research shows that women experience a wide range of transitions during their midlife years.[15] This suggests that opportunities to form new friendships may abound for many women. However, this period of life also involves shedding the weight of relationships that are no longer rewarding, beneficial, or required. These two interrelated processes, experiencing transitions that typically ripen the opportunities for new friendships to develop and clarifying and revising one's social network, can create a synergy in which friendships during this time are especially meaningful and authentic.

Just over three decades ago, George Vaillant[16] developed a yardstick, of sorts, for measuring a person's successful arrival at midlife. One necessary accomplishment was participation in an ongoing, long-term marriage as well as the presence of children and close friendships. Until the last couple of decades of the twentieth century, most midlife women would be required to have the husband and all the trimmings to be considered worthy or deserving of friendships, in fact. Contemporary society's mores, however, have perhaps irreversibly altered the landscape of how the life trajectories of *successful* and *fulfilled* women now manifest themselves. Marriage is no longer a prerequisite—nor has it ever been a guarantee—of midlife happiness and fulfillment. As Western culture ever more willingly embraces alternative paths to personal happiness, no longer are women who opt for cohabitation, same-sex relationships, divorce, and single-by-choice life paths likely to be left rejected and friendless at midlife with only the stereotypical feline form of companionship. We are, as a society, much more tolerant of diverse choices and we are more likely to offer support, not censure, to friends who follow different life paths than our own.

Asked to share their thoughts about a message they would want to convey to their daughters about friendship, midlife mothers frequently echoed a similar sentiment. They would like their daughters to maintain a nonjudgmental stance when meeting potential friends. Many women had grown up with an admonition from their mothers to "choose friends wisely." This was interpreted as a warning to carefully choose only friends whose backgrounds and lifestyles were mirrors of their own. These women now believed that their careful choices may have kept them from opening themselves up to possibly even better friendships in their younger years than they actually established. One woman strongly avowed that the advice she would give her 19-year-old daughter would be:

Don't be judgmental! Don't be judgmental! There have been people I've met that I didn't like right away, like they were snobs or different in some way, but I gave them a chance. One of them is now like family. If you meet someone you don't like at first, you don't know what someone else is going through. Give them another chance.

Taught for so many years to judge others by their parents' or husband's standards, midlife women today are eager to relax, open up to potential friendships, and see how new relationships might develop.

FRIENDSHIP MAINTENANCE

Little has been studied, explored, or shared regarding how a midlife woman might best find and maintain the type of friends that she would like to have grow close. This noted deficit of attention to friendship maintenance strategies used by midlife women may be a symptom of the pervasive invisibility of women "of a certain age." Although the middle years of life are gaining increasing focus—both the popular and the academic forms of attention—there remains a sense of "social invisibility" that is attached to this demographic. Midlifers exist in a state that could be characterized as "no longer young, but not quite old." Women, especially, seem to have been left on the sidelines long enough for them to recognize the slight. In fact, there is a social organization that by its very name and customs demands that midlife and older women be noticed: the Red Hat Society. Although the right to wear red officially begins at 50, women in their 40s are included in activities, provided they sport pink headgear. Motivated by a poem[17] that called attention to a common desire of many older women to stop worrying about what others might say, this social club became a cross-country phenomenon. Inviting women "of that certain age" to show up and stand out, women are embraced and noticed rather than shunned and ignored. Involvement in groups and organizations allows friendships to develop and to endure.

Another recent phenomenon in the business of friendships is the creation and popularity of "girls-only weekends" and women-only travel adventures. Tourist destinations, hospitality organizations, and marketing have all joined together to develop events that cater to all ages of women and their friends. The market for this form of organized travel is able to support special magazines and tour books, such as *Girlfriends Getaways*, a magazine with a circulation in the hundreds of thousands. With the increasingly isolated existence of the modern family, as described in Chapter 2, we are going to greater lengths to not only make time for, but to also celebrate our friendships with women.

A good number of our midlife interviewees noted that friendship maintenance was often accomplished via activities that were embedded within the routine activities of their lives. Women who are involved in full-time jobs frequently felt that "friendship maintenance" was important, but that the time and energy investment often limited their ability to keep up with their friends. Married women often face scheduling and priority challenges when trying to visit with friends. They are frequently stretched between the needs of their husbands and/or children, aging parents, and their jobs. Phone calls were frequently noted as the easiest way to keep in touch, but midlife women are also using texting, emails, and social networking technology, as well. Many women felt scheduled activities were the easiest way to maintain friendships and felt they were most successful keeping up with work friends, church friends, and friends in their Bunco league, a popular dice game that enjoys widespread popularity as a social event for women as the "bridge club" once did for many women, on their bowling team, or in their fitness class. Several women recounted friendships that had formed through their attendance at support groups. When asked about the activities they enjoyed with their friends, working women replied "laughs at work," or "eating lunch together during the work day." Women who were not working full-time (whether retired, working part-time, or unemployed) often mentioned lunches out, shopping trips, and volunteer work. One woman shared that her church was the meeting place two days a week, and that she probably did more socializing and connecting on those days than the other five put together. Shared activities were the most often described method of keeping a friendship going—one woman laughed and said that a daily one-hour walk with a friend kept the friendship—and their bodies—going strong. As would be expected, the activities shifted for our women as they moved across the decades of midlife.

One woman, now 52 with two children in college, said that just a few years ago that she and her husband and a close friend's family would spend the weekends together enjoying outdoor activities, whether it was skiing, camping, or boating on the lake. Now, she noted, the relationship had been altered as her own kids entered college, and the regular get-togethers were replaced by sporadic phone calls and the occasional shared activity. She said she missed the activities and the shared fun of being with close friends, but her friend still had children at home, and there seemed to be a tangible shift in their friendship as their life stages diverged. She noted that she didn't have a slew of close friends in her life, and she wondered aloud if anyone had the kinds of relationships that were portrayed in television shows such as *Friends* or *Sex in the City*. A fair share of our interviewees expressed a similar query as they tried to determine the closeness of their existing friends and the ways these relationships were maintained.

DEGREES OF FRIENDSHIP

Even for midlife women, there is a pecking order within their social circles. In any given social network, or *friendscape*, as we like to call it, there are many different "types of distances" that can separate us from our friends. Some distances are literal and geographic. Some distances are metaphorical and philosophic. Other distances may be chronological, generational, procreational, or even socioeconomical. Some interviewees had clear understandings of how these distances influenced their relationships; others had to hunt for the right words to explain how they perceived the differences between friendships.

Are Acquaintances Our Friends or Our Quasi-Friends?

An interesting phenomenon was revealed during our interviews as some women struggled in the effort to articulate their connections with certain groups within their friendscape networks. When first asked about their friendships, they would begin to describe a set of individuals that they knew at their workplaces, or perhaps in their churches, or even their neighborhoods. As they more clearly tried to describe the relationships, they frequently moved from the word "friend" to the word "acquaintance," which they realized changed the flavor of the relationship significantly. Several women pondered whether these "acquaintances" could really "count" as their friends. Visibly perturbed by her confusion, one woman expressed her dawning realization that she may, in actuality, have *no* real friends. This woman was not alone in her sense of having quasi-friends, those people with whom she would "do things," yet with whom she did not feel comfortable enough to "confide things." Another woman described the difference as "when you have problems with the choices a friend is making in her life, you can take it up with her, but you wouldn't do that with an acquaintance."

Hartup and Stevens described the difference between friends and acquaintances, or what are perhaps better-termed quasi-friends, in that

when we are interacting with our friends, we are more engaged, mutually oriented, and the interactions reflect a more symmetrical balance over
the length of the relationship.[18] All of our interviewees could sense and
understand the difference, although being able to articulate the nuances
left some women feeling upset, disappointed, and, in one case, somewhat
ashamed of her lack of *real* friends. Acquaintances were abundant for virtually everyone, but real friends were in short supply for a surprisingly
large number. Many of the women who fell into this group expressed
their desire for a close friend and their sense of somehow "missing out"
on something important. They were interested in finding a way to build
real friendships with some of the quasi-friends to whom they felt close.

Close Friends and Best Friends

When we asked women from childhood through older adulthood to
name their first best friend, the question was met with virtually immediate recognition of what we wanted and clear recall of their early friend's
first name. Asking midlife women to name their *current* best friend was
frequently met with another response altogether! Although many would
enthusiastically bubble out one or two names with solid assurance, another group of women responded with a moment or two of total silence
and a perplexed, quizzical look as they prepared a response. This latter
group acknowledged active friendships, but didn't believe that any single
friend was any closer than any other. They noted that they shared at an
equal depth with their friends, but none of them stood out as a single
"best" friend. Sharon, 42 years old, noted that she had different friends for
different activities, but that they all seemed equally close.

Many of the women who could quickly name their best friends chose
women with whom they'd been friends for decades. They described a
depth of friendship that had grown over time, through shared experience, and, quite often, through difficult times. One 39-year-old, Virginia,
named a friend she'd known since her elementary school days and as she
described how close they'd always been, acknowledged how strong the
relationship was and how important her friend's needs had been to her
when her friend's mother died. Virginia said that her whole family was
affected by the loss and that she had felt like she'd lost her own mother, so
close had she been to her friend's mother through the years. This lifelong
connection had created a friendship that was durable, reliable, and able to
not only withstand, but also ease, the suffering and loss met in a lifetime.

The gift of a best friend in life might come through a move into a new
neighborhood, striking up a conversation with a person walking the same
route as you do, or smiling and engaging a friendly face in conversation
at the grocery store, the library, or the post office. A woman who had

moved into her current neighborhood some ten years earlier shared her story of "best friend instant recognition," or the "click phenomenon." Annette, now 48, recounted that the day after she'd moved into her new home, the next door neighbor, Carla, stopped by to welcome her to the neighborhood. Annette said that she and Carla clicked right away and she felt confident she had met her new best friend. And ten years later, they have just grown closer over the years. Another woman, Joan, now 52, shared that about four years earlier, she was trying to find an "exercise buddy" of some sort. Her daughter was now in college, her son was a busy high school student, and her husband worked long hours on his job. Joan's husband had recently noticed an unfamiliar woman walking in the neighborhood each morning as he drove to work and he encouraged his wife to connect with her as a potential walking partner. Their paths finally crossed with some astute timing by Joan and they began a daily walking routine. As Joan noted, if you spend an hour a day walking with someone, you share a lot about yourself and your life and you can become surprisingly close friends. We don't have to be socially driven adolescents to need, or find, a new best friend. We just need to be aware of the various opportunities that exist for locating this treasure.

PARTNERS AS BEST FRIENDS

Not unexpectedly, married and partnered women within this demographic often consider their spouse or partner as their best friend. Numerous women shared that they, as a couple, had been through so much together—the challenges, the obstacles, the rough patches, and the rewards—and that they had grown closer together as a result of the shared life experiences. Renee and her husband have been married for more than 20 of her 43 years, and when she was asked to describe what she valued most in her husband, whom she described as her best friend, she replied, "Consistency. Yeah, consistency, just always being there. Loyalty. We've had hard times and there have been *plenty*. We always work it out. We know we can." Their friendship, unlike that of many couples, had thrived throughout the toughest times, including their experience of losing a child. To fully express the depth of their friendship, which Renee emphasized was perhaps the most valuable component of their marriage, she laughed and said, "[My husband is] my other half. We share a brain! We joke about it all the time. . . . He'll say half a sentence and I'll say the other. We can start at opposite ends of the store, and we come back to the cart with the same thing."

For many of the women in midlife, it is apparent that there is a deep appreciation and need for friendship and companionship from their partners. For women like Renee, who are in marriages that have stood the test of decades of wear and tear, including the birthing and raising of kids, in-law stress, and personal tragedy such as job loss, illness, or financial crises, there can be a sense of connection that is perhaps broader, and deeper, than wedding vows might predict in this day and age. One woman, whose husband had faced off with—and beaten—substance abuse and addiction, felt without question that her husband was her best friend and was able clarify how this relationship stood apart from others:

Right now, my husband is my best friend. I have a lot of different friends. Some of them I feel closer to than others. But my husband has gone through a lot of crises that we have gone through together. There's something that binds me now. He would only want the best for me. We're very accepting of each other.

Such a large number of the women we heard from described their partners as their best friends that a later chapter of the book, chapter 19, will present suggestions for helping build and strengthen the friendship between couples.

RELATIONSHIP WITH MOTHERS

As women grow into mid-adulthood, friendships with their mothers tend to be more easily developed than in earlier years. The relationships between midlife daughters and their mothers are typically positive with the presence of warmth and positive regard.[19] As older mothers recognize the need to call on the next generation to handle family celebrations and maintain family traditions, midlife daughters experience a rise in their hierarchical status within the family. Echoing the sentiments of many of the women interviewed, one woman noted that this transition represented a feeling of "finally being seen as an adult!" And as she and others claimed their adult status, their relationships with their mothers also transitioned. Similar to the deepening friendship that typically results as a woman first experiences motherhood herself, midlife women begin to see their mothers in a different light. Midlife daughters often begin to recognize that the shift in matriarchal responsibility is often accompanied by an impending shift in caretaking responsibility down the road. One 47-year-old woman shared regret about this challenging transition:

We were finally at a place where we could let the drama go. My anger for all of the things I felt like she'd done wrong to me when I was young. Her need to always be right. Always so much alike; finally that could be an asset! And then she became ill, really ill. All my hopes about this new best friendship just evaporated. When she passed, I felt like that woman who sings the song about "sometimes I feel like a motherless child," but I also felt like I'd lost my best friend. It's been ten years now, and some days I still miss her so much it is a physical ache.

On the other end of the mother/daughter friendship continuum are the relationships between midlife mothers and their young adult daughters. For a few of the interviewed women, building friendships with their daughters has created a surprisingly rewarding affiliation between a once frustratingly challenging and struggle-filled pair. As one woman described the shifting relationship with her daughter:

It's not as if we are "best friends" today, but now that my daughter is out on her own, creating an identity separate from just being "the second child and oldest girl" in our family, I think I can say that I really do like who she's becoming. She's finished college; she's got her own apartment, dating a very acceptable boyfriend, and beginning to really understand responsibility, adulthood, and the importance of being accountable. This works great for her in terms of friendships with girls her own age, but also with me. I really appreciate it when she calls to ask me questions about life—whether it's about recipes, dealing with her boyfriend, whatever. I know that I am finally being recognized for who I am with her—and after the terror she caused as a teenager, whew, it's nice to realize that we can actually be friends.

This perspective was a "happy ending" to the mother–daughter discord that had strained much of this woman's relationship with her daughter as an adolescent. Many women, however, are unable to reach this feeling of a "matured relationship" so easily with their daughters.

Whether it is the storm of adolescence or personal characteristics, other midlife women experience the disappointment of an unmet desire for this type of relationship shift. Joan, the 52-year-old mother of two young adults, acknowledged that her desire for friendship development was apparently stronger than that of her own young adult daughter. When asked about her relationship with her daughter (now in her early twenties), she shared the following:

I know I've read about how you shouldn't try to be friends with your kid—you hear it on TV, "You're their parents, NOT their friends." I know that. But, still, I'd really like to be friends with my kids, with my daughter. I was friends with my mother, my grandmother. Maybe she's just too independent, but I would like for her to be open . . . and receptive to friendship.

Another woman also stated that she considered her daughter, now 24, married, and a mother of two, as a friend, but cautioned that "my daughter may not see it that way." And in a separate, later interview, her daughter did suggest that her mother probably considered her a close friend, but that she wasn't quite ready for friendship yet; there was still too much of the past between the two women.

WOMEN FLYING SOLO—SINGLE AT MIDLIFE

The traditional cultural message that women are incomplete without a man has been receiving much less widespread broadcasting in recent years. Marriage rates in virtually every demographic group have been falling in recent decades[20] and the cultural acceptance of the choice to go through life solo has been rising. Based on our interviews, it appears that friendship networks for single midlife women are frequently viewed as the "family of choice." These women often have friends with whom they are in regular and very frequent contact, whether by face-to-face visiting, phone calls, texting, or email. This supports the research finding that unmarried women are able to depend more easily on time together—or, in some cases, personal communications—as a way to keep a friendship strong.[21]

Sandra, who is 42 years old and never married, shared stories of travel adventures she and her core group of friends had enjoyed and she noted that if there had been a man in her life, it might have curtailed some of her fun. She also noted that although she did have "men friends," she really counted on her woman friends for emotional support and social activities. She described her two best friends as successful single women who both held graduate degrees in a field similar to her own. One of Sandra's friends had made the choice to adopt a daughter several years ago, and Sandra—by nature of her professional position—had been instrumental in helping her friend get the process underway. Sandra said that whether or not she might have had initial misgivings was immaterial—the two women were friends and Sandra was committed to being supportive and nonjudgmental of her best friend's choices. Sandra also laughs as she describes her pleasure at how the friendship has turned into a family relationship, as the little girl adopted five years ago now looks to her as Auntie Sandra. She rounded out her friendship story by emphasizing how complete her "friendscape" truly has become as she's entered the middle years of life. Aside from her frequent meet-ups with her two closest—and also single—friends, Sandra is active in her church community, including years of service as a Sunday school teacher; she visits with family friends and old friends when she's making her regular visits to her parents, who are still in the house in which she grew up; she gets together a few times a year with friends from her college and graduate school days; and she says that she sees herself as a friend for life when she decides to commit to a friendship. Her world is a series of connecting relationships and her career in public service really seems to serve as a shorthand description of how Sandra has populated her friendscape.

Although she acknowledges that she has a social network, another midlife woman, Rhonda, wishes for more close friends. The daughter she raised alone has reached her early twenties, so the mothering role has receded and left her with more time for personal pursuits. "I see my daughter now with her group of friends, living her own life now. It makes me realize that I'd like to have more friends . . . I'd like to have friends to do some travelling with." But having been hurt deeply by a close friend, there is a hesitance to reach out to potential new friends. Rhonda also feels that her married or partnered friends see her single status as in need of "fixing," and she feels judged by the women who would count her as a friend. Not totally ruling out a possible romantic relationship, she stated that she would have to be friends with a man before she would consider the next step in a relationship. Rhonda likes her life as it is now, but feels that there is a richness that is missing that she would like to experience.

For some women, the choice to forgo a romantic relationship with a man has been based on sexual orientation. Whether a woman "comes out" in her youth or in her midlife years, it can alter the course her friendship development may take. Fifty-three years old, Gayle lives in a rural area and acknowledged the accuracy of the old joke that in a room full of lesbians, all of the women are either former lovers or former best friends with everyone else in the group. She shared that her very best friend today was also her first lover, and that although their romantic relationship had died some 20 years before, their friendship had mellowed and deepened with time. She believes that friends are the real treasure in life and they should always be treated with care. She was proud that she seldom allowed friendships to wither away. Currently unpartnered, Gayle shared that she has many close friendships—with fellow lesbians, for the most part, but she also counts among her close friends her sisters, several straight women, and a few men she feels have proven themselves worthy of friendship.

Another midlife lesbian, however, had a very different perception of how lesbians' friendscapes might look. Janne, now 51, shared that she had come out only within the past couple of years and that she felt that honesty about her sexual orientation would threaten and end a number of her friendships. When she was invited to talk about her friendships, her first response was to request clarification about "which" friends—the ones that were aware of her recently claimed sexual orientation or the ones who assumed she was straight. For Janne, living such a dichotomous life presents challenges, she said, but she felt it was the only choice under her circumstances. She also noted how hard it was for her to develop friendships with other lesbians because she felt that she would run the risk of "outing herself" if she was seen at public events with her lesbian friends. She sadly summed up her situation: "When I finally had the courage to admit that I loved women, the liking of women friends became that much more complicated." Janne said that she would very much like to be in a romantic relationship, but feels that this step would complicate her life more than she feels ready to face at this time.

The percentage of midlife women who have never married continues to climb,[22] and for these women it is important that they learn to like who they are and feel good about the choices they've made. Strong relationships with supportive friends can be essential as we ripen during the second half of life, but these relationships sometimes feel much more difficult to find. By increased self-acceptance and recognition of our own limitations, we often grow more tolerant and accepting of others, which can make us noticeably more acceptable to potential friends.

FRIENDSHIP TERMINATION

By midlife, as noted in an earlier section, women seem to be more sure of who they are, what they are about, and how they would like to invest their available time and energy. Many of the women interviewed noted that they were ready to let go of friendships that no longer felt "right" for them or worth the effort to maintain. Sue, a woman nearing 60 years old, eloquently shared her perspective on friendships:

They flow through life like waves in the ocean, coming and going, and some, like those heavy stones on the beach, just stay there no matter what. I can count them on my one hand. My grandmother used to say that, and I pooh-poohed her, in my days of women's groups, and, more recently, online groups, and really close girlfriends.

[Years ago], I had a completely different view of friendship. I had friends then I thought would be part of my life forever. One is dead, one is probably a bit crazier than I acknowledged at the time I was with her, but still a friend, one is still my lifetime friend, one refuses to remain my friend, even after many many promises of lifetime friendship. The women's group friends are all faded, due to distance and time, I guess, but I never thought that would happen. Online friends I have never met, another whole story, as close as the computer screen, and as ephemeral as electrons floating in the universe. Funny you should bring this all up right now, Suzanne, because it has

been something that I have been thinking on a lot lately. Especially as I pack and go through all my old stuff and photos, clearing, deciding what to keep, what to let go of. Parts of me are going in boxes, and parts of me are going to goodwill, and parts of me are going into the trash pile. It's a big sifting process that has to do where I am in my life right now.

When Friends of Convenience Are No Longer Convenient

The years that stretch from early adulthood through midlife are often crammed full of "doing" and "acting," whether this busy-ness revolves around work, our romantic partner, family obligations, or children. Thus, many of our friendships are forged on specific activities and expectations related to the hub of where the action takes place. This has been attributed to the time constraints that this period of life presents.[23] However, many of us in midlife find that our children are growing up and moving out and our lives and lifestyles may be shifting and morphing into a new incarnation. The "friends" we counted on to share soccer game snack duty, middle school carpool duty, or high school dance chaperone duty are no longer a regular, rotating part of our lives. As some of these "pseudo-friendships," as one woman termed them, fall away, we enter a stage where we can more clearly explore the person we are and the friendships that would best energize and more fully satisfy us. Letting go of our children and the friends that were a fundamental element of the childrearing period of our lives can be painful for some of us, but cathartic for others. One woman described it as totally liberating. She said that she was eager to cut the ties to her daughter's friends' narrow-minded and rigid parents. She felt that the putting away of her daughter's high school cheerleading uniform was the opportunity to tuck away a treasured part of her own identity that had reached fruition and a necessary ending. By gracefully exiting friendships that were built on shared calendars rather than shared authenticity, we are better positioned to develop genuine and more personally fulfilling friendships. One woman anticipating the last of her children leaving home said, "I was looking forward to it! It gave me more time!" And Barbara used this time to sort through her connections and relationships and *choose* the ones that were worth keeping. Friendships built on convenience, not connection, frequently simply fall away when life stages shift and alter.

One woman, Nancy, said that the first month or so after her youngest child was at college was a treasure—she felt a luscious freedom she had not quite anticipated. Able to cut back on grocery runs, able to enjoy last-minute dates and getaways with her partner, she felt rejuvenated. Until, she said, she realized that the house was much lonelier than she'd expected and that many of the women she had assumed were friends were really just "companions" in the raising of children. Her son's extra-curricular events had also served as her social connecting ground—she loved sitting with other parents to cheer on the band at various contests, football and basketball games, and the hometown parades. She assumed that the other parents were as much her friends as they were fans of their own children! But with her tuba-playing son now out of the house, the calls from other band mothers ceased and Nancy realized that she may have been living vicariously through her son. She decided she needed to determine whether the relationships with other mothers were really friendships or acquaintanceships. Nancy proactively and assertively contacted the women and suggested getting together for socializing beyond what they'd experienced when socializing was organized around their kids' activities. Some women were responsive and eager to build non-child-centered friendships; some others just didn't seem interested or available. Nancy noted that it took her a few months, but that she was able to let go of the hope of seeing friendships develop with some of the women whose company she had enjoyed and to appreciate the women who were as interested in growing a friendship as she was herself.

Learning to Let Go of Unclaimed Baggage

Many midlife women were raised in an era when good manners included tolerating and excusing another person's misbehavior. Women have been taught to please others even to their own detriment. More than a few of our interviewees spoke of friends who had done them wrong; although they felt the need to forgive, they found it hard to forget. This is shifting, however, as women move into their fifties and edge toward their sixties. Ridding ourselves of relationships that only serve to hurt us or compromise our integrity can bolster our self-confidence and our self-esteem. Unlike the broken friendships of younger women and girls that frequently involve episodes of jealousy, competitiveness, or gossip, and betrayal of others, our midlife interviewees saw their friendship end due to dyadic, more than group, interactions. Betrayal was not so much about sleeping with a husband or partner, but more of the nature of not taking personal responsibility for fulfilling promises and expectations.

The inability to remain nonjudgmental was perhaps the most frequently cited reason for friendship termination. One woman complained, "The friendship was great—until I made a choice that was right for me, but not tolerated by my ex-friend. It is no one else's business how I choose to live my life, and I've reached a point where I will not tolerate others' judgmental attitudes." This was shared by a 42-year-old woman who had made the choice to pursue single motherhood via artificial insemination. Another woman had allowed her daughter to spend a college semester abroad, but she lost a friendship when she was remonstrated for allowing her daughter to visit a country where, according to the ex-friend, they "channel the devil."

Refusing to accept others' judgments, bad behavior, and negative opinions is a perk of reaching midlife. It is a time when we can fully become the person we are meant to be and determine how our social networks work best for us. Freeing ourselves from the period in life in which we were serving the needs of those around us, we can now focus on how we want to live our lives, who we would like to have in our lives, and what we feel the rules of friendships should be.

CONCLUSION

As noted, there is scant empirical research exploring or explaining the midlife friendship process. From what we know of the midlife experience, it is clear that these women are experiencing shifts and transitions that have the potential to catapult them from one theoretically "predicted" life stage to one totally uncharted in academic literature. Turning 30, turning 40, and turning 50 may all be milestones in themselves, but they may also mark the start of the decade in which we find ourselves single or find ourselves taken. We may be setting up housekeeping with our first true love or breaking up a household with the one we'd assumed would be the love of our life. We may find ourselves battling the loneliness that comes from an empty nest or battling the busy-ness that comes with a new baby. The changes and experiences of the contemporary midlife period suggest that friendships are an invaluable resource throughout these decades; however, the precise function and value provided by these relationships may vary vastly based on the circumstances we face. We are free to choose the lifestyle and friendships that best serve *us*, not the expectations or conventions of the prior generations.

10

Ǝ୨ Ƨ₰

The Long Road Home
Community and Friendship
in Older Adulthood

Current research underscores the positive influence that strong social support systems offer older adult women in terms of emotional and physical well-being. Some women are easily able to remain socially active and engaged with others as they move through the challenges that accompany the aging process, whereas other women seem to close in and increasingly shrink their social circles. Here we explore the research related to friendships during later adulthood and share stories of women who are on this journey.

Once we get past the initial shock of our arrival at midlife, we are then in preparation, regardless of whether we know it, for our movement into that nebulous period called "older adulthood." Although debate about the exact chronological age that heralds the end of the middle years and entry into the golden years continue to sound, social scientists now divide this next stage into the "young-old," the "middle-old," and "the old-old" periods. Physical health rather than psychological health probably provides the true distinctions between categories. The gender advantage in longevity goes to women; approximately a third of the women who are 65 and older live alone in our country.[1] Women in their sixties and older presumably rely more on their friendship networks than men might, and research continues to provide evidence of these women's keen appreciation for a strong social support system. It is clear that women enjoy involvement in social activities throughout their lives, whether engaging with family, friends, acquaintances, or through a host of organizations or institutions (e.g., volunteer work, churches, social clubs, activity centers).[2] In fact, when older adults were asked to rank the importance of the social roles they played in their lives, "friend" was ranked higher than any other role.[3] We consistently value and honor our place in social relationships throughout our lives. And, unlike the case of midlife women, there has been a fair amount of research regarding friendship development and engagement of adults in their later years.

WHAT WE KNOW ABOUT THE FRIENDSHIPS OF OLDER WOMEN

For years we have heard about the strong relationship between healthy social relationships and overall physical and psychological well-being. This is likely one of the driving forces behind the profusion of research into the friendships of older adults. Staying connected to others keeps us connected to life, it would seem. As we age, the qualities that bind us to our friends include devotion to one another, active reciprocity between ourselves and our friends, closeness and understanding of one another, the sharing of lived experience, and a feeling of attraction to our friends.[4] Parallel to a growing awareness of one's own mortality, older adults typically show a growing awareness of the likely consequences of the loss of a friendship. With a lifetime of relationship experience, older women can easily appreciate the value of genuine, reciprocal friendships. In fact, it is during older adulthood that our friendships undergo the greatest amount of transition.[5] The presence of friends and the ability to maintain strong relationships with these special people actually enhance our self-esteem—it feels good when we can count ourselves among a group of friends.[6] And we enjoy this benefit whether we have a slew of good friends or just a single close friend.

A Garden of Friends or a Patio Pot?

We know that the size of our social network decreases with age and it makes sense that older women would have a smaller social group as they move through inevitable transitions that may bring closure to some friendships. But there are, of course, variations in the original size of a woman's friendship circle. When you think about your own friendship circle, is it populated with just a small number of close friends? Or do you picture a large, bustling crowd of people? Research suggests that older adults fall into one of three categories[7] of social network landscapers, or *friendscapers*. The first type is the *independent* friend; she has little interest in developing deeply connected relationships or very close friends. She is content to have friends that she meets for specific activities or events, such as church groups, volunteer activities, or leisure activities, such as bowling leagues or exercise classes. One interviewee, 84-year-old Betsy, a retired social worker and widow, personified this category with her description of her week's worth of typical social interactions:

Well, on Sundays, there's always church. I go to the one that I began attending after college. On Mondays, there's a senior club that meets in the mornings that I like to go to. Tuesdays, well, one week it's the church circle from my church, and the next week, I go to the circle from the church I used to go to when I was younger. Let's see, on Wednesdays, I like to help out the Meals on Wheels people, visit as they take in the meals to the homebound folk. Thursdays, well I like to rest a little bit, I suppose, most weeks. Fridays are for a social group of little old ladies just like me. We chat, talk about our lives, whatever comes to mind of a morning. Saturdays, sometimes I visit people, sometimes people stop by, sometimes I just enjoy my own company. But I don't really have the sort of close friends you sometimes read about, no real confidants. I believe I've spent my life helping other people do that through my career.

The second type is the *discerning* friend. She is the friend who develops strong and rich attachments to a relatively small number of women, but truly invests herself in the friendships. This category is illustrated by the sharing from Elsie, 71, who revealed, "I just have two really close women friends, but we see each other regularly—twice a week at our quilting and knitting circles—and we like to chat on the phone, talk about what happened at the get-togethers, who said what, gossip a bit, and talk about what's going on at home. I share a lot with my husband and children, too. I really care about the people I'm close to, but I just don't make a lot of friends. I'm just a little shy." Elsie's regular meetings with her two closest friends underscores earlier findings that regular contact, structured around shared activities, is perhaps the easiest pathway for friendships to develop.[8]

The third type is the *acquisitive* friend who nourishes friendships from years past as she continues to add to her friendscape. This is how 65-year-old Beleta described herself. "I make new friends often and very easily. I look for opportunities each day of my life to add a friend. My life would not be different with more friends, because I cherish the friends I currently have. But friendship, for me, is a constant process of discovering and unfolding each day."

Perhaps the most salient influence on the shrinking size of older women's social networks is the limited opportunity to make new friends to replace the ones that leave their circles. Aiken[9] noted that the older we get, the more geographically constrained our lives become, which results in fewer

opportunities to meet new people who might be potential friends. He also
noted that as we age, we tend to become more introspective and inner-
focused; this might limit our interest in adding to our social landscapes. In
fact, one study showed that older women with smaller social groups were
actually happier than those with larger networks. It was suggested that
more friends might just mean more headaches or conflicts—having a large
social circle may be more detrimental to well-being than having only a very
few close friends.[10] Other research, describing the Socioemotional Selectivity Theory, shows that older adults focus on maintaining the relationships
that bring meaning to their lives, letting go of relationships that seem
unproductive or unhelpful, and handling their responses to problems in
relationships more effectively.[11] Positive engagement is integral to overall
well-being, especially for older women. This means that we don't need to
round up a social support system of massive proportions; we just need a
solid, supportive, and accepting nest of good friends. Even with decreased
contact, we may still feel connected to friends we do not regularly see. Research shows that just knowing there is someone who cares about us can be
a strong emotional uplift, according to Hess,[12] as cited in Aiken.[13]

Growing Friendships in Older Adulthood

In years past, the most salient factors found to be elements of older
women's social landscapes were egalitarianism, sociability, and religios-
ity, according to a study completed a little over two decades ago.[14] This
may reflect a generational influence, as the import of religious or spiritual agreement was not mentioned by more than a few of older women
interviewed. In fact, many women noted that their friendships included
a widely diverse collection of individuals in regards to age, ethnicity, religion, and, as one woman termed it, "station in life."

Some studies suggest that our socioeconomic standing (SES) actually
influences the role we expect our friends to play in our lives.[15] Women
who are at the higher end of the SES ladder typically have markedly
different friendship needs and, usually, a larger number of friends than
those at the lower end. Women in the former group typically focus on
leisure activities with friends, whereas those in the latter group look for
instrumental support from their support networks. This is no different
for lower-SES older adults who seek physical and practical support from
their closest support network members.[16] Actually, women in the lower
economic levels typically have a much larger proportion of their support
networks populated by family members than by friends, making the need
to request instrumental support perhaps a little easier.

Age also influences the forms of support that we seek from our best
friends. Physical, social, and emotional problems are the areas for which

the oldest of us are most likely to ask assistance from a best friend; the younger "older adult" is much more likely to turn to their close friends for discussion of mental, financial, and spiritual concerns. We value our best friends, our close friends, and our quasi-friends for different, but equally valuable, reasons. Although they don't scrutinize the bank balances or the birth certificates of prospective friends, older adults do tend to be drawn to those who are similar to themselves, just as younger individuals tend to be. In older adulthood, especially, we are often more likely to share the same perspective on the world and the same morals that were prevalent during the years in which we were coming of age. This shared history and worldview often bring together unlikely friends. However, one 94-year-old woman noted that she had always sought out independent thinkers and people who were different from her in experience, age, and race. She took great pride in her small role in helping break color barriers during the 1950s when she became fast friends with a person of another race and enjoyed challenging others' prejudices through social outings to restaurants or local markets in the company of her friend. As she recounted the pleasure she took in stepping beyond the rigid race barriers, she also described associated losses that resulted from her commitment to her new friends. She noted that she had to sacrifice a number of her early friendships when these friends refused to accept her racially diverse friends.

However, for many older adults, it is often those people who are most similar to them that are within striking distance for friendship development. The housing choice or residential situation of an older woman often determines her friendship pool. By remaining in the family home, limited transportation may narrow friendships down to the existing neighbors or new families that move in. The move to a retirement home or assisted living center brings older adults into contact with potential friends who often reflect a strong similarity in demographic characteristics and interests. Connecting with people who have already made a transition that we are now facing is often very helpful in our own successful navigation of the event. Whether it is a new home, a new status, or a new identity, we value role models who can show us how things are done.

OLD-MARRIEDS, SINGLE LADIES, AND THOSE IN-BETWEEN

It's probably not surprising that older married women spend significantly less time with their friends than their unmarried age-mates. The marriage bond, especially with a retired partner or one in poor health, can require a significant investment of time and energy that may deplete the resources we might otherwise invest in getting together or connecting with our friends. Research reports frequently tout the health and well-being benefits that accrue to the monogamously partnered throughout the lifespan. Yet it is married men, not their wives, who benefit the most from having a partner in their lives. Married men typically receive the greatest socioemotional support from their wives; their wives look to their children, their friends, and other relatives.[17]

In addition to the expectation that wives devote their leisure time to their spouses, older women also tend to shoulder the caretaking responsibilities of other relatives, as well. Caretaking for older relatives is often seen as a mandatory obligation by women and without the financial means to employ paid assistance, caretakers' lives narrow down to a small sliver of what they once were. Unwilling to burden other family members and feeling the need to be present for those in need of care, women may begin to feel as if they were single-handedly responsible for their own and others' well-being. It is important to note the connection between the perceived isolation that can accompany caretaking and its potential physiological effects. Research shows that just believing that you do not have a high level of social support is related to increased levels of depression.[18]

One woman, Becky, who was caring for her disabled husband, began suffering from debilitating migraine headaches and a "growing sense of doom," as she termed it. She was close to 65, working full-time, and caring for her spouse and her own mother who lived two doors down. Becky acknowledged that she had expected failing health to be a part of growing older, but she never realized how lonely she would feel as she spent what little leisure time she had running back and forth between "one invalid and another," as she baldly described it. She said the loss of friends and the feeling of being solely responsible for two other adults was overwhelming to her and she blamed this, in part, for her somatic complaints. Becky was dealing with both social loneliness, which is the sense of not having companionship, and emotional loneliness, which relates to a feeling of having no close friend with whom she could openly and honestly share her feelings. She finished her story with a surprising twist—she sought out medical help for her headaches and was referred to a counselor who was able to give Becky a place to vent about her feelings as well as help her learn better coping skills. Becky said that she was hoping that she would be able to seek out respite care for her family members so that she could make time for the socializing she so clearly needed. If you, too, are in a caretaking role that prohibits spontaneous socializing or interferes with your ability to connect with your own support network, it is essential that you contact local agencies that offer respite care services. Join a support group for caregivers, as well, to help normalize the experiences you are having. Taking advantage of online support groups for caregivers is another option if travel from home is truly compromised.

Widows typically prefer the friendship of other women who have lost a partner.[19] Truly, a strong social support system can soften the pain felt at the loss of one's spouse, and research shows that widows benefit most from friends who are not invested in a significant monogamous relationship. Single women have more time for friends and more flexibility in their availability for activities including travel, something many of our interviewees enjoyed doing. However, the loss of a partner can leave many women feeling like a third wheel among their coupled-up friends. This may lead them to retreat from social engagement and isolate themselves at a time when this often only deepens their sense of loss and bereavement. One woman said she was only half-joking when she shared that she and her best friend have decided that because they would most likely outlive their husbands, they were already planning to take up housekeeping together some year in the future when they found themselves both widowed. Even though family ties may hold precedence over friendship ties for older adults, when children and other relatives live far away, close friends are essential to a healthy and satisfying passage through life.

Mary is a 94-year-old widow and divorcee who has lived alone for close to five decades, she guesses. She regrets that her two living children each live on opposite ends of the country while she resides in its heartland. She shared that she had outlived her husband, her ex-husband, and all of her close friends. She poignantly stated, "I'm not getting old, I am becoming fossilized." As often happens to older single women who have no children or close relatives at hand, Mary must depend on younger neighbors for both instrumental support (such as transportation or bringing in her mail) as well as for emotional support. Although Mary appreciates the assistance her neighbors and the meal service delivery volunteers provide, she holds conflicting feelings about wishing for a friend closer to her age. She communicated a longing for a close friend who could understand the world as she saw it, but she laughed and said that she wouldn't wish her old age on anyone she really cared about.

For Michelle, who states her age as "not quite four score and ten," her identity as a divorcée still carries a personal stigma in her mind. She feels that it has hampered her ability to build a healthy social support system. Even though her divorce had occurred many years before, she noted that it was not common among her circle of friends to opt for divorce, and she had lost most of her close friends after her husband moved out. This provides unfortunate support to the reported feelings of isolation experienced by women when they undergo a relationship breakup.[20] There is a sense of identity and dignity attached to the role of widow that remains unavailable for many older women who came of age during a time when divorce was simply not acceptable under even the worst circumstances. Regardless of how "free and easy" or "open and accepting" the world may be today, the values that are learned in our youth are often the ones that we embrace and by which we are judged. Dignity and self-sufficiency are of utmost importance to many older women. Unable to totally divest themselves of the sense of shame or perceived judgment by others—and sometimes by oneself—these women face a difficult struggle in their pursuit of social connections.

Not having relatives nearby for support can place older women in a difficult situation. Being required to lean on friends and neighbors for help with household chores or transportation needs can take a toll on some women's pride. However, it can become a necessary development in our relationships with younger, more able individuals, whether family members, neighbors, or helpful friends and acquaintances. Researchers suggest that the need to call for assistance without being able to offer it in return creates an undesirable imbalance in relationships with less close friends or acquaintances; there is less concern about inequity of giving in close relationships.[21]

BEST FRIENDS: DO WE NEED THEM THROUGHOUT OUR LIVES?

Best friendships differ from other friendships for older women according to consistent research findings.[22,23] Within an earlier chapter, we discussed the concept of a social exchange system being created within our relationships. Although this system is typically not verbalized between friends, it is often an underlying expectation that governs the course of the relationship. However, in the case of older adult women, the relationships they have with their closest, best friends specifically do *not* rely on a sense of equity exchange. The relationship, itself, may be the only reward necessary for a feeling of satisfaction from the friendship.

As with younger women, older women often consider their partners to be their best friends. The shared struggles have truly polished the relationships between some couples. Jessie, who is 63 years old, described her best friendship with her partner: "She is wonderful and I am blessed to have her in my life, but that does not preclude having . . . other friendships." One woman in her late sixties shared that "my best friend is my husband and has been for many years"; yet as she described some of the barriers that she felt kept her from making new friends, she acknowledged that "my husband does not want to be around [me when I'm with] a girlfriend, so I honor his wishes" and, unfortunately, she limits her efforts at establishing new friendships. This is an extreme example of how we might create a self-imposed version of social isolation. She did acknowledge that she wished she also had one or two close girlfriends with whom she could share "the good and the bad" in life. In fact, over half of all women experience a period of time in their lives when they are without a close or best same-sex friend.[24] Another woman specified that her "best *male* friend" is her husband, but she also noted close female friends with whom she could share most everything.

Those studies noted earlier in this section indicated that women who enjoy the presence of a best friend in their lives do, indeed, experience a unique relationship. Best friendships are not paralleled by less close friendships in which equity is so prized. However, as has been noted previously, conflict in a relationship—whether between best friends or less close friends—is a strong detractor from friendship satisfaction, and some women may limit their friendships in order to limit conflict. As a case in point, some women we interviewed noted that they did not have a friend that really measured up to their own definitions of best friends. One woman, a 67-year-old divorcée, shared that she really had no close friends at all: "My world is my children. Family is all that matters in the end." She defended her choice by affirming her belief that "no friends can really be trusted to be there when you need them."

Yet no matter how important strong family ties may be, research confirms that the presence of a best friend really makes a positive difference in our well-being. And because each generation seems to be more geographically mobile than the one before, the presence of reliable, close friends nearby can be undeniably important. Older women who had best friends were found to have lower levels of depression and higher levels of overall life satisfaction.[25] The need to share our lives—both exterior experiences and interior perceptions—with another person who cares about us is a "shelf-stable" need. Friends who are closer than acquaintances or quasi-friends are able to bring a sense of belonging and connection to our lives, especially when we may believe that the world is moving in directions we find surprising, if not disturbing.

Adult Children and Older Relations

Older women may be reluctant to utilize their children's assistance as frequently as they might, due to their hesitance to appear dependent or useless. Older women's daughters are more likely to visit than their sons, but the visits are more frequent by both sons and daughters if a woman is widowed.[26] Relying on one's children not just for care, but also for friendship, can be challenging for some women who have enjoyed the role of caregiver and nurturer themselves. However, it is often well worth the effort.

As the relationship between an adult daughter and her mother grows into a satisfying friendship, women have felt that they are reaping unexpected benefits from the raising of a daughter. As noted in the previous chapter, maturing women are often highly responsive to a friendship with their mothers. One interviewee, Beleta, shared with pride, "My current best friend is my youngest daughter, because I love watching my morals, ideals, and teachings being bounced back to me" and her daughter affirmed that she felt the same way about her mom. Another woman described the process as "striving to become an adult friend with both my daughters," and she looks forward to the blossoming of these new connections to her children.

When asked about her best friends, Sue, a currently single woman in her mid-sixties, shared the following:

My kids have also become my best friends, even my son, who's now in his forties. I don't understand him much—he is a redneck boy from Missouri—but we talk on the phone at least every week and sometimes more. My daughters are the friends who don't leave. Maybe we get angry, or frustrated, or busy, but we don't leave. I find that now with them in their forties my role as protector is lessened, but the role of listener never ceases.

The connection between listening and friendship is a constant in most strong friendships.

In a twist on the mother–daughter dyad friendship experience, one woman, 68-year-old Jane, described a friendship she had with her 88-year-old friend, Zona:

Well, I just love Zona. I look forward to playing bridge with her, getting lunch with her at the club, when we get together on our bowling league. Not only is she my best friend, but because I lost my own mother when I was so young, I feel like Zona is like a mother to me. And it warmed my heart when Zona actually mentioned her recognition and appreciation of the "mother–daughter" aspect of our friendship.

Becoming friends with your children—or your surrogate children—is definitely one reward of cultivating enriched relationships in older adulthood. In fact, establishing a healthy relationship with your adult children is even more important to many older women than the quality of their friendships. It is difficult for many of us to request instrumental assistance at all, but good relationships with our adult children may give us an advantage in feeling comfortable enough to ask for the help we need.

Wishing for someone to truly hear us and to care about us are basic needs that begin at birth and stay with us for life. The value of easy communication could not be understated by Mary, who acknowledged that she had become increasingly hard-of-hearing as she approached her seventy-eighth birthday. Mary shared that the loss of her hearing was the hardest part of aging for her and research shows that age-related hearing impairment is a much greater blow to women than to men.[27] Men generally have wives who serve as interpreters and communicators for them. Mary's children live several states away, her husband died almost 20 years ago, and she says that the hearing loss had brought a sense of isolation and loneliness to her life she was not expecting. Anything beyond surface, basic communication with others—storekeepers, librarians, and friends—was a challenge and she felt that much was lost in her relationships. It can be the deep, mutual communication that affirms who we are and what we mean to a friend.

Research shows that sisters have the strongest and closest bond among siblings, and they are more likely to maintain contact—and deep friendships—through the years.[28] Thus, the strong sisterly bonds that weather the decades often provide the most treasured friendships for older adult women. An example of the closeness of sisters was described by Mae, a woman in her mid-eighties. She and her three younger sisters had grown up during "hard-scrabble times" and had to find simple ways to entertain themselves in the evenings after they'd finished working on their parents' farm. They would spend the hours learning folk dances and singing tunes their parents and older relatives had sung to them through the years. Now, 70 years later, when they all get together, they still roll up the rug and show off the "buck dancing," or "clogging," as it's more commonly known—just as they'd done when they were young. Mae appreciated the tight-knit bond that she felt with her sisters, Blanche, Irene, and also with Ruth, who had died several years before. Mae recalled that they learned to be close friends as young girls, living somewhat isolated out on the farm as they did, and today, the remaining three sisters are close friends out of choice. And just watching them carrying on, laughing, dancing, and singing communicated volumes about the sisterly love and genuine friendship that runs deep among the women. Another interviewee, 63-year-old Paula, shared that her closest women friends are her six sisters. She noted that their friendships were solidified when they lost their mother 34 years ago and, at that point, decided they would meet once a year to honor their beloved mother and to share a weekend *as friends*. The value of their friendship has become more and more apparent with the passage of time.

When the Children Make the Rules for Your Friends

With contemporary economic challenges, it is frequently the younger members of the family who move back home before the older generation needs to move into the younger family member's home. However, the experience of moving into an adult child's home can present many unexpected difficulties. Though it certainly can bring an end to the burden of home upkeep, it can also bring a loss of self-esteem and autonomy. Conflict is expected to flare up occasionally when there are two families and multiple generations under one roof, but it was a surprise when a move brought conflict to the existing friendships of women who'd moved in with their children. A couple of women interviewed noted that they didn't mind so much the sharing of their lives with their children's families, but they did mind the discord that it brought to their social relationships. As one 72-year-old described:

I didn't really think about how the move would influence my activities with friends. My bridge friends and I would love to get together and play cards and laugh until midnight or so; all of us are retired and don't usually have to be anywhere early in the mornings. But my daughter complained that our laughter was keeping the grandkids awake and she wanted us to keep it down or start earlier. Now, I tell you, I have been hosting bridge clubs since before she was born! She grew up just fine, and it just feels uncomfortable asking my friends, women my age, to keep it down for the children. And, yes, I know it's not smart or "politically correct" to smoke these days, but it was embarrassing to have to ask my friends to chew gum or something instead. I love my daughter and I treasure our own friendship, but I just didn't expect her to have such a say-so in my friendships with women I've known for decades!

Keeping in mind that our friends are experiencing the same life stage events that we are facing may help us take these changes in stride. Knowing that our genuine friends love us for who we are—not the home we live in, the car we drive, or the clothes we wear—can also help us handle the perceived loss of self-esteem or sense of autonomy that may arise out of a move into our child's home. Humor is one of the most valued qualities in a friend, so being able to laugh at the ups and downs of our life circumstances will ease the tension we may feel when we are blazing a trail through new life-space topographies.

Losing Friends

Older women frequently see their neighborhood friends leave their homes to move in with children or into smaller, downsized homes or into assisted living or care centers. This loss of nearby friends can be especially difficult for older women, as research shows that older adults value long-term neighborhood friendships more than other age cohorts might.[29] Without good friends in close proximity, many older women may lose their mobility, as well. If we've come to rely on companionship for safety, as well as pleasure, this loss can be especially isolating. As aging limits physical mobility, it can also take away the capacity to drive, thus further limiting a woman's social world.

Illness keeps some women from interacting with others as regularly and as fully as they once did, which may negatively affect their physical well-being. There is a positive relationship between friendship interactions and health—the healthier older women are, the greater their involvement with friends. Having friends seems to provide some sort of immunity factor that promotes good health. Friendships—or at least social interaction—are also helpful in helping us dodge depression. Older adults who spend the majority of their time alone may display symptoms of depression as well as carelessness and apathy.[30] Sadly, as we lose interest in others and ourselves, our self-esteem drops, along with self-care, making it harder to maintain our social connections. It is vital to both our physical and mental health that we stay engaged in community, or at least in one or two strong friendships.

Death, of course, can all too often rob us of friends in our older years. The grieving process may become a perpetual cycle for older women as they come to terms with the loss of one friend only to lose another. Friends offer companionship, of course, to older adults, but they also offer the motivation to engage in social activities and community functions. This combination of factors is especially important to overall well-being during the aging process.[31] It is essential that older adults maintain social ties to members of their communities and that interaction is maintained throughout their lives. Mutually engaging relationships are one of the key factors in successful aging.

For one woman, 77-year-old Grace, watching a close friend, Laura, lose her battle with illness left her with multiple layers of grief that resembled those felt at the loss of a spouse. Grace, Laura, and Thelma, another friend, had met on the first day of elementary school more than 70 years ago, as Grace proudly noted. The three of them had been inseparable throughout their school years and the friendships continued as they graduated college and began their adult lives. Although her two friends had married, Grace remained single throughout her life. Laura lost her husband in her mid-fifties, so that was the point at which Grace and Laura's friendship grew even closer. The three friends and Thelma's husband became an adventurous foursome as they entered retirement and finally had the time and resources to enjoy travel across the country and aboard many cruises. Grace did not miss having a husband, she said, until the loss of her friend, Laura. Grace shared that at her age, she expected death to be a part of life, but she was surprised at the layers of grief she felt at this loss. As she elaborated:

Aging is not easy under any circumstances, but having a dear friend who is going through the process alongside you makes it easier. I still have some friends left, but being a part of a pair made it easier to travel with Thelma and her husband; it gave me someone to share a room with, someone to share adventure with. I never wanted to be a "third wheel," but that's how things have ended up. I may never grieve a husband's death, but I feel like this loss has changed my world almost as much as I imagine becoming a widow might do.

Sadly, many of our interviewees looked to their husbands as their best friend, and as noted above, the difference in male and female life expectancies leaves many women very much alone in their older adult years.

Financial strains may also limit our social activities. As we move into retirement, our disposable incomes often take a significant downturn, resulting in fewer leisure options. Not only does retirement often signal newly limited financial freedom, but it also often signifies newly limited social interaction. Retirement takes us away from the work setting, which is an important locale for meeting friends throughout most of adulthood. Ending one's professional career often brings an end to a good deal of one's socializing, as interests beyond work may not be enough to sustain friendships after retirement. As one 68-year-old newly retired woman described it, "My work girlfriends had been there for me for over 25 years. We'd get together for the annual departmental summer pool party and our Christmas luncheon; we shared our breaks, our heartaches, our joys. Everything. Now, though, I'm retired and, unfortunately, we don't get together very often anymore—maybe just a couple of times a year." She knows she will need to seek out new friends, relying on her new identity as retiree, which she feels she is still getting used to. Although some aspects of older adult friendship have been well studied, there is still limited attention to the ways in which older women respond to the loss of friends and social support in later life and the ways in which they fill the gaps.[32] As Jessie, 63 years old and retired, described it:

Making friends has been a bit of a puzzle for me recently. I still have my strong enduring friendships from my time in Houston. I value these deeply. But finding that sort of friendship recently has been problematic. I think part of that is due to ill health. Not getting around as much impacts the types of social connections I can have. I have tons of acquaintances, but scarcely anyone with whom I can discuss my life at an intimate level. I miss those types of conversations, and pray that someone will fill that void soon. What I seek are deep friendships, something that goes beyond the casual chit-chat. I'm part of a friendship group where that is supposed to happen, but it seems to be slowly falling apart.

Still hopeful, Jessie concludes, "So I am open to friendship when it comes along, enjoy visits when they happen. I may join some group for the elderly, since these are the only people who have time to develop these kinds of friendships, it seems." Being willing to invest the energy required to pursue social relationships through active engagement, Jessie, like many women her age, will be able to reap the multifaceted benefits authentic friendships have to offer.

CONCLUSION

We need our friends, whether we are just learning to walk or just learning to use a walker. Women who are able to maintain and establish new friendships even into older adulthood have a significant edge over others less willing to reach out to potential friends. There is no doubt that a strong social support system is a harbinger of a more pleasurable experience with the aging process, but there is no magic number of friends or special type of friends that are requisites for optimal well-being. This number or type varies for each woman. You may be content with fewer than a handful of friends, while other women need a roomful. Romantic partners, confidants, best friends, family, neighbors, and acquaintances can all serve a health-promoting function in your social network. Friends who can meet instrumental assistance needs are as essential to a healthy friendscape, as are those friends on whom we can lean for emotional support. It is also clearly wise to avoid friends who bring with them a tendency to create negative interaction patterns, as this can be more detrimental to our welfare than the absence of friends might be. As we shift into the silver or the golden years, we can ease the passage and maintain higher levels of overall well-being with the support of our friends.

III

MAKING FRIENDS—
STARTING WITH YOURSELF

11

❧ ❧

Understanding Who
You Are as a Friend

How did you learn how to be a friend? Who taught you the informal rules about social interactions and personal relationships? Who were some of your role models? Are you pleased with who you have become as a friend? Exploring past patterns in relationships will raise your awareness of the role you play in your relationships today.

Have you ever found yourself saying about a friend, "I can't believe she *did* that! I never would have expected that of her!" Sometimes we get mixed messages from our friends. Maybe you expect more from them than they are willing to give. Maybe you are given more than you feel you deserve, whether in time, attention, energy, or patience. Maybe your expectations seldom match your experiences in your relationships with friends. Maybe you feel that you are not attracting the sort of friends that you would like to have. Our expectations, however, can definitely influence the types of friends we choose and those who choose us. If you don't believe that your friendship network is all that it could be or if you just want to better understand how your social relationships are structured, it can be helpful to assess the roles you tend to play in your friendships. As one astute woman has noted, we teach people how to treat us.

VISUALIZING YOUR CONNECTIONS

Friendships invite you to open your heart and your mind to others. Friendships encourage honest communication and creative expression

143

of your thoughts and feelings. Giving yourself space to explore the ways in which you relate to friends—both past and present—will provide you with an opportunity to acknowledge and connect with who you are as a friend. To help with the process, you are invited to engage in a guided visualization activity. Prior to the visualization, gather some colorful pens and markers and a few sheets of paper. On one sheet of paper, use a compass or a plate to trace a large circle in the center of the paper; have the outline of the circle reach to within an inch or so of the edges of the paper. Now, find a place where you can relax in peace and solitude for an hour or so. If you'd like, turn on some soft music if it won't distract you from the visualization exercise. When you're settled, take a few deep breaths, letting go of a little more stress or worry each time you exhale until you are completely relaxed. When you feel calm, safe, and grounded, proceed with the following activity:

Reflect on the term "best friend." What images appear to you when you think about best friends? What are the feelings that are attached to these images?

When did you find your first best friend? How old were you? What drew you to one another? What made the two of you best friends? Did you mark or celebrate the friendship in any way? What did it mean to you to have a best friend at that point in your life?

Now, think about other best friends you've had throughout your life. How were these friendships different from other friendships? What made these relationships special?

Think about your current circle of friends. How satisfied are you with the support network they provide? Are there relationships that you work to maintain that might be better off ended?

Are there relationships that need to be strengthened?

Are there relationships that need to be redefined?

Are there spaces or gaps in your friendship network that you would like to see filled?

There are many words that are used to describe sets of friends, such as "system," or "network," or "web," or a variety of others. Take a moment and reflect on your own relationships with your friends and let your imagination create a visual representation of those relationships.

What image rises up for you?

How do you see yourself in the role of friend? What do you see as your contributions to your relationships with friends?

How would you choose to symbolically represent who you are as a friend? Would it be an emblem? A symbol? A phrase?

Imagine the form, the design, the colors, and the shading of the design as the image takes shape in your mind and grows clearer and clearer . . .

*Now, using the art supplies you gathered, give form and life to that
image.*

After you have completed your visual representation of how you see
yourself as a friend, take a moment to gaze at the finished work and then
reflect and respond to the following questions—it's most helpful to write
down your responses.

- What features of your work stand out as you view your art?
- What colors did you choose to complete the image?
- What feelings arise as you look at your artwork?
- If you were to title the image, what would that title be?
- Write a paragraph or two about the part of yourself you have cap-
  tured in this image.
- In 15 words or less, how would you sum up your personal belief
  about friendship that you have depicted in this image?
- Describe what you like most about who you are as a friend.
- Describe what changes, if any, you might like to make in yourself as
  a friend.

After completing these questions, take a fresh look at the artwork you
created and note if there are any fresh thoughts or revelations that arise.
Friendships are dynamic constructs in which periods of growth and still-
ness are interspersed. As you work through the exercises in this section
and the next, you will be encouraged to develop your abilities to make
and maintain the friendship network you desire. Use the image you created as a baseline for measuring your personal development as a friend.

TAKING STOCK OF YOUR READINESS
FOR FRIENDSHIP DEVELOPMENT

There are times when once-warm friendships grow cool, new friendships fail to develop fully, and potential friends remain acquaintances.
As we try to figure out what led to a failed relationship, we sometimes
jump first to judge the behavior of the friend, rather than our own.
Perhaps we forget that relationships rely on mutual interactions. It
is important to examine the way that we, ourselves, contribute to the
working of a friendship. It is only our own behavior that we can control
and change and there are certain personal qualities and characteristics
that are essential to cultivate if you would like to build healthy, lasting
friendships.[1] A baker's dozen of personal traits were derived through
focus groups and surveys of women who spanned the life stages from

adolescence through older adulthood. This set of "friendship qualities" is similar to a list of traits that were determined to be the "most likable" personal qualities in a seminal study completed by Norman Anderson almost four decades ago.[2] These 13 traits could be broadly categorized into the areas of integrity, acceptance, and congeniality; they reflect both the ability to interact with others in a healthy manner, as well as the presence of a healthy sense of self.

For most women, past experience with friendships influences the level at which they believe they currently exhibit each quality. For instance, many women shared that one significant incident of broken trust can alter their willingness to open themselves up fully in another friendship; therefore, they score themselves lower on trust. Other women noted that they are uncomfortable when a friendship is "out of balance," and they find themselves giving—or receiving—distinctly more support or energy in a relationship. Women who believe they receive more than they provide may mark themselves lower in categories related to support of others. It is doubtful than any woman could be a perfect friend in every situation, but it is possible to work toward self-improvement in areas in which the greatest self-determined need exists. Following are descriptions of the ways in which these traits can affect a friendship. After reading these sections, complete the Friendship Readiness Self-Assessment Scale to determine your own strengths and weaknesses.

Traits of Integrity

This quintet of traits includes trustworthiness, honesty, dependability, loyalty, and, as an interrelated quality, the ability to trust others. These five qualities are related to core values held by most cultures. If they are not firmly established in individuals as adults, it is often due to inadequate role models and disappointing childhood experiences in which we were let down by others.

Trustworthiness. This is often the "make or break" element in a friendship and has been shown to be one of the most important qualities in many key relationships.[3] If you lose your credibility and a friend believes she can no longer trust you, this can signal the end of the relationship. Trustworthiness also relates to being able to keep the confidences of friends and being true to your word. A breach of trust can range from sharing information that a friend has asked you to keep private to canceling out on plans in the absence of a plausible explanation. Any breach, regardless of perceived magnitude, can devastate a relationship. It has been determined that trustworthiness is made up of several components; these include *honesty, dependability,* and *loyalty.*[4] Although each of these traits is important to successful relationships (including friendships, romantic relationships, work relationships, etc.), dependability and honesty have been identified as the most vital in the realm of friendships.

Honesty. In relation to sharing ideas, thoughts, and feelings, this virtue requires that we speak openly from the heart and incorporate objectivity into our words. It is important that we own our feelings and beliefs as just that, *our own,* and to feel comfortable in sharing these with our true friends. Being honest can be a challenge in a variety of ways. Many women worry that some types of honesty will hurt their friendships. Concern about the self-esteem and feelings of friends may limit the level of honesty in a relationship. However, friendships can be irreparably damaged when there is intentional dishonesty for any but the most rare and altruistic purposes. We may fear rejection and the loss of friendships that can result in holding different beliefs, especially as they relate to politics, spirituality, and religion. This can lead us to choose to remain silent, to stifle our expression, or to support ideas that are contrary to our own belief systems; this ultimately leads to friendships that are based on false identities, which, are not, in essence, true friendships at all.

Dependability. There are times when we are forced to "call in the troops" and ask for help from friends. We need people in our lives that we can count on to be there when they say they will be, to do what they say they will do, and to be willing to stand up for you when you can't stand up for yourself. If a friend is just as likely to let you down as come through for you, the relationship often becomes superficial, less engaging, and resentment-provoking, if it doesn't end altogether. Because dependability is one of the most desired traits in friends,[5] if this is one of your lower scores, it is an excellent area for primary focus to improve your friendship readiness.

Loyalty. Loyalty is valued early on in our relationships as evidenced in such diverse and age-defined forms as secret handshakes, sorority pledging, and even gang-related membership rituals. Expectations of intense loyalty peak in the adolescent years,[6] but women at all stages of life express a desire for this quality in their close friends.[7] Women want a friend who will not spill their secrets to others, gossip about their latest fashion faux pas, or let others badmouth their childrearing practices behind their backs.

Ability to trust. Being able to trust another person involves being comfortable with vulnerability. Women seem to gather at opposite ends of the pole; either we trust too easily and too freely, leaving ourselves open to being hurt, or we have been hurt before and stand resolutely steadfast in a refusal to trust again. As Marilyn, a 43-year-old, shared:

I used to be so trusting of everyone—I grew up in a home where religion was a big part of our life. Mama taught us kids the importance of turning the other cheek, following the Golden Rule, believing the best of everyone, ya' know. Well, I was in my early twenties and a group of us women from work loved to hang out after work on Fridays and enjoy the happy hour snacks and complain about our jobs and bosses and talk about our men. Now, none of us were married yet, but I felt like me and my man were starting to get serious and I was hoping that it might work out. One Friday, he decided to pick me up for dinner from the bar we were at. I told him where we'd be and what time to show. He got there a few minutes earlier than expected and I left the group to run to the restroom before we left. While I was gone, one of my so-called friends started hitting on the man, and I didn't know anything about it until another of the girls told me the next week. Now harmless flirting is one thing, but this woman went too far—she even called the man over the weekend! I confronted my ex-boyfriend first and he admitted that he'd picked up the call. Then I confronted the woman and she made up some excuse about it's all okay since there wasn't a ring and the guy chose to take her call, whatever. Anyway, I dumped the guy and dumped the friend. It just took that one bad experience with a friend to change the way I looked at people. Trust still is harder to come by for me now, when it comes to making new friends.

When any of these integrity-related traits show up as a weak spot, it may be helpful to do a little self-exploration and journaling related to the feelings, experiences, and thoughts you associate with trustworthiness and trust in others. What does it mean for you when others put their trust in you? What does it mean when you risk placing your trust in others? Friendships are built on reciprocity, and being willing to offer the foundational properties of trustworthiness, honesty, dependability, and trust to others is integral to enriching your friendships. Reflect on the feelings you experience when let down by important people in your life. Recognize how you, yourself, may be leaving others with similar feelings when you compromise their faith in you or forget a promise. By beginning to acknowledge the effect your choices have on others, you will find the motivation necessary for change and growth. Learning to trust will require that you begin to take small risks in placing your trust in others. As your positive experiences build, trusting others will grow easier.

Traits of Caring

This cluster of traits includes empathy, the ability to withhold judgment, good listening skills, and the ability to offer support in good times and bad. These require personal insight, self-discipline, and unconditional positive regard for our friends. These are the qualities that women seek in the friends whom they want to invite closer into our lives.

Empathy. Empathy is the ability to understand what is going on for a friend, to recognize how she is feeling, and to interact and respond accordingly. According to the neuroscientific research outlined earlier in the book, women enter this world pre-equipped to offer empathy to their companions. Research shows that even in infancy, we are already beginning to practice empathy by vocally joining in with the other babies in the nursery who are crying.[8] As women, we have built-in antennae for picking up on what is going on with our friends even if they don't share their feelings aloud. It's also important that we recognize that our friends' reactions to events may not always mirror our own. Even though women have the inborn capacity for empathy, it is still an important skill to cultivate and develop to the fullest extent possible. Taking time to really "get" what a friend is experiencing and then responding to her based on this knowledge is vital to enjoying a successful friendship.

Ability to be nonjudgmental. This trait speaks of our ease in the acceptance of a friend's choices. Many women have difficulty in accepting friends who make choices or engage in behaviors radically different from their own. Women who choose divorce over remaining in a destructive relationship often lose friends who disapprove of this choice. Some women have been hurt by friends who have been brutally honest in a judgmental way. These friends may suggest that they are telling you something "for your own good," but it may be an opportunity for the friend to air their personal judgment calls about the choices you are making. Learning to be okay with another's limits and faults can go a long way in improving your ability to make and maintain friendships. To overcome the tendency to judge, it is important to be able to objectively evaluate your own choices and to acknowledge your own faults and missteps. For example, remembering the times you, yourself, have made choices that have disappointed significant others in your life and their negative responses may help remind you to stand steadfast by your friends when they make their own unexpected choices. Recognizing that there are many different paths to a satisfactory outcome can help you appreciate the uniqueness of the friends in your life.

Good listening skills. A hallmark of women's friendships is the sharing of intimate thoughts, feelings, and experiences. This sharing is a gradual process of give and take. As one woman shares her story and her truths, the other woman must practice good listening skills, which include being present, attentive, and encouraging of deeper communication. Being able to focus on another's concerns and needs is integral to a balanced relationship. Women turn to their friends to listen to their problems, to know when to offer advice, and to know when to just be present. These skills are part of the glue that holds friendships together, as Lindsay, 24, described:

I always have a hard time making decisions in my life, whether I'm with a group of friends trying to pick a restaurant or when I was trying to decide my college major. So, I was wrestling with a big decision—or at least it was a big decision to me. I had been invited to go on a cruise by the guy I was dating and though I like him, I thought that he was more into me than I could ever be into him. Sooooo, that's where I was stuck. It was all I could talk about for three solid weeks, and all of my friends knew that I'd start wrestling with my indecision whenever we hung out. One of my friends listened to me day after day, never telling me to be quiet, never telling me that she didn't want to hear me talk about it again. She was just real patient, and then she said to me, "Lindsay, really it sounds like you DO want to go on the cruise, and that you probably like the guy more than you want to let yourself realize." Okay, she listened, she heard me out, and I went on the cruise and had a blast! Seriously. And I'm still dating him, kinda serious, maybe permanent?

Supportive of others in their bad times. This is one of the defining qualities of a good friend. Having someone who will be there for you when you are in trouble or up the proverbial creek without a proverbial paddle personifies what friends are simply expected to offer. When a relationship becomes unbalanced, and one friend feels that they are constantly bolstering up another, the friendship can derail, resentment can build, and the relationship can fail. In most cases, you should plan to be supportive in rough times, but if a friend hits rough times far too frequently over the years, then you may want to *very gently* encourage your friend to seek professional assistance in regaining balance. If you are the friend who seems to repeatedly lose your own paddle, you may want to take the initiative to get professional help.

Supportive of others in their good times. The saying goes, "everybody loves a winner," but for some of us, this just isn't so. Especially when adrift in distress or misfortune, some friends have a hard time celebrating another's happiness or good fortune. Sometimes these friends want to warn us that good times seldom last or they may show resentment of the success that we have earned, found, or had dropped in our laps. These friends have been termed "toxic friends" for their ability to sour even the most succulent moment of joy. If you recognize yourself in this description, it may be a helpful exercise to construct a personal gratitude list. Take a sheet of paper, title it "Things for which I am thankful" or "Counting my blessings" or "Gifts in my life." Then just begin listing the people, places, things, and beliefs in your life that you hold dear. Gaining awareness and appreciation of the things that are going right in your life will open you up to the ability to share in another's celebration of their good fortune. Janita, 27 years old, experienced a lost friendship due to this challenge:

Me and a couple of good friends finished our graduate school program together, which means that we all were hunting for jobs at the same time and in pretty much the same geographical location, give or take 20 miles. We were all proud of our great grades, our glowing letters of recommendation from our professors, and our self-confidence about being ready to enter the field. But because of the limited number of open positions in the area, we knew that all three of us might not find jobs right away. Well, I was blessed by a job offer and I felt really thrilled—I was getting married in June, and my fiancé really hoped I'd have a job before the wedding! But I also knew that it meant my two good friends' job hunts just got a little tougher. One friend really handled it well; she was excited for me and glad that job hunting would be one less stress on my new marriage. My other friend, though, seemed a little distant with her congratulations when I told her about the job. I figured she was a little disappointed, and could really understand that. But when my wedding day rolled around a few weeks later, this particular friend didn't attend, and it's been a couple of months, and we still don't get together or talk like we used to. I don't know if it was the job or maybe even my getting married—she's still single—but I feel like this friend just wasn't there for me when things started going really good for me.

To offer empathy, acceptance, and support to friends requires that we step outside of our own limited perspectives and allow ourselves to see our friend's world through our friend's eyes. All of us will make choices that end up disappointing someone—whether it is a job we choose, a hair color we try, or a romantic partner we start seeing. Being able to offer friends support when they experience similar events is necessary to healthy friendships. Virtually every culture has a version of the Golden Rule,[9] and by offering your friends each of these important attributes, you are providing people you care about with what you, no doubt, would like them to offer when you are seeking support and understanding. By withholding judgment, offering support to your friends, and trying on their shoes, you will be creating the framework for a relationship that can strengthen and deepen. If these are traits you recognize as shortcomings in yourself, work toward self-growth through the increased practice of active listening skills with your friends. A good way to start moderating your tendency to judge, to withhold empathy or support, and to tune out, is to respond to a friend with a request for more information. Invite your friend to tell you more about their perspective, to share where they are coming from in a decision, and to open up and help you learn more about how she sees the world. As you listen to the backstory shared by your friend, metaphorically step into her shoes, and look around—you may be amazed at how different the landscape looks.

Traits of Congeniality

Each of these three traits, self-confidence, the ability to see the humor in life, and being fun to be around, enhances anyone's appeal as a friend. This trio of traits has also been associated with overall well-being and happiness in life.[10] We look to friends for support and camaraderie, and these qualities describe a person who is prepared to offer solid support and enjoyable companionship.

Self-confidence. Studies show that a high level of self-confidence is related to high levels of overall well-being and happiness.[11] It has also been connected to creativity, which is a quality that can enrich relationships in numerous ways. Self-confidence is an appealing characteristic in a friend and may even be contagious—when we are in the company of self-confident individuals, we may feel our own confidence rise. Lower levels of self-confidence can drain a relationship of equality and energy if one friend is always looking to others as measures of self-worth and self-esteem. Elizabeth, 46, shared the following story that had haunted her since high school:

> When I was in high school, I cared intensely about my grades! I was driven to do really well academically and was always obsessing over every assignment and exam. I had a good friend, even my best friend for a couple of years, who was also really smart. Smarter than me, and I knew it. When I was around her, I was always doubting my abilities, questioning my performance and even comparing myself to her out loud! I don't know why grades mattered so much, or why I felt that I could not do as well as she did, but my self-doubts eventually got in the way of the friendship. I still remember what she wrote in my high school yearbook, "I'm sure you'll get to the top eventually, even if you have to step on others to get there." Ouch! And it was ironic that it was a lack of self-confidence, not over-confidence, that was the real problem in the friendship.

Fun to be around. From time to time, we all go through some pretty rough patches in life. Some days we may wake up and think that just getting out of bed will be a losing battle. These are times when interactions with and encouragement from friends can really be beneficial to lift us up out of the darkness. Yet if someone is walking around with a cloud of doom always hanging over her head, then chances are good that she is *not* fun to be around, and she is less likely to have healthy, positive relationships as has been noted in studies of subjective well-being and friendships[12,13,14] Friends who are fun to be around are those who enjoy life, handle challenges in proactive ways, and keep negative experiences in perspective.

Ability to see the humor in life. Life has a way of making us all look a little foolish sometimes. Not only that, but life can also throw curveballs and spitballs, to borrow an analogy from the tomboys in the world. Yet having friends who are able to laugh at their own limitations and embarrassing moments helps make a friendship less likely to strike out. Blessed is the friend who can help us laugh at ourselves and/or our circumstances.

FRIENDSHIP READINESS SELF-ASSESSMENT

Take a few minutes to respond to the items on the Friendship Readiness Scale. You are encouraged to be totally honest with yourself as you reflect on how well prepared you are to offer each of the listed qualities to current and potential new friends. If you have a close and trusted friend that can be honest and more objective than you might be, invite her to work with you as you respond to the assessment. Inviting others to provide new information about how you "show up" in relationships can often provide the new perspective needed to better understand who you are as a friend.

Research shows that there are specific qualities that we seek in our friends—and that new friends expect to find in us. Table 11.1 lists qualities that have been found to be important to successful friendships. On a scale of 1–4, rate yourself on your level of agreement with the statements in the table.

Table 11.1   Friendship Readiness Self-Assessment

I believe that I am . . .	Not much of the time	Some of the time	Most of the time	All of the time
Honest	1	2	3	4
Supportive of others in their good times	1	2	3	4
Supportive of others in their bad times	1	2	3	4
A good listener	1	2	3	4
Trustworthy	1	2	3	4
Fun to be around	1	2	3	4
Able to see the humor in life	1	2	3	4
Empathic	1	2	3	4
Loyal	1	2	3	4
Nonjudgmental	1	2	3	4
Self-confident	1	2	3	4
Dependable	1	2	3	4

NEXT STEPS

After completing the assessment, list the traits in descending order based on your self-assessed rating to see where your strengths and weaknesses stand. The majority of the traits that are integral to healthy friendships are also the traits that are associated with personal resilience,[15] which is the ability to successfully meet and manage adversity and challenges in life. Although the adage that "misery loves company" may be accurate, we still need friends who won't allow us to wallow too long in our own sorrows and who won't always drag us down in their own! Developing your own resilience will allow you to be a more desirable friend as well as to live a more satisfying life, in general. As you review the traits that you most need to develop, recognize that the effort invested in the change process will pay off with a more satisfying and gratifying path through life.

Take a moment to reflect and journal on the following questions as they relate to your self-assessment results:

- What are your areas of strength in friendships?
- Describe a time when a friendship was improved because of one of your strengths.
- What are the areas that are weaker and less well developed?
- Describe a time when a friendship was damaged because of one of your weaker areas.
- How would you like to be able to rewrite this friendship story?
- How would you prioritize the areas that need improvement?
- What will be your first steps in addressing these areas?

12

❧ ❧

Roadblocks to Friendships

What keeps us from looking for new friends? What keeps us from letting acquaintances become close friends? Barriers to forming friendships typically fall into one of two categories: internal or external. In this section, we share stories from women who continue to face these barriers, as well as some helpful stories from women who have overcome barriers and developed strong friendships.

The urge to pursue a socially interactive life is pretty much genetically programmed in all of us, as we explored in the first section of this book. There are variations, though, in the levels of interest and need we have for companionship. Some of us desire just a few close friends with whom we are intimately and deeply connected. Others of us want lives loudly crowded with many friends—some close, some less so, but connected to us nonetheless. In between the extremes are those of us who need a couple of close friends who really understand us and a wide variety of others on whom we call for as wide a variety of reasons. Regardless of the type of friends or the ideal number of friends we would prefer, there are many of us who have trouble cultivating friendships. Our interviews revealed that just about all of us have difficulty making friends at some point in our lives. We have also discovered that these difficulties, or barriers, to friendship fall into one of two categories: internal challenges or external challenges.

"IT'S NOT YOU, IT'S ME": INTERNAL BARRIERS TO FRIENDSHIP

Who has not looked back at a decision made in the past and wondered how things might have turned out if the "other" choice had been made? These choices may run the gamut from choosing the Frappuccino instead of the nonfat latte to saying "no" to adventure when you might have said "yes." Or maybe there was an opportunity to approach a prospective friend, but you let the moment pass due to the fear of possible rejection. We face many choices in the course of a day, and many of us spend too much time playing the "what if" game with ourselves after we've settled on a choice. In the case of pursuing potential new friendships, there are heaps of questions that might arise. What if I'd followed up the smile with a greeting? What if I'd invited the woman I pass on my daily walk to buddy up for a walk sometime? What if I'd been more willing to risk being turned down than I was? The list could stretch for miles for many of us! Fear of the unknown keeps many of us from moving forward—especially in regard to relationships, which are already fraught with a fair amount of uncertainty, in general.

Fear

A lengthy list of internal barriers to pursuing friendships was provided by the women we interviewed and the most frequently cited barriers were related to *fear*. Women expressed fear of being rejected by potential friends; fear of being judged by new friends; fear of being betrayed; and fear of loss, in general. All of these fears are simply elements of the existential human condition. Women's apparently inborn need to be liked and desire for others' approval may also keep women from putting themselves in a position in which they may receive rejection or disapproval from others.

When most of us hear the term "fear of rejection," we tend to connect this fear with romantic partners, rather than friends. But women who have been hurt by friends in the past can become increasingly unwilling to risk pursuing new friendships due to the fear of rejection. Research shows that even young children who have experienced rejection by peers were much more likely to anticipate future rejection and show more distress in social situations.[1] One of the women we interviewed could clearly remember the feelings of rejection she experienced 50 years earlier in her kindergarten class:

I was only 5 years old at the time and we'd only been in kindergarten for a few days. This particular day was going to be the first "free play day" outside on the playground and everyone was full of excitement and chattering and, of course, grouping up together as the teachers were trying to get us in line. As we were shepherded out onto the inviting playground, I realized that I was the only girl standing by herself in the midst of numerous pairings or little groups. I went up to one group at the swings and was immediately treated to a girl saying, "All the swings are taken. Sorry." And the girls standing by the swings turned their backs to me. I went to a teacher and said that my stomach hurt and I needed to go inside. When I think about that day, I still can feel that hurt in the pit of my stomach—and, today, 50 years later, when I have to walk into a situation where everyone knows everyone else, I can still feel that fear deep inside.

Rejection may happen before we even begin a friendship, as described in the previous story, or it can be something that occurs further into a relationship. In a reversal of sorts, some women know going into new friendships that these will be time-limited connections, at least within the paradigm in which they are begun. Women who must relocate frequently for their own or their partner's career path may have a difficult time continually making the effort to find new friends in new geographic locales. Women who must uproot themselves and their families every couple of years may learn to protect themselves from the potential pain of lost relationships by limiting the number of friends they make in a new town.

A past experience of betrayal by a friend can also limit our willingness to try to find new friends. For some women, the betrayal can be perceived as a single incident, but for others, it colors all potential new relationships. A 30-year-old woman we interviewed, Jen, described a betrayal by a friend that had happened in high school. She related that she had been devastated when the friend broke her trust by spreading personal information that Jen had asked her to keep confidential. Jen said that she had been furious at the friend and ashamed of the news that was spread. Although it took months for her to finally work through the betrayal, she said that she is now much more careful in what she shares with friends as well as more careful in choosing her friends. As she summed up, "You really can't know what anyone will do with the secrets you share, but that works both ways. Trust has to be two-sided or it's no good. I am more careful in the levels that I self-disclose with friends and I don't rush into intimate sharing like you do when you're in high school. Choose your friends wisely— but don't let past problems keep you from choosing any!"

When we have been hurt in the past, it can be difficult to pick ourselves up and try again in social situations. Learning to toughen our skins can be the first step toward building friendships. Just as thoughts of rejection, betrayal, or eventual loss can become obstacles to making friends, the fear of judgment by a friend is also an effective barrier. One woman, Rhonda, 42, shared that she had been involved in a close friendship for over a decade when it came to an ugly end a few years prior to our conversation. Rhonda's friend had dedicated herself to making rapid upward movement in her career and was disappointed that Rhonda, who worked in a social service field, was content in the less upwardly mobile career choice she had made. According to Rhonda, her friend's disappointment eventually moved into disgust when Rhonda was unable to keep up with her friend's expensive taste in activities and "bling." Rhonda said that her friend judged her career choice and many other aspects of her lifestyle and that the conflict led to a rocky and emotionally charged decision to end the friendship. The experience of being judged and found lacking was enough for Rhonda to be turned off from friendship for a number of years. During our interview, she acknowledged that she was ready to begin looking for a new close friend. She believes herself to be in a space in her life where her own confidence and self-awareness will guide her to finding better friends. She also has the skills to keep a level head and balanced demeanor if a friendship starts to deteriorate in a way similar to her earlier experience.

If your fears keep you from seeking out new friends, it is possible to successfully master these self-imposed barriers. One way to do this is to use the "worst-case scenario" exercise. First, imagine the worst thing that could happen if your overture to a potential friend were turned down or disregarded. Would it involve money, time, well-being, or just a little bit of personal discomfort? Now, imagine how you can successfully respond to this worst-case scenario. Even if it is humiliation, we can live through that. Just remember that our own missteps or errors always appear worse to ourselves than they do to anyone else. Once you've successfully played out your fears in your head and created a successful response to each "worst case," you are ready to move forward with a potential friend.

Judgment Calls from Our Own Perspectives

Among the women with whom we spoke, there were several who openly acknowledged their own tendencies to pass judgment on others, sometimes a little too quickly. Ownership of this trait can keep women from pursuing friendships even when they were interested in doing just that! The tendency to judge others may be part of a lifelong pattern or may have developed as a response to a past episode of poor judgment. Among the women we interviewed, this trait was most frequently acknowledged among mothers with young children. One woman, 32-year-old Erin, described the changes she had experienced in her expectations after having her second child a few months earlier:

When I was single and up until I had kids, I didn't worry too much about the things my friends were doing with their lives. Having my kids has made me more selective of who I hang out with. Like before, I would hang out with people who were drinkers, who wanted to go out all the time. Having kids forced me to grow up, to say when we go out that no-body's drinking and nobody's smoking.

And if she were in the market for a new friend, she feels that she would definitely steer clear of people who make choices that she doesn't feel are optimal. She attributes this new level of caution to being a parent, but some women have had their judgment tested and honed by poor friend-ship choices in their pasts.

One married and devoutly religious woman, Bobbi, noted that her experiences with faith and spiritual transformation defined who she was today. Her commitment to her church leads her to choose only companions whom she believes to be equally devout. Bobbi shared that she had tried to befriend less pious women in the past, but they viewed her eagerness to share her religion as a case of "Bible-thumping." One friendship ended when Bobbi was asked "to leave her faith at home." Somewhat reluctantly, she made the choice to keep her friendships within the circle of her faith. She admitted that she probably came across as judgmental of others, but she affirmed that a commitment to faith led her to this path. She was surprised, however, when one of the friends who had passed her self-described "faith test" began talking behind the back of a mutual friend. Bobbi acknowledged that perhaps she needed to look more closely at her friends as individuals—not just at "faith" value.

For those of us who are quick to judge others, we might be ruling out potential friends that we ought to "rule in." Research shows that when we first see a new face, we pass judgment on a number of traits within *fractions* of a second.[2] This means that we, ourselves, have a very short win-dow of opportunity to make a positive and engaging first impression. Yet so many of our true qualities and best virtues can be communicated and shared only through deeper interactions than initial meetings and surface exchanges will allow. We need time to get to know a person on a more genuine and empathic level. Opening up the door to deeper connections can require that we let go of an initially negative judgment of a person. First impressions can determine how a situation or meeting unfolds, but be careful not to be too hasty in cutting short conversations that could possibly lead to friendship.

Unsure of How to Take the Leap

Poor communication skills and a lack of assertiveness were two barri-ers that often worked in tandem to keep women from establishing new relationships, according to our interviewees. One woman described her challenge as "just not knowing how to be a friend." She was referring to the dynamics of give and take and personal interactions expected in friendships. She attributed some of this, she said, to her upbringing as an only child. She spent most of her time with her parents or other adults and had little experience in the unstructured interaction between peers. She said that she learned to communicate with her parent's clear and rational communication patterns as models, and she never learned how to navigate more informal or emotionally laden discussion dynamics. It can also be difficult for some women to be assertive enough to make initial overtures to a potential friend.

Another group of women, who acknowledged their longing for close friends, admitted that they were unsure exactly how to connect with potential friends. Crystal, a 27-year-old graduate student and full-time computer tech, described her current frustration and her track record with friends by beginning with a story from her childhood:

For me, it was kind of struggle for friendships with me. I remember being back at 4 or 5 and . . . asking my mother how to make friends. She responded that all I needed to do was act and be myself and people will draw to me and my personality. Through the years, I would find myself trying to befriend others and working harder than anyone else.

Not feeling confident of the relationship-building process can lead to a feeling of being out of sync with potential friends. There is a communication rhythm that begins in the early stages of friendships, as we described in Part I. To learn the rhythm, you must be willing to enter the dance. Focusing on the other person typically gets a new relationship moving along. By inviting a potential friend to talk about herself, you are giving her the chance to focus on the subject we all love most to talk about: ourselves. Listening to her cues of depth and topic will help you determine the appropriate level of self-disclosure. As your relationship brings you closer together, the depth of self-disclosure will intensify and the breadth of topics is likely to expand.

"One at a Time, Please"

Women were often quick to share stories of how friendships had withered when a new romantic interest entered the picture for themselves or their friends. Leisure time is already at a premium in our lives, and when we must choose between investing time deepening a romantic relationship or cementing a friendship, our friends too often place a distant second. This may be attributed, in part, to our biology—as the saying goes, "biology is destiny"—but it may also reflect the culture's strong support and glamorization of romance and sexual relationships. One young woman, 20-year-old Ginger, was several months into a new romantic relationship when she was interviewed. She said that her boyfriend was really her best friend at this point and that her closest female friends were all busy with their own boyfriends. She explained that most of her friends were also in college and held part-time jobs, too, and that left little time for social interactions if they were also involved in a romantic relationship. When she was asked about couples getting together, she shared that it was hard with everyone's schedule, that some of the guys didn't get along together, and that some of the girls didn't necessarily like the others' boyfriends. This situation wasn't a problem for Ginger—she believed that just as relationships come and go, friendships need to change, too.

Most of us probably expect romance to edge out friendships during the first half of life when finding a life partner is such a strong social and biological drive. However, we also heard stories from midlife and older women who were been willing to let friendships take second place to romantic interests. One woman, 60-year-old Lucy, shared that she was much more interested in spending weekends with her boyfriend on his boat than she was in keeping up with her "woman friends." Lucy said she loved the excitement and anticipation she felt as the weekends got closer and she described how the feelings reminded her of what it was like to be young and in love. She believed that "friendships will keep," and figured that once the seasons changed, there would be less time on the boat and more time at home with other couples.

Friends left behind in the wake of the new relationship often feel hurt, angry, or betrayed. Others may accept that this is the natural order of things and assume that the friendship will come alive again when the newness of the romance wears off. If you are unsure whether you are in the habit of playing "romance first, friendship second," it might be good to do a check-in with your friends to hear their perspectives. Love can be blind—not just to the faults of our beloved, but also to the realities of life. If love fails and you've let your friendships grow cold, you can be very lonely after a breakup. Friendships need nurturing and making time to be with friends can actually positively affect your deepening romantic relationship. Isolating yourself away with your partner precludes the interaction and time off with others that helps keep problems or disagreements with your partner in perspective. If you're in a new relationship or looking for love, make sure you bring your backup group—your friends—along for the ride. They can share and reflect your happiness when the road is smooth or offer you support and companionship along the way, if things get rocky.

An Independent Streak

Another fatal friendship flaw, according to our interviewees, was the drive for total independence. Some women were proud of their fierce independent streak but shared that this often kept them from establishing a strong support network. A few of our independent interviewees believed that they were missing out on an important part of life through their choice to go it alone in most things. Others, however, strongly affirmed that relying on others was a sign of weakness—whether it had been drummed into their head by their families or taught by some prior, unfortunate experience. One woman, Elizabeth, 47, described her own experiences with her desire to be seen as independent and ambitious:

When I was growing up, I had a semidysfunctional childhood—and I took on the "super achiever" role in my family. I had to be careful making friends when I was young and I couldn't always expect things to go smoothly at home when friends were visiting. The shame I had about my family problems led me to be super independent, super responsible, and, as a result, super lonely! I spent so much time learning how to take care of myself and my family that I began to believe that being independent and not needing close friends was a really positive trait! I left home, went to college, and still carried that belief that independence and having a lot of good friends were incompatible. In fact, I was married, in my mid-twenties, and 400 miles from where I'd grown up before I let myself need others in my life. It hit me, one day, that aside from my husband, I had absolutely no one in that new town to call on if I needed to do more than just borrow an egg or a screwdriver or something! Independent, yep, totally lonely, yep, too. I decided right then that I was going to force myself to break out of my independent, isolated shell and pursue friends—for the first time in about 20 years, I guess.

"If only she were more like me . . ."

Other women described as *internal* some barriers that were actually anchored in the *external* interactions between individuals. These included "life space" challenges, which describe difficulties that might arise when two people are in different places in their life stories, so to speak. An example would be the gulf between women in significant romantic relationships and those who are single. For some women, these basic, often demographic, differences are enough to curtail efforts at forming meaningful friendships. One woman, Mandi, 24, shared that she'd like more friendships in her life, but that as a mother of two preschool children, trying to form friendships with childfree women was just too much trouble, "They just don't understand—or if they have grown kids, they don't remember—where I'm at in my life. I can't just up and go for a bike ride and leave two young kids alone at home!"

Other women named their relationship status as a barrier to friendship formation. One woman felt that being in a committed relationship took priority over developing new friendships and she also believed that what she and her partner needed were "more couple friends, not single friends." She described her desire for friendships as strong, but her opinion about the single women with whom she worked was that "they are fun to work with, but I don't know if it would be worth it to try and move from co-workers to friends since they don't have boyfriends or partners." In both of these examples, women are locked into the belief that social/demographic identity—meaning the roles you play in your relationships and your world—define the type of friends that you can have. However, we did hear a different perspective on the "life space" issue, when Jackie told us about her friendships at her first job after college:

When I first got hired at the communications company, I felt really clueless in some ways. I hadn't worked in an office environment before. Well, there were half a dozen women in my department—each of them older than me or else already married. I felt we were worlds apart! One evening, though, when we were working on a high-priority project, three of us stayed late to help our manager put together the final proposal. The manager had sandwiches delivered, and as we took a break to eat, two of us were trying to find the veggie meals—turns out that Marnie, a woman with two teenagers and a husband, and I were both into vegetarian eating, green living, that kind of thing. I realized then that to make adult friendships, I had to get the belief out of my mind that I could only make friendships work with "sorority sister"-type women. Marnie and I have become close friends at work and in our personal lives, too.

The encouraging aspect of internal friendship barriers is that they are within your ability to overcome. It is not always easy to change your social patterns or your "go to responses," but the joy of friendship is a great motivator and gratifying reward in itself. Some of the barriers, though, may require a different approach than the examples described previously when it is outside of your own control.

"IT'S NOT ME, IT'S YOU": EXTERNAL BARRIERS TO FRIENDSHIP

Although many of the reasons we are reluctant to begin new friendships are clearly located within our own mindset or attitudes, external obstacles also exist. These barriers frequently revolved around two areas, logistics and personal circumstances, for our interviewees. Logistics challenges included scheduling issues and physical distance between women and their existing or potential friends.

Logistics

Angela, a thirty-something mother of an only child, laughed about the possibility of establishing new personal friendships at this point in her life as she stated:

> *My life is all about my daughter's social life right now! I spend my time taking her to dance and gymnastics a couple of times a week, to play dates on weekends, and soccer starts up again in a few weeks. Yeah, I see the same faces in the lobby at the dance studio or on the sidelines at soccer games, but it's just not worth all the bother of trying to get to know people right now. These years are about my daughter. I'll have time for making new friendships later in life when she's in high school or college.*

When asked if she was content with her current friendships, Angela affirmed that she didn't have time for more friends in her life than she already has. She also emphasized that most of her friends lived in her neighborhood as these women were the ones with whom she had the most contact. Time and geography work together to limit the development of any new friendships. Additionally, reciprocity is an essential component of friendship and women like Angela are often hesitant to try and extend their groups of friends for fear of not finding time to give to the relationship in equal proportion to what they might receive.

Personal Circumstances

Women described a variety of personal circumstances that factored into their hesitance to establish friendships. A lack of adequate financial resources can hinder friendship development at any socioeconomic level. As one woman in her late sixties said with regret:

> *I'm a widow, now, and I wasn't left as well off as other widows in my social circle. There's a group that loves to travel, take cruises, just go, go, go! And as much as I'd love to do that, I just cannot afford the kind of trips they take. So, when a new woman joins the circle, I wait for a bit before I make plans to become friends. I need to know where they'll fit in with the group. It just doesn't work out all the time, where financial resources are concerned.*

Other barriers included conflicts that can arise from holding different values or belief systems. Depending on where you live and the climate around you, these differences may involve any number of different issues—including religion, education, and politics, among others. Living in an area in which there are strong opinions on either side of these hot-button issues can create rifts in relationships that have barely begun. Learning to accept another person who holds diverse beliefs or values can take practice and time. We often uphold the belief systems of our parents and their parents before them. Expanding your definition of "friend" to include the multiple layers of identity a potential friend possesses can help you let go of the tendency to see people as only their spiritual belief system, their political leaning, or their sexual orientation. Reading about a different way of life or belief system (in fiction or nonfiction sources) can be a good way to ease into the process of diversifying your friendscape.

Child care can also be a barrier to the development of new friendships. Many of the mothers we spoke to acknowledged that their young children take special priority over their time and their closest friends typically come in just one flavor during these years: other mothers with kids of similar ages. Culturally, the sharing of child care has been a bond that defined the existence of friendships in nonkin networks. Without readily accessible child care, significant limits are placed on women's opportunities and availability to create new relationships. Single working mothers can be especially hard pressed to establish friendships on their own without a partner at home to help share child-care responsibilities. Financial resources also play a significant role in restricting a mother's opportunities to socialize without children along.

A few of our interviewees shared that domestic violence was the circumstance that most hindered their ability to create relationships with potential friends. This wretched dynamic, whether involving physical or emotional abuse, wreaks havoc on a woman's social support system. She is often cut off from her family and friends by a controlling partner, isolated in her home, and kept away from situations in which she might be able to establish social connections.

One woman, a past victim who asked not be identified, revealed that her abusive ex-partner had brainwashed her into believing that she was unworthy of healthy relationships or friendships. It took ten years, and the birth of two children, before she was able to get free. Only through the support of friends at her workplace did she feel able to begin to believe in herself again. She said these women helped her gather the courage to do what she had to do for the well-being of her daughters, as well as herself, and to exit the relationship. Other women described their experiences with trying to build friendships with women they suspected of being victims of abuse. They shared their fears about the safety of these women and a feeling of futility in their efforts to promote connections.

The desire for friendship is often outweighed by a variety of barriers that can be successfully overcome. However, one external barrier that seems to be faced by each of us at one time or another is lacking the knowledge of where to find potential friends. Many women have a hard time figuring out a good place to meet women who might be good matches as friends. Regardless of where you are in your life, finding friends can be a challenge. In the next chapter, we will share ideas for locating potential friends to help you expand the vistas of your friendscape.

IV

TAKING A CENSUS
OF YOUR CIRCLE OF FRIENDS

13

⟡⟡⟡

Mapping Out
Your Friendscape

This chapter gives you an opportunity to create a visual representation of your social connections. We've termed this your "friendscape," which is like a landscape map of your relationships. This image will include you at the center, with your friends and connections placed around you depending on your relationship with them. This activity will reveal the relative closeness of your friends and supporters. A second exercise will help you recognize the types of support you access from friends—whether you count on a friend for emotional support when things are stressful or for active, or instrumental, support when you need help with a task. At the end of the exercise, you will assess the areas in which you need to make some shifts in the landscape to create a more supportive and rewarding system of support.

Reflecting on the images you developed to represent your roles in your friendships in Chapter 11, how did you conceptualize the interrelationships between your friends and yourself? Understanding the different roles that people play in our lives and the levels of closeness we allow them can help us understand how we can maximize our friendship support systems. Some of our friends may be lifelong, true-blue friends to whom we feel about as close as one person can to another. Other friends may be ones in whom we don't confide but on whom we rely for assistance in daily living (e.g., carpooling or borrowing the proverbial cup of sugar). Some friends may be those with whom we just make casual conversation over the counter when we stop for our morning cup of coffee or pick up the groceries for dinner. By creating a visual image to represent the energy and time you spend interacting with each of these people, you will be in a better position to create the friendscape that best suits your needs—and your wishes.

There are many metaphors for the groupings of friends that we assemble over the years. These include a *web* of friends, a *convoy* of friends, and a *network* of friends. These descriptions are helpful as we seek to understand our relative proximity to others, to describe the interactions we have with others, and to determine the overall size and shape of our social support systems. We tend to have many different layers and categories of friendship, as illustrated by the many stories shared by our interviewees. We have friends to whom we may be very emotionally close, yet seldom have the opportunity to see. There may be friends with whom we interact on a daily basis but have yet to share much intimate information. We may have friends with whom we feel our lives and paths have so fully intertwined over the course of time that it seems impossible to imagine a separation. Each of our friends has a unique relationship with us, and as we attempt to create an ideal friendscape, it is essential that we understand the relationships we have today.

The concept of a social convoy was developed several decades ago to explain a person's social support network. The conceptualization includes three concentric circles positioned around an individual located at the center.[1] Each of the circles represents the degree of closeness felt for the supportive people in our lives. People to whom we are closest reside in the inner circle. The outer circle contains those people to whom we are least close. Women we interviewed used a variety of descriptive images to clarify how they perceived their own social worlds. One that seemed to resonate with many of our interviewees was the image of a landscape. One woman described the image she had of her friends and acquaintances as a forest of people. Some women imagined an interconnected map of relationships. Others described a garden with a variety of plants including perennials, annuals, and, of course, a few weeds.

In keeping with the notion of our relationships as living, dynamic entities, we invite you to contemplate your own collection of social connections using the model of an outdoor landscape. By following the guided imagery instructions, you will be encouraged to visualize the areas of already strong growth as well as the open spaces in your own relationship environment, or *friendscape*. Before beginning, find a comfortable place where you won't be disturbed; if today is a beautiful day, sitting outdoors would be ideal. Have available a journal or notebook so that you can complete the written portion of this exercise after the visualization is complete.

Sit back into a comfortable position and let yourself relax. Take one or two deep cleansing breaths as you feel yourself unwinding. If you are outdoors, listen to the ambient sounds of nature around you. If you are indoors, relax and let an image of yourself sitting outside arise for you and imagine the sounds that you would hear in your favorite outdoor place. Feel yourself rooting into the ground as a reflection of how you are rooted into your life today. Once you feel sufficiently rooted into your place in the world, open your inner eyes to see the panorama around you. What is the climate of the environment in which you are planted? What does the earth look like? What sort of sky do you see? What does the landscape offer? What elements are represented in your environment? What are the feelings associated with where you are planted?

As you become familiar with the topography of your environment, allow your support network members to become visible to you. First peer around at your immediate surroundings and notice who is closest to where you are rooted in your life. This is home to your very closest supporters—friends, family, and any others you feel belong there. These are the people you feel are essential to your happiness and your satisfaction with life. If these individuals were not in your life, you would likely feel bereft and at a loss. Notice the sort of living entity that represents these individuals and note their strength and their sturdiness. How would you describe them in this climate where you find yourself? What connects you to these individuals and what do they ask of you in order to sustain or thrive?

Moving your gaze a little further away from where you are rooted, who are the individuals you feel are important to your life, but not as closely intertwined as some? These are the people whose company you enjoy and those with whom you might self-disclose to some degree, but not as intimately as you would with your very closest connections. How would you describe their place in your personal landscape and the type of support they provide? Reflect on their contribution to maintaining the landscape and how well they thrive in the location in which they are currently rooted. Do you feel that they are planted in the best spot for maintaining the relationships you want with them? What do they ask of you in order to sustain or thrive?

As your awareness of your own social topography is heightened, continue to gaze further and further into the distance around you—looking in all directions, north, south, east, west, up, and down. Notice the individuals who are planted at the periphery of your environment and the type of connections you have with them. How do you represent their relationships to yourself? How firmly rooted are they in your life? What forms of support are they providing to you? What do they ask of you in order to sustain or thrive?

After perceiving the variety of supporters in the landscape you have created, take a moment to center your thoughts on where you are rooted and how verdant and alive you feel in this environment. Where do you find your nourishment? What is the life force within you like? With whose roots do yours intertwine below the surface? Are you providing shade and protection for others? Do others offer this to you? Are there weeds growing around you that are choking you out? Are you standing tall and facing toward the sun?

When you feel sure of your vision and ready to create an illustrated representation of your personal habitat, slowly open your eyes as you hold onto the visual image.

Now, using the supplies you gathered, draw your perception of your friendscape as it currently exists. You may want to use the grid in Figure 13.1.

Include yourself, your close supporters, and each of the others in your world with whom you feel connected and worthy of inclusion. After you have developed an illustration of your social environment, reflect on your visual image and the diagram you created as you journal your responses to the following questions:

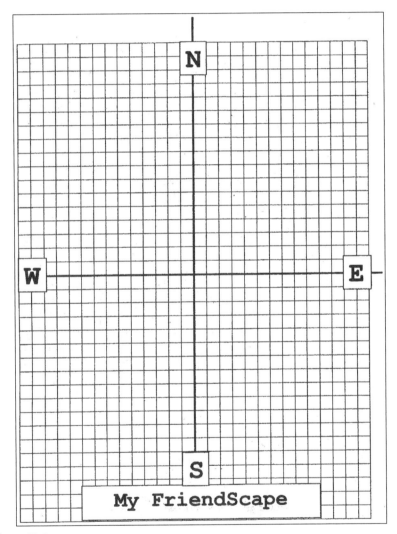

Figure 13.1.

1. How would you describe your environment?
2. What is the climate of your existing friendscape? Lush and vibrant? Arid and dry? Heavy and humid? What is the atmosphere like?
3. Is this environment as healthy as you feel it can be for you? If not, what would you like to see more of? Less of?
4. What imagery did you use to visualize yourself and the people in your life?
5. Turning your attention to your drawing, where did you place yourself in relation to the others in your life? Are you in the center, the top, the bottom, or off to one side or the other? What were your thoughts as you placed yourself within your friendscape?
6. Focusing on your own personal qualities and characteristics, how strong do you feel your roots to be? Keeping within the sphere of social interaction, how healthy do you appear to others? How healthy do you feel yourself to be?
7. Who are the people who are closest to you?
8. What is the relationship between you and those nearest to you? Is it one of healthy symbiosis? Do you feel that you and your closest alliances are thriving in this environment?
9. Do you feel choked by the proximity of any of your connections? Do you feel as if you are competing against one another for any resources?
10. Make a list of the people you have included in your drawing. For each person, include the following information:

   - Name
   - Visual image that came to you as a representation of this person
   - Key thoughts or feelings that the image/location brings up for you
   - Qualities and traits you most value in this person
   - Types of support they provide to you
   - Types of support you are providing to them
   - Level of satisfaction you feel with the relationship

Once you feel you have completely assessed and described your current friendscape, take a moment to imagine the most fertile and beneficial environment you could experience. Review the drawing that you prepared, reflect on the mental image that inspired it, and then follow the guided imagery instructions that follow.

As you survey and explore your current environment, as you perceive it, consider the changes you would like to see happen in order to improve the atmosphere and enrich the landscape. What could be done to make things healthier? More conducive to healthy growth? More wholesome and healthy? Are there changes you would like to have happen in the climate of your friend-

scape? Are there geographical barriers that you would like to have removed? What needs to happen to make the environment more hospitable to new growth or continued stability?

As you look around, do you see friendships that need tending? Spend a few more minutes imagining how you would like to tend your friendscape. Repositioning? Replanting? Transplanting? Weeding? Pruning? Are there open spaces that need to be filled? Is the growth too sparse and spread too thin? Or is there overcrowding that needs thinning out? Do you have too many of one type of social connection and not enough of another?

There are no limits to how your friendscape can be organized in your imagination. As you gain clarity of how this personal habitat could grow and flourish, solidify that image in your mind so that you may translate it into a graphic representation of your ideal friendscape. As you slowly open your eyes, hold the image of this newly created vista.

Now, take a moment to capture this new, revised image on paper. After you have sketched out a diagram or drawn its image, please journal your responses to the following questions.

1. As you look at the revised image, what feelings arise for you?
2. As you look at the revised image, what thoughts arise for you?
3. What basic changes in the overall friendscape do you imagine?
4. As you look at your drawings, have you changed your own location between the first and second diagrams?
5. Comparing your new drawing to the original, are there people who are no longer in the picture? If so, please note the following for each missing individual:

   - Name
   - Your feelings about their removal from the picture
   - How you believe your well-being would be improved by their removal from your friendscape
   - Any needs that they are currently meeting for you which you would need to recruit support from others
   - Any needs that you are meeting *for them* and how you believe it would be if you were relieved of this responsibility

6. Comparing your new drawing to the original, are there new people in your friendscape now that were not there before? If so, please note the following for each new individual:

   - Name (if you know it or their role if you don't, such as "Close Friend")

- What needs you hope they would be able to meet for you
- How you believe your well-being would be improved by their appearance in your friendscape

BASIC TYPES OF SUPPORT

There are two basic structures of support that we give and receive in our social relationships: instrumental support and emotional support. Our instrumental needs are about the "nuts and bolts" of survival in our environment and might include such tasks as giving a friend a ride to work when her car is in the shop; lending that cup of sugar to the next-door neighbor; even lending a co-worker a dollar or two to help cover her lunch when she's short of cash. Our needs for instrumental support shift with each passing life stage, but we all need to have individuals in our friendscapes who can offer the support we need *when* we need it.

One young woman, 17-year-old Katie, described a time when instrumental support was essential to what she believed to be her health and well-being. Katie had been taken to a party by her boyfriend where there was a large group of teens, some she knew and some she didn't. When she realized that her boyfriend and his friends had been sneaking alcohol into their energy drinks, she became fearful about the prospect of getting home safely and by her curfew. Another young woman that Katie described as "a not-so-close friend" quickly volunteered to help Katie out with an early ride home. This kept Katie from landing into trouble with her parents, kept her safe, and became an opportunity for an "instrumental support friend" to shift into an "emotional support friend," as well.

Instrumental support was especially valued by another interviewee who is at the opposite end of the age continuum. Mary, a 78-year-old widow, can no longer drive safely after nightfall, but she still greatly enjoys attending the poetry and prose readings held at the state university in her town. She has a neighbor who is retired from the English faculty at the university who willingly provides a ride to the readings that catch her interest. Mary described this individual as "just a neighbor, not a close friend," which expresses just one flavor of the relationships possible with those on whom we rely for instrumental support. Mary's story also supports the research finding that as we age, we require more instrumental support from others while increasing the level of emotional support we offer in exchange.[2]

Emotional support is what we look for and expect to find in our closer relationships. Our need for love and hunger for comfort drive us to seek emotional support from the people in our lives. Requesting emotional support from others, however, might be much more difficult than asking for instrumental support. For many people, the need for emotional support implies an emotional vulnerability that some of us have difficulty exposing. A relationship that allows the give and take of emotional support requires a level of self-disclosure and intimate sharing that not all friendships reach. To ask for emotional support is to risk the pain of rejection at a most basic level.

When we are turned down in a request for instrumental support, such as needing a ride somewhere or help with an outdoor project, it is easy for us to rationalize that the denial was based on circumstances beyond our control. It is easier to believe that our friend's car was low on gas, their schedule really was too full, or they had crises of their own to manage. Being denied a shoulder to cry on or a comforting word can provoke in us a much different response that can be difficult to rationalize beyond accepting that the relationship is not as deep or as mutual as we had believed. Thus, emotional support is a special aspect of personal relationships that is not inherently found in quasi-friendships, friendships, or even close familial relationships.

As the research shared in earlier sections has shown, emotional support is integral to our overall well-being and satisfaction with life. Developmental scientists have suggested that patterns of emotional attachment are ingrained in us through early interactions with primary caregivers by the time we're out of diapers. However, what has been learned can definitely be unlearned with a little practice. Learning to ask for emotional support will open up a world of deeper personal connections to those people already in your friendscape—as well as pave the way for bringing in new emotionally supportive friends. The first step is in the process is evaluating your current support systems to determine exactly where you need to enhance your connections.

ASSESSING YOUR FRIENDSCAPE SUPPORT SYSTEM

Now that you have visualized your current and your ideal friendscapes, it is time to clarify your next steps in reshaping the support system you have. Follow these instructions to create a clear plan for friendship development:

1. Review your journal responses related to the "Ideal Friendscape" visualization. Focus on the instrumental and emotional support needs that consciously or unconsciously guided your development of the ideal support structure.
2. Take a sheet of paper and divide it into two widthwise columns. Label one Instrumental Support Needs and the second one Emotional Support Needs.

3. List the Instrumental Support needs that you identified as important or essential to you.
4. List the Emotional Support needs that you identified as important or essential to you.
5. Review each list and place a checkmark by the needs that you believe are adequately met by the individuals in your life. Note the name of the person(s) you count on to meet each need.
6. For each of the remaining needs, circle the need if there is someone in your life that you feel would be able to meet the need and note the name(s) of who you believe could help you meet the need.
7. For the final group of unmet needs—the ones that you do not believe could be met by any of the people among your current group of friends—write each need at the top of a separate sheet of paper. Describe an example or two in which you felt this need. What stands out for you? What was the lack you felt without having the need met?
8. Brainstorm the type of person you feel you need in your life to meet this need. Would a new friend be able to meet more than one of your unmet needs? What sort of qualities would you look for in this person?

Acknowledging Those Who Meet Our Needs

For the group of individuals whose names appear on the list as actively meeting your needs, take a moment and reflect on the ways they positively influence your life. How do they make your day better? Your life easier? How do you express your appreciation for their contribution to your world? What needs of theirs are you able to meet? If you were to imagine a seesaw holding your needs on one side and your friend's on the other, how balanced would it be?

Friendships rely on mutuality and an overall, though not necessarily immediate, balanced level of giving and receiving. If you believe that your friends are giving less or more than you are to a relationship, you may need to assess the commitment level and the satisfaction level for each of you. If both of you feel satisfied with a relationship, identify some ways to acknowledge the worth of the relationship to your friend. Pen a quick note expressing your appreciation for specific ways in which your friend offers you support. Drop an email or send a text message. As a 50-year-old interviewee emphasized, "You really *do* have to be a good friend if you want to have good friends."

Preparing to Reshape and Realign Your Friendscape Support System

Many of our interviewees mused about types of friends that are absent in their lives today. Corinne, who is single, mourned the lack of a best friend in her life—the kind of friend, she said, that would be willing to listen to her moan and groan about a bad day at work or listen to her ramble on about possibly pursuing a new career. Her daughter had grown up and out and into her own apartment, so Corinne has the time and energy to devote to friendships. She just isn't sure how to go about finding a new best friend. Another interviewee, when asked if she had enough good friends in her life, replied firmly that whereas she had plenty of friends that would better be described as "acquaintances;" but when it came to true friends, she simply stated, "No, there is just a lack of good friends. A definite lack in that area."

Another woman felt that some of her friends were "too much into my business" and that she needed more privacy and space. One newly engaged woman said that she loved spending quality time with her fiancé, but that she desperately missed spending time hanging out with her girlfriends. She missed the easy give and take and girl-talk and she expressed a strong desire to find a way to put some "social space" between her fiancé and herself.

Friendships and social relationships are open to dynamic transformation. There are times in which we may choose to draw closer to someone under certain circumstances and times when we feel called to step back. Being confident in your ability to be a good friend and understanding the needs you have regarding your social relationships are two key elements in being ready to move forward and transform your friendscape. In the following chapter, we will share the experiences and advice of women who have managed to purposefully reshape their social connections to better meet their relationship needs.

14

⚜

Redesigning Your Social Support Landscape

In this chapter, we address the process of fine-tuning your connections to existing friends. Whether you would like to transform distant friends into closer friends or to find ways to step back from friends who may be too close or feel too stifling, you can create the friendscape that best meets your needs with a little bit of effort.

As we continue to shape our lives and our identities over the years, our friendship needs undergo corresponding shifts. Sometimes we find ourselves wanting to deepen the relationship with a particular friend or acquaintance or longing to put some distance between ourselves and friends who may no longer fit into our perceived social schema. Friendships tend to shift as we enter new life stages, develop new interests, enter new romantic relationships, and relocate to new neighborhoods. There is a popular saying that friends enter our lives for reasons, seasons, and, in rare cases, lifetimes. Whether it is coincidence or fate that brings people into our lives, we are responsible for choosing whom we invite into our inner circles and who we continue to keep at a distance.

WARMING UP ACQUAINTANCESHIPS INTO FRIENDSHIPS

Rebecca, who is in her early forties, was forced to uproot her family to move halfway across the country when her husband received a promotion. She shared, "I have so many friends I left behind in Florida. Those friendships defined who I was as a new bride, a new mother. Now that we've moved up here to a new state, I have had to force myself to allow new acquaintances to grow into friends. And that's not always easy—at least for me." For Rebecca, moving across multiple states and several climate zones with a husband and three children created significant challenges, but she felt the most difficult was the collapse of her friendship network and the struggle to rebuild a new one. Taking a teaching position shortly after the move, however, provided Rebecca with opportunities to shore up her local support system. Although a fairly private and reserved woman, she realized that as the newcomer to the school, she might have to make the first move to build relationships.

One of Rebecca's methods for transforming colleagues into friends relied on paying careful attention to others' conversations; this helped her figure out who shared her interests or experiences, including motherhood. Feeling the loss of nearby friends, normally reticent Rebecca forced herself to strike up conversations with the colleagues with whom she felt the most compatible. Knowing how important her own kids were to her, Rebecca began conversations with potential friends by asking about their own children and their partners. Initially, Rebecca sought connections with women who could empathize with her desire to work as well as with her longing to be more available to her children. By inviting others into conversations, she began to populate her friendscape with acquaintances who would eventually blossom into friends. Rebecca widened her net after a couple of initial successes and now counts several of her colleagues, from a variety of life stages and ages, among her friends.

Life Stage Changes

In a similar situation, Morgan was a new bride who had left her job shortly before her wedding and subsequent entry into graduate school. She felt that being a stay-at-home-wife-but-not-yet-mother left her feeling "odd woman out" as the first semester of classes began. She said that she worried about the impression she would make, as most of her classmates were talking about their jobs and, in many cases, their kids. Morgan related that she relied on the art of attentive listening as others discussed their lives and their interests. She realized that she was not the only student feeling the need to find a way to plug into friendships within the group. After she "zeroed in" on classroom acquaintances that she judged to be potential friends, she suggested they go out for coffee after class. This willingness to make the first overture moved her one step closer to developing friendships. And as the after-class coffee break became a weekly ritual for the group, casual conversations deepened into honest self-disclosures that set the stage for authentic friendships to develop. According to Morgan, one of her new friendships has grown into a *best friends* relationship. She attributed this development as a result of the choice to include their partners in their shared social activities. Both women were ready to become more connected and their mutual appreciation for each other's company allowed them to deepen the relationship into a bond between families.

Another young woman, Jenni, had always smiled and nodded at the women pushing strollers through her neighborhood when she took walks or runs along the streets. As she and her husband had hoped, she became pregnant and began planning for an extended maternity leave. She realized that she would need to populate her friendscape with other at-home mothers for daytime companionship and who might have flexibility to swap babysitting and participate in play dates with their kids. So as Jenni's due date grew closer, she worked to grow closer to the other moms in the neighborhood. Her greetings morphed from just a smile and a nod into questions about pregnancy, newborns, and toddlers. As women shared their stories, Jenni was able to reposition several of her neighbors closer into her central support system. Once you are able to identify your friendship needs, you are better prepared to reshape your friendscape with relationships that enhance your life.

Being at the opposite end of the childbearing/childrearing arc requires similar friendship seeking skills. Marchetta is a single parent whose only child, a daughter, chose to attend a college far from home after high school. Because Marchetta and her daughter had been so close, she experienced a deep loss of companionship after her daughter moved out. Sure that other women at her church might be feeling a similar reaction to children's newly exercised independence that autumn, Marchetta organized a "WMC (Women Missing Children) Group." The bi-weekly meetings provided a setting where individual friendships could take root between group members. As new friends were made, the group meetings became less frequent, but Marchetta was definitely delighted with the deeper relationships she had formed. And she was especially grateful that she had been able to develop a "deep and abiding friendship," as she termed it, with a woman whose "missed child" had actually passed away two months before Marchetta had first organized the group.

New Trends in Friendship Opportunities

Women are able to connect with new friends in many expected places, such as shared neighborhoods, shared workplaces, shared classrooms, shared walking trails, and so on. However, one young woman, 26-year-old Dana, shared an unexpected story of how she and her current best friend had initially connected and their first conversation focused on a particular designer handbag. "For a couple of weeks in a row, on my weekly shopping trips to the discount store, I saw another woman about my age there carrying the same lime-green Coach bag I carried. I figured that two people who both chose the stand-out color would have to have more in common, so I just struck up a conversation one day and we just clicked."

Being Open to New Possibilities and Renewed Relationships

Connection and social interaction are basic needs and one woman we interviewed experienced a "slipping away" of friends due to a change in her residence and entry into a new romantic relationship. However, she has been successful in adapting to the changes in her friendscape, as she clarified for us:

As I have moved through life and its occasional challenges and obstacles, I have learned how to shift my social support system by allowing more acquaintances to have a higher level of importance than before. I would say that I enjoy the company of any person that expresses warmth and appreciation to me/for me. If I need a lift, a brief but sincere conversation gives me a much-needed boost. That additionally allows my closer friends some respite from always taking the "up lifter" role in the relationship. My newest friend is my next-door neighbor's girlfriend and as their relationship has gotten more serious, our own friendship has deepened from acquaintanceship to friendship.

Most of us have had the experience of feeling a chasm develop between ourselves and a friend, whether it is an intentional or unplanned shift. As a previously close relationship unravels, we may view women in the outer edges of our friendscapes in a new light. We may notice a new, or newly perceived, similarity in attitude, interests, disposition, or life stage in women with whom we have not been especially close. As a new perspective materializes, it can be the impetus to invite an acquaintance closer into our networks through social invitations and more frequent efforts at contact. We can also find new close friends within the middle circle of our support networks. Making the first move to grow a relationship into something deeper and more meaningful can both reward and sustain us as we experience the satisfaction found in ripening friendships. And drawing back friends from the outer edges to our inner circles can bring new joy as one woman described, "About 15 years after a middle-school argument that ended a friendship, I called to wish this friend a happy birthday and asked to have lunch . . . that friendship has continued now for 24 years—it is an amazing friendship! I wanted the friendship more than I wanted to be right."

Steps for Cultivating Friendships with Acquaintances

1. Identify individuals in the outer circle of your social network with whom you feel compatible or to whom you feel attuned.
2. Determine a focus that will provide the path to a deeper friendship. These might include things you enjoy doing now, things you would like to try, shared cultures, mutual acquaintances, and so on. The list is as varied as individuals can be!

   - Shared interests (gardening, cooking, TV programs, books, music)
   - Shared activities (sports, exercise classes, meditation, concerts, theater)
   - Life stage (single, partnered, parent, expecting, widowed, divorced, retired)
   - Neighborhood (city, country, suburban, high rise, gated community, tract housing)
   - Career path (professional field, employer, college-bound)

3. Research something current that is related to what you have in common to use as the conversation starter (extra tickets to an event, new magazine, online news story, garden show, whatever you feel is relevant) and open up the path for sharing at a new level and, if the friendship warms, move more deeply into honest communication and appropriate self-disclosure as you build a strong foundation for the new relationship.

Rebecca, whose story opened this section, described her efforts to bring friends closer using the metaphor of an approach toward a fire: "You can appreciate a bright roaring fire from a distance and enjoy the view. It adds a nice touch and you can imagine the warmth that is coming from the flames. Kind of like enjoying the presence of colorful, entertaining acquaintances. Yet to truly feel the warmth of the fire and benefit from the energy it produces, you have to move closer—just like with building friendships. You have to let yourself get close before you can enjoy the warmth and bask in the glow."

CREATING SPACE AND ROOM TO GROW

For some of us, taking the initiative to invite friends closer is a challenge. For others, it may be more difficult to weed out friends who are no longer beneficial or nourishing to us. We may worry that a request for more space in a relationship will cause hurt feelings, burnt bridges, or self-imposed guilt later on. However, there are definitely times when we must root out those friends who choke out other relationships or demand more tending than we feel prepared to provide. One woman described herself as being "tired of lopsided relationships. If a person does not consider me important enough to take the time to help maintain the friendship, then I am no longer willing to put out extra time, every time, either. I don't mean in the everyday give and take. I am strictly talking about relationships where people constantly expect things but never give back or always find an excuse why they can't do whatever might need to be done."

Taking Advantage of the Geographical Cure

Deciding to trim back a friendship can be easier said than done, but moving to a new neighborhood or city often coincidentally provides an opportunity to readjust or retire less rewarding relationships. As Miriam, 52, noted, "Friendships that I have let go are now 'long-distance friendships' started during a previous relationship with someone in another city. I don't know that I have so much let them go, as I have just stopped taking time to cultivate them and now make no effort to see these past friends even when I go down to visit the town and other old friends." She acknowledged that the friendships no longer served a need in her life and that the physical distance supports the emotional distancing she sought. Other women also shared a similar sense of relief when presented with an opportunity for a "geographical cure" for unsatisfying or disappointing friendships, much as it is sought for romantic relationships that go awry.

Being Purposeful in Friendship Revisions

When we invited women to share stories of friendships that had undergone deliberate and purposeful distancing, we often heard accounts of friends who had become too needy or clingy. Melissa, in her mid-thirties, noted that she had kept up a friendship from her high school years, but as time went on and her life grew to include a husband and then children, her old high school friend's claims on her time began to feel uncomfortable and suffocating. Melissa shared that she had always prided herself on being a tolerant person and a loyal friend, so she felt significant conflict at the thought of having to step back from this friendship. She prayed over the dilemma and recognized that she would need to put distance between herself and the friend. Being a straightforward woman, Melissa made a lunch date with the friend and was able to communicate her need to honor her commitment to placing her own family's needs first. Melissa admitted that her friend was openly upset during the conversation and accused Melissa of betrayal. Melissa felt aggrieved, as well, at the harsh words from her friend, but she followed up the meeting by dropping her friend a card in the mail. She hoped the message she wrote conveyed her appreciation for the friend's role in her life through the years and the sincere hope that she would understand Melissa's need to focus her energy on her growing family. Melissa said that the few times she has run into the friend that the conversation was a bit brusque, but Melissa still hopes that time will smooth away the jagged edges of the relationship's transition.

Many women are much less inclined to go to the lengths that Melissa felt necessary in placing boundaries on a relationship. Popular methods of "disconnecting" from friendships that had run their course included screening calls and not returning calls from these individuals. Not surprising is that many of the women who use these methods do express shame at choosing this "quick, but dirty" trick. Many of these same women also noted that they do their best to avoid conflict; they don't like to create scenes; and that they wish they could be more honest in their relationships.

Another woman took a middle path in disentangling herself from an unhealthy friendship. Not as openly up front as Melissa, but not as cowardly, perhaps, as the "call screeners," here is how Elaine handled a "thorny" friendship situation:

I realized that one of my former close friends was terribly negative and downright mean to me much of the time. My life situation changed as I entered graduate school and she stayed in the work world, so I didn't see her often. When I did see her, I was struck by how selfish she was and how she always seemed to try to put me down. I'm not sure why I didn't notice it before or if it had changed drastically, but I decided that I didn't need a friend like that. In order to distance myself, I stopped calling her and tried not to be overly friendly when she would contact me. It is more difficult now that we are thrown together due to a shared obligation; however, I still attempt to avoid the fake friendly game. I am choosing to be friendly enough with her but not friends with her any more. I would never go out of my way to hurt her, but I know that I have the right to choose those individuals whom I let into my circle of friends.

Artfully Transplanting a Friend

Another method of introducing distance between yourself and a friend who no longer "fits" your life is to facilitate connections between her and others of your friends that you believe might be good matches or good company for her. Catie, fresh out of a local college, shared that this was one of the best ways she had found for dealing with friends who she felt didn't suit her new life style as she negotiated a transition from partying and exams to a full-time nursing job. Because one of her "party friends" was having trouble accepting Catie's consistent rejection of offers to go out clubbing, Catie organized a get-together at a popular nightspot for the persistent friend and a few other old college buddies who were still into the night scene. Catie showed up early, made sure everyone was introduced to each other, and then pleaded the "early-morning job commitment" as she headed for the door. Catie knows that her friend may still try to convince her to go out, but she feels good knowing that she has done what she could to help the friend transition into a new social group that better matches her friend's interests than Catie now does.

Sometimes we change, sometimes our friends change, and sometimes the friendship changes. These are all normal aspects of healthy development, yet it is important that we do not lose sight of the benefits and positive experiences we have enjoyed in a once-close friendship. Just as all of us can remember a time when we were unceremoniously dumped, snubbed, offended, or ignored by someone we thought cared about us, it is essential that we avoid these tactics as strategies for moving friends out of our inner circles. The following concise steps might serve as a guide in helping you untangle yourself from a no longer thriving friendship:

1. Acknowledge to yourself these things:

   - You have the right to choose only mutually supportive friendships.
   - You have the right to determine your own personal boundaries and the responsibility to honor those of others.

2. Make an honest assessment of whether the relationship in question has run its course or is potentially salvageable.
3. If you believe the friendship is worth an investment of additional energy:

   - Prepare a list of the changes you believe would improve the relationship.
   - Set up a meeting with your friend to openly discuss your needs and invite her to share her own needs and perceptions of the relationship.
   - If she is committed to working with you on the friendship, co-create a plan of what each of you needs to do next. Possibilities might include:

     - Lessening the frequency of contact
     - Revising expectations of each other's contribution to the friendship

- Developing new communication patterns to guide future interactions

- Agree to reassess the success of the changes at an agreed-upon future date

4. If you believe there is truly no future for the relationship, honor your own needs by personally communicating your feelings and related decision to your friend. Ideally, you should plan a face-to-face meeting, but if distance and scheduling are obstacles, a telephone call is a much better option than email, texting, or posts on her Facebook wall.

Being honest with yourself about what type of relationships offer support and what type places the burden of support on your back is the first step in uprooting unhealthy friendships. Although familiarity may breed contempt and absence may make the heart grow fonder, each of us has the right to determine just how close is *too* close in any of our relationships.

UNEXPECTED BEAUTY IN UNPLANNED FRIENDSHIP

To close this chapter, we share a story that illustrates how close friendships can bloom between diverse individuals:

My friend, Jane, and I met at work. We did not think we had anything in common and did not interact beyond the necessary requirements of our job duties. But after working together for a time, both of us needed a new place to live. We decided to rent a house together, even though we did not know each other well or even think we had much in common. We rented a house and realized while being housemates that we had more in common than we thought. We both enjoyed following the same sports teams, music, and many other things. We taught each other things that we needed to know. For instance, she taught me how to be more responsible and not look at everything as a party; that some things are important. I taught her how to loosen up and let go every now and then and to enjoy life as it came to you. Together we taught each other the balance that one needs for a complete and full life. We are still friends today, and even though we don't spend a great deal of time together, we talk whenever we can and consider each other integral parts of our lives. I would not give anything for the experience I have had with Jane and treasure her friendship dearly.

In summary, we encourage you to assess your own friendships and determine whether you need to create space between friends who have grown too close or draw nearer to acquaintances with whom friendships might flourish. As you survey your existing friendscape, look carefully at those people who populate your social world. There may be some unexpected joys to be found in the least expected places. Weed out the people who drain rather than sustain you and invite closer those people who offer you understanding, support, and connection and to whom you are happy to offer the same.

15

꧁ ꧂

Finding New Friends

Innovative strategies and tried-and-true tricks for finding new friends are described in this chapter. These tips are organized by life stage so that you will be able to find specific strategies for making new connections that fit your life space.

"I look for opportunities each day of my life to add a friend" is how one woman described her attitude toward friendship development. At 62, she is open and eager to invite new women into her social world and she offers a warmth and acceptance that any of us would appreciate. Some of us seem to be "friend magnets" who can find new friends in just about any setting. Others of us, however, meet with obstacles before we even enter a path that might lead to new friendships. Finding new friends can be as easy as the proverbial walk in the park if you know where to start, so here is a collection of ideas to set you on the right path.

Keep in mind, however, that once you locate a new potential friend, it will be up to you to follow through the process of friendship development, from striking up an acquaintanceship to cementing a friendship. There are many circumstances and places where you might connect with others, and each has a built-in conversation starter inherent in the locale. Use the meeting place as the focus and open a conversation that identifies your shared interest. For instance, if you run across the same woman at every garage sale you visit on a particular morning, open up a conversation with something like, "Well, either we're both looking for the same elusive treasure or we're both determined to hit every garage sale in this morning's paper."

If the conversational opener is met with a friendly response, be willing to keep the interaction moving. How the dialogue develops from there depends on whether you are in a setting that will provide regular contact (class, club meeting, etc.) or a likely one-time meeting. If it's a "now or never" opportunity, and you feel like a friendship is possible, you may reference a possible future meeting or event. In the case of the garage sale meeting, you might follow up with something like, "If there's something in particular you're searching for, let me know. I'm heading out to the big flea market in a couple of weeks and could drop you an email if I find it." Trust can be a little slower to develop in our society today, so be patient with potential friends who are reluctant to divulge freely. If you feel like someone could become a good friend, let the relationship develop naturally, but don't despair if it doesn't move forward as quickly as you would like. Recognize that all relationships move at different speeds.

The rest of this chapter is organized according to life stage, but you will want to read about stages other than your own—your interests or circumstances may be different from our interviewees. And although we include several age/stage-specific groups for meeting potential friends, many women we interviewed also noted that support groups for any life challenge provide an excellent place to meet friends struggling with the same issues you may be. Whether you are an adolescent or an older adult and whether the group is related to mental health, physical health, life stage, or life event, you are entering a group of people who already understand some of the unique challenges you are facing in your life—and who are ready to provide and receive assistance and connection with others.

ADOLESCENTS

This time of life may be both the easiest and the most challenging to develop new friendships. Young women spend most of their waking hours in the company of others—school and extracurricular activities and part-time jobs all involve social interactions. However, the harsh judgments of peers can play a guiding role in friendship choices. As we seek to develop our own unique identity, it is especially important to figure out the type of people you want in your life. The use of technology has amplified the opportunity to "meet" potential friends, so being clear on who you need in your life will help you better choose your online and face-to-face companions. Some of the best ways to meet new friends, according to our interviewees, are presented here:

School-Related

- Take classes in subjects that you really care about and check out who is as passionate as you are about the topic.
- Get involved in as many clubs as you can comfortably fit in your schedule. In a high school with hundreds of students, there are bound to be some students who are fun to be around that aren't necessarily in your classes or from your neighborhood.
- Volunteer for service projects—if there's a food drive, blood drive, or similar event, inquire about helping out with organizing or running it. It's a great way to get to know other people who care about helping others.
- Consider "group projects" as opportunities to get to know new people and be willing to join a group with unfamiliar members. Scary, perhaps, but it can be fun.
- Go out for a team or be a part of the scorekeeping squad.
- Audition for a play, or if you don't feel comfortable on stage, sign up to run tech or crew. It will give you a chance to spend time with new people working toward a common goal. And there will be impromptu after-practice doughnut runs and cast parties, too.

Outside School

- Get a part-time job. This is probably the easiest way to get to know other people your age that you don't typically see at school.
- Volunteer for a community cause and invite along someone you would like to get to know better. Walk dogs at the animal shelter. Spend one evening a month at a homeless shelter helping prepare/serve a meal. Volunteer at your local food pantry.
- Join a church youth group.
- Spend a summer as a camp counselor.
- Learn to play the guitar or drums and invite other musicians to join your band.

COLLEGE-AGE WOMEN

Whether you choose to attend a university, a two-year school, or take a class here and there, getting involved in higher education provides rich opportunities to get to know new people. The best part about meeting people in classrooms is that they either have the same interests you do or, at the very least, have to suffer through the same class you do! Beyond the person in the desk next to you, here are some additional ways to find new friends:

- School-based student organizations are great places to meet people and can range from service organizations to honor societies to purely social groups.
- Once you've joined a new group, get involved in its activities. If they are planning a fund raiser, volunteer to man the event. If they are planning a ski trip, sign up before all the places are filled.
- If you have an interest, but there's not a club or group to support it, find a faculty member who is willing to be the advisor and start making and distributing flyers.
- Work-study or part-time jobs anywhere on campus will provide opportunities to meet new people.

WORKING WOMEN

When we leave school, the next step is usually a full-time job that opens us up to a whole new order of life. Regardless of where we rank in the social world off the job, we often find ourselves banding together with our co-workers. There are still pecking orders and hierarchies, but the shared culture at most jobs can create unique new friendships. Spending a third of your life in the company of strangers can be exhausting and lonely, so friendships with co-workers can be crucial to on-the-job satisfaction. Being attuned to any politics that pervade your workplace is essential to making good friendship choices. For most of our interviewees, workplaces presented opportunities to make strong friendships with at least one other co-worker, and some of our interviewees counted numerous close friends among their colleagues. Here are some ideas to get you started:

Friends through the Professional World

- Find out about any "Young Professionals" or "Working Women" meetings in your community. Look into the communities nearby if you're in a small town with limited resources.
- Get involved in local branches of any professional organizations connected to your field.
- Look into any entrepreneurship classes in the area—the people who attend these events and trainings are usually creative and interested in networking in the community.
- Look for Chamber of Commerce–sponsored events like "Business After Hours" gatherings that encourage networking—of both the business and social types.
- If your company is running a volunteer campaign (e.g., United Way, health-related activities like walk-a-thons), offer to be part of the steering committee or organizational team.

Friends from Off the Beaten Path

- Attend events sponsored by the local chapter of your college alumni association. If there's not a local chapter, contact your school and offer to help organize one.
- Look into the civic events happening in your community and choose to attend something where it's easy to go solo. Art shows are great opportunities to explore on your own and when you stop to admire the art, engage artists in conversations about their work, their experiences in the local art scene, and so on. And when you find yourself admiring a piece of art that has drawn another's attention, use the shared interest to open up a conversation. Your public library may offer a range of interesting free events such as poetry readings or independent film viewings.
- Taking noncredit classes will also open the door to new faces. Courses may be on the local community college or university campus, but some high schools offer adult interest classes like photography or technology, as well.
- Attendance at open board meetings for libraries, community events planning, or fund raisers/charity events is a way to get to know people who care about your community.
- If you're a dog owner, don't just tramp through the local streets. Find the nearest dog park or shoreline or animal-friendly park and be ready to meet other dog lovers.

Half of a Couple

For many of our partnered interviewees, finding other couples for possible friendship seemed especially daunting. One thirty-something woman said that she and her husband were close to putting out a personal ad along the lines of "couple interested in finding other couples for friendships," but laughed and said she was worried about just what sort of people might respond. In addition to the previous suggestions, we offer the following ideas for finding other couples for friendship:

- Take walks through your neighborhood together and be sure to stop and admire the lawns of other same-age couples who might be potential friends.
- Sign up for a ballroom dancing course at a dance studio or the local recreation center. Suggest going out after the class to couples you both feel drawn toward.
- Depending on your interests, get involved in a sport that lets you play as a team. This could be a bowling league, a mixed doubles tennis league, golf league, or similar.

- Learn to play bridge and find a local bridge club or weekly game.
- Get involved in a religious education class for couples in your age group.
- Attend charity events in your community—silent auctions, wine tastings, police auxiliary dances, and so on. Even if you don't find new friends the first time out, you may begin to see the same couples at these events and this would give you an easy entry into conversations.

Moms on the Go

Once you enter the world of "expectant mothers," your status in your social world may begin to change. You may leave behind late nights in smoky clubs or afternoons shopping for the perfect wine selections for your perfect multiple-course menus. Your focus naturally shifts to the future care and feeding of your unborn child, and with this new of focus often comes a parallel new focus in your social life. However, women who may have never spoken beyond a brief greeting may now be ready to engage you in lengthy conversations as they recognize your new arrival into motherhood. When a baby arrives, the strollers roll out and your "instant introduction" to the neighborhood is set. Our interviewees all agree that pushing a baby carriage down the sidewalk is a great way to find the other mothers in a neighborhood—especially if you are making the shift to full-time mom and you are strolling the streets before the baby's afternoon nap. Other ideas include:

- Carpool lines. One woman said she would walk in to get her child and try to memorize a few of the names on the cardboard signs in the cars, so that when she saw a parent at a class party or walking in their child, she could say something like, "Oh, so you're Tyler's mom."
- If you're a working mother, look for women who have pictures of kids on their desks and follow up to see if they are also parents. It's nice to have work friends who can understand how hard it can be to balance work and family.
- If you stay home, find a club or activity that offers on-site child care. There are many types of mothers' groups—both secular and church- or synagogue-related. You might do an online search for groups in your region or ask other mothers you meet at the grocery store or discount store if they know of any. One woman shared that when her third child was born and she was juggling the baby and two preschoolers, she joined the "Homemakers' Club" that met at a church once a week and provided a paid sitter in the church nursery. She said that the "two-bucks-a-kid fee" was the best investment she ever

made and that she is still close to the friends she made there, even though her youngest child is now 17.

- If you attend church, volunteer to help in the nursery for children the same age as your own and strike up conversations with the children's mothers.
- When you attend "parent's night" at the school, follow up a smile to the other parents in your child's classroom with a greeting and question. If you're in the algebra classroom, ask if the other parent is any better at helping their child with the new math than you are.
- When you take your child to the skate park, hang around awhile and admire his or her tricks and chat with the other mothers there.
- Talk to parents of your children's friends whenever possible. Invite the parents inside when they come to pick their child up from your house after a play date. Use children's birthday parties or their sports practice to connect to other parents instead of running errands or reading your magazine.

Midlife Freedom

Many women have more time to focus on their own interests and activities once they reach their forties or so, which provides a wealth of opportunities to become more socially active and to develop rewarding friendships. As we become more comfortable with ourselves, we are generally able to see others for who they really are and to be less caught up in the exterior trappings of another. As several of our midlife interviewees emphasized, they are able to value diversity in others much more readily than when they were younger. So as you reach the point where you know who you are—or are ready to start exploring different interests to help you get to know yourself better—take advantage of opportunities that will bring you into contact with others. Don't just read about a possible new interest—experience it! Here are some ideas to get you started:

- Take a cooking class in addition to buying a new cookbook. Strike up conversations with fellow students about the new recipes you are trying at home.
- Take up a new sport—there are beginner-level classes available in tennis, golf, racquetball, and so on at local recreation centers and clubs. There are often beginner leagues or open clinics that you can attend, and when you do, look for potential sports partners.
- Take kayaking or scuba classes from an outdoor outfitter. Sign up for trips that are planned to practice your new skills.
- If you've been attending a gym or fitness center for a while, but don't feel like there are any potential friends in your current class, attend

at a different time. Shake up your routine and see if you see people from a different perspective.

- Volunteer to "adopt a library shelf," help with the "Friends of the Library," or work at a book drive at your local library. If your library doesn't offer any of these opportunities, volunteer to help organize one.
- In general, just volunteer, volunteer, volunteer. You will meet people with similar interests and the willingness to get involved and help others. Check out the lists of nonprofit organizations in your area online or in the "Volunteers Needed" section of the local newspaper. You can meet others who share your passion for everything from abandoned animals to preserving the wetlands to helping less fortunate community members.
- Feel like breaking free from the everyday grind? Find a "women-only" adventure camp or travel club and spend a weekend off the map.
- If you've ever been fed up with the way "city hall is run," volunteer for the political party you feel could do a better job.
- If you work full-time, seek out other women who might like to start a weekly lunch tradition. This could include any of the following: bringing pot luck to the office break room for a "lunch club," trying different restaurants once a week, playing cards, taking a walk, or having a 30-minute cardio workout in an unused conference room.
- If you work, but have no time to schedule a lunch event, think about something you might like to do outside office hours. One teacher put up a flyer to locate colleagues interested in going to the theater downtown once a month. She ended up with half a dozen regulars who were from disciplines as diverse as drafting and drama!

OLDER WOMEN

The role of older women has changed dramatically in the past few decades. We may laugh about the saying that "60 is the new 50," but many older adults are truly living a life much more active and dynamic than generations past. If you are unable to be as active as you might like or are unable to leave home easily, we suggest that you take advantage of services available in your community for homebound adults. Inviting neighbors to stop by, asking neighborhood children to help with small chores, or chatting with the person who delivers meals to your home each week are activities that will allow you to maintain social connection with the local community, even if your family is not nearby. If you are relocating from your family home to a new community, there will be numerous opportunities to get involved in activity groups at the new location. Be willing to give the new residents and the residence a chance—engage in activities you've always enjoyed, but try out new things, as well. Whether you're in the same home you've lived in for decades or at a new place, if you are able and willing to get out and make connections, below are some ideas for getting a social fire kindled:

- Find out about the local resources in your community. Most towns, even small ones, have a center where activities for seniors occur fairly regularly. If pinochle is the only card game going, but you'd rather play gin, ask if you could organize a new activity.
- Volunteer for causes you care about—whether it's helping out at a food pantry, delivering meals to those who are not ambulatory, or serving as a docent at a local museum, you will be interacting with others with similar interests.
- Attend any senior programs for exercise and fitness at the local YWCA/YMCA. Even if you are not yet in shape, they will be able to help you get moving. Water aerobics is easier on your joints and popular with older adults.
- If you are a caregiver for a relative, seek out any support groups for other caregivers. Connecting with women who are dealing with the same struggle can be an emotional and social lifesaver—even if your obligations limit your interactions to mainly telephone or email.
- Always wanted to travel? Some organizations offer inexpensive trips. For instance, the South Carolina Cattleman's Association offers educational trips related to the beef industry. Other organizations specialize in trips for women. You may need to ask around or search online.
- If you are home during the day, spend some time outside and chat with your neighbors. If they work, plan to be picking up your mail or paper at the same time they are leaving for or returning from work.
- If you attend church services, get involved in women's group meetings or church school classes.
- A local church may have a group of volunteers eager to visit people who are homebound. Either join the group as a volunteer or ask to be put on their visitation list.

V

STRATEGIES FOR SURVIVAL— BUILDING AND MAINTAINING LASTING FRIENDSHIPS

16

⚜

Building Strong Friendships
from the Beginning

What are the skills that some women have that allow them to make friends quickly and easily and to keep them close throughout the years? In the previous chapter, we presented ideas for finding new friends, and in this chapter we share tips for laying the foundation for lasting friendships.

In the first part of the book, we explored the science behind the development of friendships, and in the second part, we shared a chronology of the ways in which our connections to friends develop as we move through each new stage in life. Now, we offer ideas about some effective ways to build strong friendships regardless of your age.

During our interview with Cindy, a yoga teacher in her early fifites, she revealed that when she was only 10 or 11 years old, she had an epiphany about friendship—that she must be a good friend in order to have good friends. Although a sentiment we usually hear when we are young, its salience endures generation after generation if the girls and women we interviewed are to be believed. Following are interviewees' suggestions, in their own words and arranged by developmental stage, for establishing friendships on strong footing from the outset.

TWENTIES AND YOUNGER: SOCIAL LIFE IS IDENTITY

- Most important, be yourself! Don't try to fake your identity, your likes, or dislikes—friendship is about honesty, and getting started on the right foot is the only way to build a friendship that will last.

- Establish boundaries early on with new friends to avoid causing hurt feelings later. Let your new friends understand the limits of your "comfort zone" and honor their own expressed boundaries.
- Communicate expectations of how you would like to see the friendship develop—close friends, workout buddies, or campus/classroom friends. Letting someone know how much room you have in your life is good for you and your friend.
- Follow through on any commitments you make, whether they include communication, meeting plans, or something similar. Demonstrating trustworthiness is really important in solidifying a new friendship.
- Take time to get to know the person—so many new friendships now start with text messages or communicating through a social network. These networks are helpful because they give you an informal way to communicate with people you aren't yet close to as friends. As you get to know them, you can invite potential friends to group get-togethers or activities that interest both of you.
- Invite friends to accompany you in normal, everyday activities like running errands together or going to the gym together.
- Have fun trying out new activities or going to new places that your new friend recommends. Share your favorites, but don't be afraid to try new things.
- Find time for frequent conversations and getting together often early on to get to know each other better. Talk about important topics and insignificant things—don't be shy about asking questions of your friend. Learning about a person helps you understand them better if the friendship grows and deepens and also lets you know if they are someone you would really like to have as a friend.
- Invite them to hang out with your existing friends. This allows them to get a good sense of who you are. Also, let your new friend meet your family and loved ones and then ask for a chance to meet their family and loved ones because you learn about a whole new side of each other.
- Keep the communication path open early on if you would like the relationship to keep building. Feeling like you're being ignored is painful no matter what excuses you have for not staying in touch.

THE THIRTIES: WHEN TIME IS SCARCE

- Listen and make yourself available when it fits your schedule or you feel it is necessary, but also set guidelines early on so that everyone is on same page from the start. One woman shared that she did not over-extend herself in the early stages of a relationship because that would set a precedence that she might not be able to follow. As she clearly stated: *you want to remain as true to form as possible when developing a friendship.*

- Invite new friends to join in activities with your existing friends— this helps maximize the little bit of free time we have available each week.
- Talk frequently with your potential friend and really listen to them as they share their interests and their strengths. Find commonalities that provide opportunities to engage in activities and interests that appeal to both of you. Shopping, specific cuisine restaurants, walking/hiking trails, and book clubs are all easy ways to spend time together while engaging in an activity you know you will enjoy.
- If you both have children around the same age, arrange for play dates where everyone can enjoy the social activity.
- Many women shared the dilemma of spending their workdays on the phone or interacting with people, which made maintaining contact with new friends seem like another chore. These women often relied on email or texting in lieu of phone conversations. One woman revealed that when she is drawn to a new person and makes the effort to converse on the phone or in person, she tries to reveal enough of herself so that friends recognize that she is making an effort to further the friendship.
- Be open in sharing information about yourself, which will create an environment for your new friend to be open. You must get to know a person before knowing if the friendship will be long-lasting or for just a season.
- Be open to sharing! Sharing of time, sharing of your listening skills, and sharing of stories are important.
- Be genuine, be real, and be yourself. As one woman noted, she is *drawn to people who are willing to share their trials and tribulations*, because, as she so plainly asks, *who wants to be friends with someone who is perfect?*

MIDLIFE: WHEN SELF-ACCEPTANCE GROWS EASIER

- Friendships are different now than when we were younger and connection can happen on so many different levels! Because we know ourselves better and tolerate differing opinions more easily, it's finally a pleasure to engage in active discussions with new friends about their viewpoints on all different topics—such as inner motivations, moral beliefs, political thoughts, and religious beliefs. We don't need "carbon copies" of ourselves in friendship anymore—difference is no longer a threat.

- Look for friends who can offer positive reinforcement and offer this to others—this helps place the friendship in a positive and rewarding perspective. The more we associate with women who are upbeat with positive attitudes and who are accomplished in their own lives, the more empowered and inspired we can be in our own lives. Successful women are not the dreaded competition we considered them to be in our younger days.

- Perhaps the most important step is to follow up with your suggestions and your promises. For example, if you say, "Let's get together for dinner sometime," then make the call and set up the event. Don't wait for new friends to call first if you would really like to pursue a friendship—be the one to pick up the phone or send an email first.

- Share stories of your past to help new friends understand how you got where you are today. Give them a peek at your struggles and your successes. You may not have a shared history, but you can bond as you each share your history.

- The basics always work best with new and old friends: Be genuine. Be open. Be accepting. Do not judge. Be positive. Be encouraging. Be supportive. Ask questions. Show interest. Give compliments freely. Smile.

- Look happy to see new friends when you meet up—give them a hug and an authentic smile.

- Zero in on what is most important to friends and offer to explore that further with them. This helps to quickly build a bridge between friends. Don't be afraid to explore ideas, beliefs, or activities that differ from your own. By the same token, look for common bonds, values, and interests and build on those, as well.

- Spend time in activities that allow for meaningful conversation—leisurely meals, long walks, and so on. By listening to what people are saying and what they are feeling, it can show that they matter and that their thoughts and feelings are important and validated.

- Offer support to the person and begin to be a part of their lives, whether she is going through good times or bad.

- When building a new relationship, it can be very important to develop a trusting rapport. Because our society seems to rely on first impressions, it can be important to be yourself from the very first encounter with any potential new friends so that there are no unpleasant surprises later in the relationship.

- Take time to really get to know people—their goals, their hopes, their needs, and their desires. If you feel drawn to a person, find ways that you can be the friend that he or she needs and that you feel comfortable being.

- Ask questions—always about them! Find out about their family, their likes, dislikes, their birthday, significant parts of their lives. If they have kids, it is almost always easy, because people love to talk about their kids. If they are younger or don't have kids, focus completely on them and any important others in their life.
- Age can play tricks with our memories, so one woman revealed that she always make notes as time goes on so that she doesn't forget important facts and interests of her friends.
- As you get to know friends better, invite them to gatherings with your existing friends so that your network of friends can grow and strengthen.
- Laughing together is important—sharing humor is vital to any friendship. If we can't laugh together, we generally can't cry together, either. Find reasons to laugh!
- Always make an effort to call, email, and keep in touch. Send the person information you believe they'd find useful or interesting—email or snail mail news articles, book suggestions, and so on whenever you run across something that you believe they'd find helpful.
- Include them in your life in informal and formal ways. Meet for coffee, make them dinner, go to a move, catch a show, or something similar.
- Make real adventures together! Experiencing new activities with new friends means no expectations or preconceived ideas about who you are or how you are "supposed" to react. Let yourself try new things as you explore new aspects of your personality.
- To help new friends know that you are a *true* friend, treat each and every one of them as you would like to be treated.

OLDER ADULTS: CONNECTION MEANS CONTINUITY

- Share confidences with new friends—as we get older and friends move away or pass on, it's important to develop new relationships in which we can be intimate and honest about ourselves and our lives. Loneliness and isolation come too easily now, so fight against these foes with active engagement with others.
- Find ways to contribute to new friendships. If new people move into your neighborhood, invite them over for coffee or lunch. If the person lives alone and you have other friends in the same situation, organize regular potluck or simple suppers for the group.
- Find activities to do together that you both enjoy. Share a meal at one another's home, work on projects together, read the same books and discuss these together, visit museums or the library, or take adult ed-

ucation classes together. Stay connected through shared experiences and let these things be events of *their* choice, not just your own.

- When first connecting with a new friend, be sure to pay attention to his or her likes and dislikes. Get to know where people are coming from in their lives and what is important to them.
- Introduce new friends to your current set of friends so that the community of older adult women can be more closely connected.
- Call up new friends instead of waiting for them to call you. If mobility for a new friend is an issue, be sure to make regular phone calls to her to check on her. This caring and compassionate interest can be a strong foundation.
- Send cards and notes—everyone enjoys receiving something other than bills in the mailbox. Clip articles from the newspaper or magazines you receive and include these in mailings—these engage your new friend and as you discuss the articles, you learn more about their opinions and viewpoints.
- Learn to use a computer—email programs allow you to keep in touch and easily forward interesting information to friends.
- Ask new friends about their accomplishments and what they are proud of in their lives. When with others, share your new friend's accomplishments, as many of us are hesitant to "blow our own horn." Celebrate your friends each day.
- Carry a camera (digital, 35mm, or cell phone) with you wherever you go and take pictures of events and friends. One woman shared: *I am forever carrying a camera, so I take shots of key events and these photos soon become memory-makers and memory-keepers when sent to my friends: "A picture is worth a thousand words."*

CONCLUSION

Whether you are at the entry point of adulthood or looking back over a half century or more of living, new friendships are out there for discovery and development. Although the manner in which we approach relationships may change with time and age, one unified thread runs through the wisdom shared by women of all ages. The elements of this thread include an unfailing authenticity, candid self-awareness, and the ability to focus on the needs and interests of others over those of ourselves. The wisdom shared by women of all ages makes it clear that presenting false fronts and holding self-centered perspectives will block the development of healthy relationships. However, no matter where you are in your life journey, there are new friends waiting to be met with a smile and embraced with open acceptance.

17

⚜

Tips to Strengthen
Existing Friendships

Here are strategies to encourage you to honor and acknowledge the friendships you have formed and to give attention to maintaining and strengthening these relationships.

Virtually all of the women we interviewed shared stories of friendships that had lasted decades as well as friendships that had ended after only a short period of time. Although there is evidence to support the adage that some friendships are only meant to last a season, there is also evidence that friendships can thrive for decades when intentionally tended with nurturing care. Some researchers have suggested that merely keeping a friendship in existence could be described as friendship maintenance.[1] For the most part, interviewees seemed to believe that "maintenance" was about keeping in touch with frequent or, in some situations, even sporadic contact with a friend. How do researchers suggest friendship maintenance can best be achieved? Canary and Dainton[2] noted that there are four basic methods of maintenance that consistently appear in the literature. These are (1) spending time together, (2) maintaining openness, (3) providing social support, and (4) avoidance. In their discussion of previous scholars' attention to spending time together,[3,4,5,6] they noted it has been clearly determined that without some form of interaction, friendship termination usually results. Today's women use a variety of methods of interacting that include virtual, voice-to-voice, and face-to-face. Each of these methods proves able to keep a pair of friends close heart-to-heart. In fact, Rawlins[7] presented evidence supporting many contemporary women's beliefs about the flexibility and mutuality of the timing and nature of contact—it's not so much regular, concrete interaction that is necessary to keep a friendship alive, but more the sense that emotional support would be provided when needed.

Openness was described as willingness to provide self-disclosure and conversations about our current life events and circumstances. Being open to self-disclosure is necessary to developing genuine relationships with friends. Women strongly endorse the value and necessity of sharing their honest and deep feelings with their close friends. However, there is often an element of risk involved in self-disclosure that acts as a barrier to the process for some women. Being open about the hidden parts of ourselves requires trust, but also builds trust.

Researchers have also noted the value of consistently offering social support to friends.[8,9,10,11,12,13,14] Just knowing that they could count on their friends for support was appreciably sustaining to all women interviewed. The ways in which we offer this support, whether through listening to a friend's struggles, giving them ideas on how to handle problems, or standing behind them in their endeavors, are integral to keeping friendship ties strong.

Last, they addressed the role that avoidance played in friendships—not avoidance of a friend, but willingness to avoid specific "hot-button" issues that might cause friction or discord in a relationship. In association with this specific method of avoidance would be the honoring of the need to avoid spending too much time together with a friend. As a little girl, I can remember my mother warning me that sometimes friends needed to take a break from one another. This was made clear during my tenth summer, when my best friend and I tried to contrive ways to spend alternating overnights at each other's home. After a couple of nights of convincing our parents to say yes to the pleas of "please let Suzy (or Betsey) spend the night tonight," I remember Betsey and I needing a couple of days off from each other's company to preempt the meltdowns and high drama that are so typical of the "tween years."

Conflict management and what might be called "damage control" are integral to maintaining friendships as well. We must be willing to own our contribution to a disagreement, and, perhaps on rare occasions, be willing to offer an apology even when we are not convinced that we were at fault. Damage control is also essential when we may have crossed a "friendship line" by breaking one of the tacit rules of friendship described in Chapter 3. We must own up to transgressions before a friendship is irrevocably damaged. If we find ourselves at odds with a friend and fear that the disagreement is a possible "no turning back" point of discord, conflict management skills are mandatory for a successful resolution. Few relationships are immune to disagreements or conflicts; being able to turn back the tide of friendship dissolution is a negotiation skill worth acquiring.

We asked interviewees how they stayed connected and maintained their friendships in our over-busy world. For the most part, women who successfully handle these tasks are a highly communicative bunch and rely on a multitude of communication methods. To transform the research data into practical applications, their successful strategies are organized into categories similar to those of earlier researchers, but based on contemporary communications technology, the category for spending time with friends has been expanded to include not just "face time," but "virtual time," as well.

EMOTIONAL SUPPORT AND POSITIVE ATTITUDES KEEP FRIENDSHIPS FRESH AND VITAL

Here are tips, in the words of interviewees, that reflect the common thread in many of the responses that addresses ways to ensure that your friends know just how important they are to you:

- Treat the special friends like family.
- Always remain positive about the friendship. Always try to be understanding of others' time constraints, as life is busy with children—or partners or aging parents or careers or any of the myriad draws on a woman's time.
- Giving opinions only when asked will show that you are not judgmental and encourages the individual to be open in sharing their thoughts and feelings. Being a good listener and gaining knowledge of the other person's interests helps us understand the individual. Being honest with this person, our friend, helps build trust and validates true friendship.
- Do your best to remember important dates and events in their lives—for happy occasions and difficult times. It is important to remember the date of your friends' birthdays, but it's okay to "forget" their ages. Keep up with the anniversaries of losses, too, whether it's the loss of loved ones, relationships, jobs, and so on. This means checking in around these dates and hearing and honoring what is *most important to them.*
- Keep in mind details about your friends' lives—this may be pets, hobbies, children's ages, whatever is significant to your friend—and acknowledge these things.
- Try to make time for your friends no matter how busy you all are and *always* be there for them when they are in need.
- Commiserate and laugh about yourselves and your plights. The burden does not then seem so heavy.

- Giving a friend a small gift or making a phone call "out of the blue" to tell her you are thinking about her can really make both your days brighter.
- Let your friends know that you love them. End phone calls with an "I love you" or a similar sentiment to remind your friend just how much she means to you.
- Do you best to lend support in times of need: whether it's that they need a babysitter or just someone to listen to them, being actively engaged in what's going on will keep you "tight."

KEEP COMMUNICATION OPEN AND HONEST

- Maintain consistent contact, offer honest communication, pass no judgment, and support friends through the good times and the challenges in life.
- When you are with your friends or catch them on the phone, be sure to ask them how *they* are doing. Don't be in such a hurry to talk about yourself. Show interest in their lives and make that person a priority at the time, no matter what else is on the day's to-do list.
- Share important personal information—trust in yourself and in your friend. Talk about the significant things going on in your life, regardless of how far away you may live from one another or how seldom you get to see one another. Laugh! Love! Live! Stay in full communication on a regular basis.
- Listen to your friend! Make yourself *available* but *not intrusive*. Listen and focus on what is the *real* issue for your friend. Ask yourself the following questions: How can I help her? How can I be present for her in her life? Then do what you can to be there.
- Sometimes take a moment to reach out and call or email when a friend comes to mind just to check in. Call at unexpected times. Call at happy times. Call at sad times. Get together at least some times. Send the occasional email. Dance together. Love each other's children. Think about your friends during the day—they'll know they're cared for. Knowing someone is thinking about us can really warm the heart and strengthen a relationship.

STAYING IN TOUCH: FROM SNAIL MAIL TO TECHNO-TALK

Still mourning the year, almost 30 years in the past, when her best friend moved some 2,500 miles away, Molly, now 50, said that the pair relied on longhand letters and enclosed photos as their lives and families grew. Now they rely on the "magic" of email and photo sharing via Internet sites such as Flickr. Molly admits that it is not the same as having her best friend next door, but they've been able to maintain a close friendship that has truly deepened and taken on new meaning as the decades have passed. "We see each other about once a year, sometimes twice, and when we do, we usually have one day where our whole families get together—partners and kids, but we also have a visit that is just the two of us. We may not look like we did when we first met in junior high, but our appreciation for each other and connection is every bit as strong and probably stronger. We have a shared history, and although our "present" isn't shared geographically, we've shared our lives and our most intimate feelings and experiences. We're definitely friends forever, just like we promised a million years ago when we were just kids." Following are additional comments from women that illustrate the role of communication in all its forms:

- I am over 80 and rely on email and phone calls. I and my friends are older now, and I find you have to work at it to keep it all going—even though we have known each other over 40 years—often because they have husbands and I don't.
- I make use of email especially during the busier times of the year . . . and I *never* miss a birthday, always send a card, and try to make a call. In addition to the expected birthday and holiday greetings, it is nice to send cards for no reason at all!
- When life gets busy with family or other responsibilities and there isn't a lot of time left to hang out, just calling, texting, or contacting through social networking tools like Facebook lets your friends know that you're still thinking about them and, therefore, that you care. These quick forms of connecting can keep the relationship open and active.
- Make sure to find time to call and talk on major holidays or other important dates. Other forms of communication work well, but on important days, it is best to always hear a voice.
- Sometimes even emailing cute little jokes back and forth can help you stay connected. (Just avoid the chain emails and the risqué/off-color jokes, unless you really know your friends well!)

HOW OFTEN SHOULD WE TRY TO CONNECT WITH FRIENDS?

Women have different ideas about how frequently they should be in contact or meet up with friends. From "constant" to "yearly," the following suggestions illustrate how variable individual timelines can be. It is helpful for friends to reach an agreement on "how often is often enough" to avoid hurt feelings and mistaken perceptions about each other's investment in the relationship. Following are some verbatim comments from our interviewees that attest to the wide range of communication frequencies:

- Keep in *constant* contact. This could be either by email, text, phone, Internet Skype—whatever. Keeping in constant contact and knowing how your close friends are doing is always a plus.
- Staying connected through *daily* texts or using social networking sites.
- I try to keep in touch with my closest friends at least *twice a week*. Whether it is a call, or a text or a message on Facebook. Staying in contact with someone and making an effort to show that you care and that you want this friendship really helps keep it strong.
- I contact my closest friend at least *once a week*. Sometimes, I stop in at her house on my way home from work. I often call her from my car on the way home from work. Usually we try to do something together, like go to a movie or to lunch once a week. I check with her when I know something is stressful in her life.
- A random phone call once *every few months*.
- Maintain some form of contact at a very minimum *once a year*. Gather for lunch and/or movie once a year; plan trips somewhere with them.
- Commit to seeing each other a certain number of times per year— whatever works best.

What appears to be most important is being in contact with one another on a *consistent* basis—using expectations that the two of you co-create. As one woman affirmed, "I believe that keeping in touch is important. With some, that might mean twice a month, and with others, it might be as little as twice a year."

Another woman hailed the value of consistency: "Consistent contact via phone, email, Facebook, cards. Stay in contact by any means—if geography is an issue—which it is with my very best friend, so we stay in touch with phone, IM, email. With friends that are local, I make every effort to have a meal with them at least once each month. Also, socializing with them is important in ways beyond just sitting down to a meal—like taking in a movie, some theater, or visiting an art exhibit."

FACE-TO-FACE NEVER LOSES ITS CHARM

We were reminded by one woman that "[women friends] should spend time together! Even though you may have a strong friendship, it can only get stronger as you spend more and more time together." Whether it is the influence of nature or nurture—we've explored both theories earlier in the book—women thrive on social engagement. The women we interviewed had no trouble coming up with ideas or reasons for getting together with their friends. For some fortunate women, neighborhood visits were virtually a daily occurrence, especially for a few of the women with young children. Keeping connected with other adults, beyond husbands and partners, was a key goal for many of the mothers we met. One woman, Kathy, a 33-year-old mother of two preschool-aged children, declared, only partially tongue-in-cheek, "If it weren't for living down the street from my best friend, I know I'd be crazy by now. Looking after two young kids, having a husband who works 12-hour days, and having given up a full-time job with co-workers I enjoyed, without daily contact with a friend, I'd be putting the kids up for adoption and putting myself back in the job pool!" The years of early career-making or baby-making may draw some of us away from frequent visits with friends, but the ideas that follow attest to the creativity of women for finding ways to connect.

- Meals are a great way to socialize:

    Breakfasts on the go on weekdays, brunches at your home on the weekends
    Lunch-hour meetings in town or picnic lunches at the park with the kids
    Milk and cookies at play dates with the kids
    Appetizers and drinks in nice clubs after work
    Dinner at a favorite restaurant with your gang of friends on a weekday
    Themed dinners, potlucks, or progressive dinners on the weekends at home

As one woman noted, "As family situations and financial situations have changed over the decades, so have the level of haute cuisine and the price of the wine. Nothing's wrong with salad forks, dessert spoons, and crystal on the table, but nothing's wrong with pizza delivery and a bottle or two of 'two-buck Chuck,' either." Another woman suggested that friends "keep rituals going like meeting for breakfast, celebrating birthdays, or seeing movies" to keep friendships from fizzling out. Similar to the encouragement to treat friends like family, the connection of ritual to friendships mirrors the value of ritual to family passages.

- The "Girls' Night Out" concept has been well-marketed and well-tested. Some of the ways in which "girls" are spending their evenings out include meals, of course, but other pastimes are being enjoyed as well. As one woman suggested, "It's great to meet with friends for different activities." Ideas we gathered include:

Movies
Bowling
Gossiping and retelling "do you remember when" stories over ice cream
Attending the theater in the city (or the university or the community playhouse)
Shopping, shopping, and shopping
Manicures and pedicures
Makeovers at the department store or local home beauty saleswoman's pitch
Parties for candles, lingerie, make-up, jewelry, kitchen products, and so on
Bunco or bridge or even gin rummy or poker
Plan girls-only getaway weekends—go to the beach, the mountains, Las Vegas, local inns, whatever your budget and interests allow!

- For an alternative, enjoy the "Girls' Night In" if you are short on cash or babysitters. One group of single women we heard from schedule one night a month to hold a "Grown-Up Slumber Party," at which they watch movies, order in pizza or Chinese, and enjoy staying up into the early morning like they did when they were adolescents. As one woman noted, "Hanging out in my flannel PJs and comfy slippers with a group of women brings back that whole teenage joy of being able to share my secrets, listen to gossip, and just be comfortable with who we were as awkward teens." Another woman shared that when she and her friends all had children that still needed babysitters, they would have all the kids at one house with the sitter while the women met for "girls' night in" at another home so that the kids could still be nearby, but they'd not be bothered by the kids and vice versa.

One woman shared that she meets up with her girlfriends a couple times a year: "These are the friends I have known since grade school and I am over 50." Another woman emphasized that she tries to meet frequently with the friends who live close by: "I make an effort to stay in touch and meet with them over coffee and discuss what everyone has accomplished in their lives." An important caveat to planning meetups was provided by one woman who enjoys "oodles" of friends, "Being flexible is important. Though it's tough to stay in touch when everyone is busy, just calling and inviting a friend out for a coffee, dinner, a glass of wine, whatever. Making a date is important. If it falls through, no biggie, make another date. Keep trying until you finally meet up! Good friends are worth the effort."

WHEN LIFE GETS MANIC, SOCIAL NATURES KICK INTO HIGH GEAR

As women, it seems that our workloads have grown both at home and on the job. What used to be leisure time is now catch-up time and finding time to maintain social relationships multiplies in difficulty at each new life stage or added responsibility. Here are several innovative ways that creative women are able to squeeze friend time into their hectic and over-scheduled lives:

- It is of my opinion that women are used to multitasking due to the many unique levels of demands they have on their lives and diverse roles they play. Creativity for me is often a key factor. When I drive to see my father, it is an hour and a half drive. If traveling alone, I always call a friend in N.C. When I arrive at the destination, I know she will understand I need to hang up. Otherwise, it is difficult for her to let me go. Since I am on a moderate length trip, I can totally enjoy the call.
- My friend and I walk "together." However, she is in Michigan on her cell phone and I am in New York on mine.
- I sometimes attend the activities that my friends' children participate in, such as concerts, science fairs, athletic meets, and religious functions. I not only get to spend time with a friend, but I also get to get a peek into their lives and learn more about what they value.
- We have made doctor appointments together or gone to each other's visits just to support each other or catch up.
- One thing I've learned from being up front and honest with my closest friends is that we're all more alike than we realize. I have one good friend who struggles with some of the same demons that I do and we now have a standing date to attend a specific support group meeting each week. Sharing the struggle and sharing the time together really help me in my resolve to handle my challenges.
- When time is tight, I just invite several friends to get together at one time—it lets us reconnect *in packs*, plus it allows different friends to get to know each other better.
- If I am going on an errand, I've called on friends to see if they would like to come along for the ride just to have some time and quiet space for a visit. This can include running to the post office, the "big box" stores, or the library, as just a few examples.

Hopefully these ideas will resonate with you or spur your own creativity in finding ways to keep your friends close. It can be a challenge, but one that is definitely surmountable, and the payback is well worth the effort.

CONCLUSION

In a nutshell, perhaps the following testaments to working at friendships sum up the heart of strong relationships:

- To maintain strong friendships, you have to be a strong friend. You need to be there for your friends through the good times as well as the bad times. Providing support, listening, and just being there are essential to maintain strong friendships. And be committed to growth—of yourself, your friends, and your friendships.
- It's hard keeping friendships strong over the years—no doubt about it! You can call, you can invite your friends to do things, but for me, the longest and strongest friendship I have is there whenever either of us needs it. It's less about maintenance activities as it is about the bond that we have forged over years and years of time and common experience.

The women who successfully hold on to friends over the years hold friends as a priority. They carve out time and energy to build and maintain these cherished relationships and clearly reap a sweet reward.

18

❧ ❧

Friendship in the Digital Age: Technology Keeps Us Connected—Sometimes!

Communication has never been as multi-faceted or as rapid as it is today. Texting, Facebook, MySpace, Twitter, AIM, and email are just a few of the social "techno tools" that support and circumscribe our social connections. This chapter provides a primer on how these technologies are used and how women of all ages rely on them to stay connected to current friends and discover new friends.

There are few people left who do not make some use of communication technology. In many homes, children learn how to use computers before they learn to speak, and technology modifications have been developed to handle the special communication needs of older adults. A generation ago, little girls engaged in make-believe phone calls on brightly colored Fisher Price toy phones. Today they practice their social skills on pretend cell phones that closely mimic the real thing. Even cell phones today are more colorful and "cute" than the typical landlines ever were!

Not only do we carry our phones in our pockets so we can "be" with our friends wherever we go, but we are also able to communicate *instantly* via text messages, email, online social networking, photo sharing, or tweets on Twitter. It's not only younger women and girls who are using social networking to connect; according to the recent Pew Internet & American Life Project data, over 46 percent of Americans 18 and older are using these sites and, of these users, 73 percent have Facebook accounts.[1] We know from research presented in earlier chapters that we fare better overall with friends, a sense of connectedness, and a feeling of belonging—and many of us may be *logging on* in order to find a place to *fit in*.

Although our availability to our social contacts has risen in the past few years, there's no definitive proof that easy accessibility has enhanced or deepened our relationships with friends. Controversy continues as to whether social technology brings us closer to others or isolates us in a bubble at our computers. What *is* certain is that women of all ages are introducing technology into their social communications. Older interviewees noted that cell phones have changed their communication patterns by allowing more frequent and lengthier calls to friends. One woman in her late fifties firmly reminded us that "cell phones are a form of technology! And as one old enough to recall when a long-distance call was an expensive and rare form of communication, liberal use of this technology serves me and my friends well."

We invited women to share their feelings about the most popular communication technologies and to let us know what they felt were the benefits and the drawbacks. Following are brief descriptions of the technology formats and their ability to meet our needs in "real time."

EMAIL

Email, short for electronic mail, allows us to correspond with any of our friends who have an email account, regardless of their service provider. Though the communications are stored electronically, much like a word processor, we are also able to print emails out upon receipt and save the sender the cost of a stamp. Email systems allow us to send attachments of files, photos, videos, music, and the like. As one woman noted, "Email allows me to keep in contact with college friends and other friends who live far away. You want to maintain the connection but calling or visiting is usually harder than normal. You can type out things you want to say *and* you can delete some things you shouldn't say." For the most part, email is seen as a great advantage to keeping friendships alive. Following are lists of the pros and cons women have shared regarding the effect of email on their friendships.

What Women Like about Email

Provides Quick Connectivity

- It allows me to maintain friendships through an often busy and hectic life. It is easily accessible and convenient for both parties involved. It helps me keep balance in my life while still letting others know that I care. It's a quick and easy way to maintain open lines of communication with people I might not have stayed in touch with otherwise—due to distance, time, life stage, etc. Easy, fast, and no postage fees.

Easy Communication to Multiple Friends at One Time

- When I had breast cancer, I was able to send information and updates on my progress to 20 people at once. It helped me stay connected and it was an easy way for friends to show me their support.

Few Constraints and Allows Archiving

- Lets me get a point across at length and it can be easier to express my true feelings via email. It's a way to fully get my point across without being interrupted. I am better at writing sometimes than I am in person and sometimes I can say things I wouldn't in person. I am also able to think through everything I want to say before I say it. I like that email is a form of archiving—something you don't get with regular phone conversations.

Great for Including "Bonus Material"

- You are able to attach things to emails for download—I share photos of my kids, my pets, and my life.

No Worries about Personal or Geographic Time Zones

- It's a great way to touch base during off-hours if your schedules don't coincide. You can email in the middle of the night if you want to and you won't have to wake a friend to listen to your story! And it can be cheaper than a long-distance call!

Although email has the many positive features listed previously, there are also significant drawbacks, as noted in these comments.

What Women Dislike about Email

Impersonal/Imprecise

- It's not as personal as a phone call or letter where you use your own handwriting, choose the stationery, etc. I used to write letters and make envelopes; now I'm too lazy to add those personal touches. Emails can lack depth and intimacy—even when a person is baring their soul, a "virtual" message doesn't carry as much weight as more personal forms of communication.

Frustrations with Timing/Delivery

- It's not in real time—my email might get read tomorrow and responded to the next day. Sometimes people don't respond, either because they do not want to or the message possibly gets filtered into their junk email and then you have to follow up with the phone call you were hoping to avoid in the first place. Or if you sent a long, personal note, you may end up feeling neglected or ignored.

Can Take Up Too Much Time

- I don't like receiving forwards, political emails, religious emails, chain emails, distasteful jokes, offensive content, huge attached files that clog up my work email, requests to pray for some person I've never met, etc. Emails that really deserve responses can get lost in the stacks!
- I'm lazy. I hate having to log on to the computer and it can be frustrating if I can't remember friends' email addresses.

Potentially Hazardous to Relationships or Reputation

- Once you've hit the "Send" button, you can't take it back! Emails can accidently get sent to wrong person and that is how rumors start or poor impressions are made. If you use it to send derogatory messages about people, remember that the recipient might forward it to that person or someone else who might forward it—people are just "one click away."

Another method of using email is to create listservs, or electronic mailing lists, for groups of people who have something in common. Whether it's a group of women who have twins or women who work the night shift or women who are cow farmers in the Northeast, there is probably an online group and listserv for them. One woman who has been overseeing a listserv for women trying to lose weight on a shared diet noted that most of the women will never meet, due to geographic obstacles, but that the friendships she enjoys with the dozen or so listserv members are equal in intensity and loyalty to the friendships she has with women she saw on a regular basis. Listservs provide an opportunity to seek and receive support, information, feedback, and most of all, connections to others experiencing something similar to what you are going through. Friendships grow strong when communications are written from the heart and shared with a group whose bond is built on being a supportive presence to its members.

TEXTING

Text messaging is similar to email in its format—we use our cell phone number pads or keyboards to type in messages (often now containing generationally codified shorthand) and send them instantly to the cell phones of others. Texting has skyrocketed in its use and its notoriety in the past few years. It has been blamed for tragic moving vehicle accidents, made illegal for drivers in motion, and been the means for teen "sexting," in which sexually explicit messages and photographs are sent. Regardless of its questionable reputation in the courts and among many parents, texting is one of the most frequently used methods of communication among friends and families, although its popularity is inversely proportional to age. As one woman exclaimed: "Why on earth would a 55-year-old woman who is interested in quality relationships text as a primary means of communicating with friends?" Yet there are many of us who depend on texting as a frequent and useful method of contacting our friends. Following are some of the ways in which texting makes communication easier among friends and some of the ways that texting gets in the way of relationships.

What Women Like about Texting

Quick and Convenient

- Easy, easy way to communicate. If you have one thing to say but you don't have time to call and get caught up chatting, you can just text.

Provides Immediate Responses

- Texting is such a fast way to communicate with friends. Sometimes you just want to know your friend's son's shoe size or if they are going to be in town, but you don't have time for an entire conversation.

No Talking/Conversation Required

- When I am in a hurry and don't have time to talk, it is great.
- It's the only way I can communicate with my friends since I'm deaf and cannot hear on the phone.

Provide Constant Contact

- It's quick and to the point. It keeps you in almost constant contact with people, especially if they live far away.

This form of communication serves a purpose with women and their social networks, but there are definitely aspects of texting that women believe limit its usefulness.

What Women Dislike about Texting

Gets in the Way of Real Life/Real Relationships

- People use texting to hide behind a shield and not own up to their real feelings that should be expressed in person.
- It's not personal. Texting a "Happy Birthday" wish is definitely different than calling and saying it in person. It gives an illusion of personal contact, but actually creates distance.

Miscommunication Is Frequent By-Product

- You cannot delve into what you really feel or want. It is too impersonal. Much of real communication is body language and facial expressions. These are lost in texting—even more so than in email. A lot of miscommunication happens during text messaging.

Not Appropriate for Lengthy Conversations

- I do not like that people utilize texting as if it were email . . . anything longer than 10 minutes of text time is considered "phone conversation or face-to-face time" in my opinion.

Practical Problems

- Spelling mistakes, small buttons, archaic phones, can't type fast enough, difficult to text in a hurry. The older I get, the harder it is to manage the technology—physically and cognitively!

Many of the same likes and dislikes of text messaging apply to women's feelings about instant messaging and online chatting, two methods of communicating via the Internet. Women like that they can instantly send out messages to their friends, carry on private conversations, and keep up with friends who are geographically distant through very inexpensive means. Yet the frustration of misspelled words, confusing acronyms, and choppy, fragmented sentences were a turn-off for many. Frustration also accompanied the unmet expectations of "instant" communication when friends were not available or were not responding as quickly as the sender desired. One woman in her mid-twenties confessed that online chatting could become addictive—especially when she and her friends were sharing gossip.

Another twentysomething noted that she felt that online chatting could be intrusive when she was not in the mood to chat or didn't have time to fully respond. She also expressed fear that she would be perceived as rude if friends issued an invitation for chatting and she didn't feel up to responding. It seems that when we choose to be alone with our thoughts, but have signed in online, people in the virtual world are more likely to "knock on the door" than those in our real world. As new forms of accessibility to our friends increase, it also means that their accessibility to us will increase—which limits how positively some view new technology. Even women who have grown up with cell phones in their hands feel the creeping crush of social technology. As one young woman lamented, "I feel like I am 'too available' sometimes—there is no escaping from email, text messages, phone calls, instant messaging and so forth!"

SOCIAL NETWORKING

Social networking includes Internet sites such as Facebook, MySpace, Ning, Twitter, Classmates.com, or Friendster. Although MySpace is typically the choice for the under-18 set, Facebook has fans of all ages. The site provides a place where we can create a virtual home and upload photos, files, and even moment-by-moment status updates. These sites are designed to help us connect and reconnect to others—whether we are keeping up with friends we met in elementary school or developing new ties to friends we first meet via online communication. We may even feel close to celebrities when we are their Facebook "friends" or we receive their "tweets" from Twitter. Research about the effect of these sites on social development/behaviors seems to vary. Some reports provide evidence that the "rich get richer," meaning that the more friends we have in "real life," the more online friends we are likely to have and the more active we are on social networking sites.[2] Other evidence suggests that socially anxious individuals may be more comfortable using online communications with their friends and that it especially increased their willingness to engage in self-disclosure.[3] These individuals may not have more friends through technology, but they may feel more comfortable in their relationships. Regardless of the lack of conclusive evidence on their value or role in relationships, these sites are clearly an embedded component of social connections.

What Women Like about Social Networking

Ease of Use and Flexibility of Functions

- Great, simple technology that doesn't take much time to learn and a nice link to share pictures and such with my friends.

Connects Us to Old Friends

- Facebook is fun because you get to see what your first-grade best friend is up to now. It's also interesting to see who finds you.

Keeps Us Connected to Current Friends

- It's a great way to stay connected to people's lives as well as to those people I wouldn't otherwise have reasons to personally email or call.
- It really comes in handy with my friends away at college. They are always just "a click and a type" away.

Helps Us Find New Friends

- It keeps me in touch with my friends while I'm away at school and helps me contact new ones.

What Women Dislike about Social Networking

Privacy Is Compromised

- I feel it can be an invasion of privacy; people overuse it and put things up there that are inappropriate. People also have the power to post pictures of you without your permission. Everyone can see if you post something on a friend's wall—and this might create problems if a friend misunderstands your comments.
- Employers are actually using online information to assess the desirability of a new hire nowadays.

Time-Consuming

- It's one more thing that needs attention and upkeep. Responding to people who leave unimportant messages, sending notes, playing online games with friends, etc., are all time-consuming and bring me no satisfaction.

Too Superficial for Building Real Friendships

- Not a good way to develop a relationship. It is too public and it does not lend itself to developing deep relationships. I dislike the senseless updates—they don't really do much to strengthen friendships.
- People ask you to be friends who you really have little to no interest in befriending but you'd feel rude turning them down.

Blogging

For centuries, young girls have been confiding their most important secrets and feelings to their diaries on a daily basis. As we move from youth into womanhood, we often continue this practice but call it *journaling*. Women keep journals of their activities, their hopes, their dreams, and their life experiences. Today, women may opt for beautiful, handmade journals they lovingly choose at their local bookseller or they may enjoy the latest version of the journal—an online blog. Although blogging may seem too personal for some women, many of us enjoy sharing our lives with old and new friends and virtual strangers via the web.

For one of our interviewees, blogging has become an important part of her life that gives her a chance to sort through, record, and celebrate the significant and the everyday events she and her family experience. She values the ways in which her blogs have added connections to her friendscape. As she shared: "I am a blogger and have made a few friends solely through the blog. We have a common bond in that we like to write and we share an interest in our blog topics. One friend I have made has so many things in common with me. We both blog, we both have two boys, and we are in the education field. Although I have never personally met my friend, we occasionally email to see how the other is doing and share stories about our boys or our hectic lives. I can appreciate what she is going through because I live it. Some blogs are very personal, including mine. Each time I write, I am giving my readers a glimpse into my life, my home, and my personal relationships. You can't help but be friends after that!"

One of the most positive by-products of the blogging phenomenon is the connections that form between like-minded individuals. When faced with personal challenges, such as battling chronic illness, or just faced with the daily challenges of making it through life, blogging online provides an opportunity to not simply connect with similar others, but also to normalize the experiences of their lives. Blogging and commenting on others' blogs allows us to feel closer to women who are our online companions. Women are able to learn from one another, share their stories with those who care about them, and feel a part of a social network or, in many cases, an extended family. Blogging requires the willingness to open up your life to public view, but it also provides a link to a chain of support that our isolated lives might not readily provide.

VIDEO CALLING

The telephone—landline or cell—is the most frequently mentioned form of "social technology," but the Internet and web cameras now offer the magic of video-enhanced voice calling at an economical rate—free for most users. Some of our interviewees who use video calling complained about the choppiness and jumpiness of images, but all of the users really appreciated the availability of the service. One woman who greatly enjoys the technology pointed out one flaw as she laughed and commented, "It's like a big tease, I can see the person but they are not really there." Another woman felt that it was far better than a regular phone call—"It's great and it allows for a more personal communication than a phone call because you can see a person's expressions!" Many grandmothers we interviewed were really pleased with this type of communication technology—it is simple to operate and has a very gentle learning curve.

CONCLUSION

Social technology grows increasingly sophisticated at lightning speed and the desire to connect to friends who are not present is a strong instinctual urge. Little girls once relied on a couple of empty tin cans connected by a long piece of string as their first "mobile phones," but today's technology has zoomed into instant access and amazing clarity in transmission. Although we might feel like we are face-to-face with online friends, it is still important to make time to actually be face-to-face with others. Spending too much time in a virtual world can isolate us in ways that negatively affect our well-being, so transfer those online buddies into real-time companions. And there are at least a few of us who might prefer that technology slow down just a bit. As one woman a little past her seventieth birthday quipped, "[I am] too old to learn all the new technologies, and deeply suspicious of the way others can use it to your discomfort." And before we assume that it is only the older generations that place little value in new ideas and new technology, let's close this chapter with a brief comment from a young woman in her twenties: "I drive my car to go visit my friends. Automobiles are technology and I think they are the best thing to help friends keep in touch!"

19

❧ ❧

Full-Time Friend /
Part-Time Lover
Making Friends with Your Mate

A surprisingly large proportion of interviewees named their husbands/partners as their best friends. Whether in their twenties and the early years of marriage or rounding the bend into older adulthood, many women definitely valued their life partners as their closest friend. With this connection so solid for so many women, we invited them to share stories about their "best friendships" with their significant others.

Although there were a large number of women who espoused their spouses as buddies, a smaller proportion noted the lack of any friendship qualities to their primary romantic relationships. When asked about the existence of a friendship with her partner, one woman grew quiet and seemed to cautiously weigh the words as she responded, "No, I wouldn't consider my husband a friend. He's very independent; maybe it's the way he was raised? He spends his time with his books, alone. When I want to do something with someone, walking or kayaking or something like that, I have to look to someone else." Many of the other women who could not acknowledge a feeling of friendship with their partners expressed a wish that they were better friends and companions as a couple. One woman complained about the many demands on her time from career to family to church-related activities and noted that it would be a boon to her if her partner *could* be more of a companion and friend.

The role our partners play in our happiness and well-being is especially important if we do not have a female best friend.[1] Having a variety of others in our social network, kin or nonkin, is important, but the quality of the relationship we have with our partner, out of any other social relationship (including both family and friends), is the one most highly associated with our well-being. Friendship with our partners is frequently noted as an essential component of marital longevity.[2] If your current romantic relationship is less than satisfying, developing a positive, dynamic, and fulfilling relationship with your partner may be the most important investment of your social capital for the moment.

One of the foremost researchers in the area of marital satisfaction and success, John Gottman, states unequivocally that friendship is the key to a healthy marriage. He believes that the strength of a couple's friendship behaviors is identifiable within a matter of minutes and that these behaviors will predict the success or failure of the relationship. Reflect, for a moment, on the most recent interactions you had with your partner—was it in the middle of a hurried morning? At the end of a busy commute from work? At dinner where the kids' chattering monopolized the airtime—or at a dinner for two where a lack of chatter punctuated the dead air? Listening to the words you use, the tone of voice you employ, and the attitude you present when interacting with your partner may be sadly surprising.

What are some of the boundaries that exist between you and your close female friends? Are there unspoken rules about how much rudeness, thoughtlessness, and disrespect you would accept—or dish out—to your friends? Would you complain about your best friend's increasing waistline by calling her out in public as she ordered a venti caramel macchiato with whipped cream? Would you interrupt her as she began a story you'd heard before with a roll of your eyes and a "Not again—you've told this story three times already, for heaven's sake!"? Do you ever find yourself treating your partner more poorly than you'd treat a clueless clerk who forgot to give you your change at the grocery story? Bringing the basic social skills back into your relationship can go a long way toward rebuilding—or building—a friendship between partners.

If you want your partner to be more actively involved in the role of companion and friend, you must be assertive enough to acknowledge this desire to your partner. Let your partner know what it would mean to you to expand your relationship to include more of a friendship component. This may be especially challenging for women who are in relationships that have stiff and inflexible role expectations. It may be difficult, but opening up about your needs is the first step toward a better friendship—open communication is one of the most valued aspects of friendship. Being able to openly and honestly express your feelings and to allow the same from your partner is essential. In an interesting counterpoint to the strong support for the value of friendship in marriage, an author of a pop psychology book suggests that choosing a partner for a best friend undoes a couple's ability to argue with one another, which he feels leads quickly to a falling out of love.[3] Using a study by Duke University researchers that notes the increasingly smaller network of friends each generation seems to have, Marshall suggested that we are too nice to our partners and afraid to fully express our feelings for fear of losing a friend. We are not suggesting that you swallow your negative feelings or unpleasant reactions within your relationship—we are suggesting that you develop ways to fully express yourself, and, if need be, to fight fair.

REKINDLING FRIENDSHIP OR *WAS* IT JUST THE SEX?

Think back to what drew you to your partner when you first met. Was it physical attraction? Was it something you had in common? Did you just *click*? Any of these reasons can provide insight to help you choose the best path to rekindle your friendship.

If physical attraction first brought you together, that's a reminder that you found pleasure in just being around your partner from the beginning of the relationship. Recalling that excitement at just being with your partner can help you recognize the "otherness" of your partner. Long-time relationships, fraught with clock punching, paycheck crunching, and kids munching, can lead us into a mindset in which we take our partners for granted. And, as all of us who have ever been there can affirm, being taken for granted by a friend can leave you feeling wounded and indignant. Remind yourself of how it felt to crave your partner's company and to go to lengths to make time for one another. Next time you're alone with your partner, let yourself recall those positive vibes of attraction. Before getting caught up in a discussion of the daily hassles, let yourself look at your partner, not with "new eyes," but with "true eyes," the ones that drew you to them years ago. Take time to recognize your partner as an individual—not just the co-manager of the household.

When Renee, 42 years old, was asked about her best friend, she named her husband with no hesitation. When asked for more information about her friendship, she shared, "My best friend would have to be my husband. We've known each other forever—we met when we were teenagers. We were attracted to each other and started dating and married when we were very young; we weren't even 20 yet. To keep our friendship and relationship strong, we do everyday things together, but we also get away for a night every few months. My mom watches the kids and we're only a half hour away, but we need that time to recharge and focus on the relationship." She and her partner have found a way to keep romantic love exciting while strengthening the friendship. Research shows that we choose friends that are attractive to us, in whatever guise that may be. Letting yourself rekindle the attraction to your partner is an important step in honoring that friendship.

Shared interests are often responsible for bringing us into the orbit of our current partner—as well as into the paths of many of our female friends. What activities did you enjoy when you were first getting to know each other? Where did you go on dates? Where did you spend time outside the bedroom during the early years of your marriage? What types of films did you watch? What type of restaurants did you visit? In many cases, we are so caught up in the feelings of being "in love" with our partner in the early stages of the relationship that what we are doing together isn't as important as that we *are* together. For others, shared interests may be the very thing that kept the relationship moving forward. One woman said that she and her partner enjoyed "the simple stuff—like projects around the house, just hanging out, and even yard sale-ing and flea marketing. We went just yesterday and spent the entire day traveling around looking at other people's junk. When we spot a treasure at a bargain price, we feel like we've won some kind of prize and we gloat all the way to the next house!"

Another woman felt that she couldn't emphasize enough the value of spending time in common pursuits. Miriam, 52 years old, revealed, "I have found that doing activities of common interest are critical to a decent relationship. Sometimes it is something as simple as going to a baseball game together or going fishing." However, another interviewee noted that it was allowing her partner to engage in non-couple-focused activities that had most helped their relationship maintain a strong friendship. Barb, 57 years old, said she felt guilty that when their children came along she asked her partner to stop his hunting trips. "I can't believe I took him away from hunting. When he'd return from those trips, he was just so relaxed, so much more at peace." She realized that demanding he forego those trips with his friends was detrimental to their own friendship. When she realized that "anything that made him that calm and serene had to be good for him," she did what any good friend would do for another—she encouraged him to get back into the activity. They developed a compromise that would help Barb feel that her partner was pitching in with the growing demands of the growing family and still allow her partner to find the zenful state that helped them all.

Some women say that they just "knew" that their future partner was going to be someone important in their lives. Since friendships are often journeys of discovery, finding ways of experiencing the friendship aspect of the relationship can be a highly enjoyable adventure. However, many of us have knee-jerk resistance to some activities that our partners enjoy. One interviewee, Elizabeth, revealed that she was the type of woman who never washed her own car whereas her partner looked forward to the first warm week-end in spring when the first car wash of the season could finally take place on their own driveway. Preparation for the task usually included a trip to the local auto supply store to check out the latest washes and waxes, scrubs and polishes. Elizabeth seldom went on these errands and thought the entire affair was a ridiculous waste of time and energy until she finally took time to see the joy the entire experience—from buying the detergent to buffing the wax—brought her partner. Although Elizabeth had no interest in actually *washing* the cars, she did finally take her partner up on the invitation to stretch out on a lawn chair by the driveway while her partner reveled in the task. It took Elizabeth a little while to realize that a clean car was a "gift" from her partner—and that by keeping her partner company, she was giving the "gift" of companionship in return.

COMMUNICATION, COMPANIONSHIP, AND SUPPORT

Partnership implies a shared responsibility for the workings of a relationship as well as enjoying the shared benefits and rewards. The incentive for pouring energy into the friendship aspect of the relationship may be the bonus of better communication, strengthened support, and pleasant companionship. Sharing our lives with another can be much more fun when we're also sharing our thoughts and feelings. Communication not only eases the intricacies of daily life with another, it also builds warmth, understanding, and connection. The primary challenge for most couples who seek counseling is overcoming poor communication. Entire libraries could be filled with the many pop psychology and academic volumes written on the topic, so we are only providing a shorthand version of key communication skills: (1) listen, (2) check in to make sure you heard correctly, (3) listen some more, and (4) respond with kindness. If a friend doesn't get something important the first time you tell them, do you resort to anger, frustration, yelling, stonewalling? Most likely, you try telling them again, but in a different way. As you and your partner make efforts to improve communications, remember to be patient with each other and avoid negative blow-ups or unproductive shutdowns. Treat your partner with respect. Yes, just as you would with a friend.

Whether we actively chase down true love in the hopes of finding a soulmate and "happily ever after" or whether we unexpectedly find ourselves smack in the middle of being smitten, relationships are, inherently, about companionship. Although there are more concerns about financial security and professional ambitions when choosing a partner than a friend, similarities do exist between the two processes. We choose partners whose company we enjoy; who make us feel good when we're with them; and who make life fun—the same way we choose our friends. Many of our interviewees shared that their friends were the people with whom they enjoyed "just being" and the kind of company that you did not have to entertain. Beth, 48, has found this kind of deep friendship and companionship with her husband. Asked to describe this relationship she responded, "[It] is not so much specific activities we share, but more it is a state of being in his presence . . . a state of calmness, serenity, oneness, acceptance, peace within myself . . . no one else can provide for me that type of comfort. My favorite activity is quite simple—watching Fox News while holding hands or a movie. We share other interests such as camping and nature, but lack time and financial means presently for the pursuit."

Support of your partner can definitely be modeled on the support you offer your friends. Earlier in the book we discussed rules of friendship that should not be broken, and one of our interviewees clearly lives these rules with her friend, her partner. In particular, the rule of providing support and protecting your friend's honor to others is clearly illustrated by Miriam's shared experience: "I have found that acting as a supporter requires common interest in seeing each other grow and to be able to be individuals, as well as a part of a unit. I also believe that our friendship has been sustained because I have willingly stood up for my partner when family members cause problems. While I believe that everyone has a right to their feelings, I am not going to allow someone to say unnecessary, ugly things about my partner. I have tried to act as a buffer at times and this action has gained respect and a deeper level of trust from my partner."

After 30 years, Sandy was frustrated with the changes that were showing up in her marriage. Her partner was semiretired, dreaming of hitting the open road for a cross-country Harley-Davidson adventure, while Sandy was newly degreed and looking forward to beginning a career for the first time after spending the past 30 years raising a daughter and running the house. Sandy realized that George was eager for the ride, but she was raring to go on her new job. Arguments, screaming, and stubbornness were getting nowhere, so Sandy listened to her best friend's advice to talk *with*—not *at*—George about her vision of the next few years. "And it was amazing! I hadn't realized that he was looking to me so much as a friend and companion now that he rarely saw the guys at the office and I was looking to him to listen to my daily struggles, just like when you'd call your best friends in high school and talk for hours. Once we were able to actually hear what the other was saying, I realized that companionship was what we both wanted from the other. Okay, I'll go out for a weekend ride with George every month or so, and he'll make time to talk with me at the end of the day."

IMPORTANT ASPECTS OF THE FRIENDSHIP

Making room for this new—or renewed—development in your current relationship lets you more fully enjoy the friendship opportunities available to you. Following are specific ways to focus on this friendship, but they require that you prioritize this element of your relationship at the top of the list. As counselors who have worked with many couples who were trying to deepen—or even locate—their connection beyond the bedroom and the bankbook, we understand how resistant people can be to new ideas or suggested interventions. Suggestions for new ways of interacting and relating might be often considered "contrived," "forced," or "hokey" at first. But when a couple is reminded that what they have been doing is not getting the results they want, they are generally more willing to try out a new idea. If you are motivated and ready to enhance your own relationship, the following ground rules and creative activities may be your own first step in the process.

SOME BASIC RULES FOR BEING FRIENDS WITH YOUR PARTNER

Just as we have unspoken rules for successful friendships, there are some important rules for ensuring a successful friendship with a partner. The essence of these rules focuses on a heightened awareness of how a partner/friend should be treated. Partners deserve love, patience, and respect—just what we offer any good friend. With this in mind, try out the following ideas as you move into a new way of being in relation to your partner:

- Encourage your partner in what they do and refrain from criticizing their efforts. Just as friends expect you to provide encouragement and support, do this for your partner. Even if you would rather see a job done right than have the luxury of not having to do it yourself, please be tolerant of your partner's attempts and accept, accept, accept.
- Be patient when your partner is dead set on making a mistake no matter how much foresight, wisdom, and insight you want to impart. We often laugh indulgently about our friends who have to learn lessons the hard way; we need to recognize that our partners might also need to go that route. Acceptable exceptions would include matters of life and limb, bankruptcy or solvency, fire or flood—a little spackle on the wall should be okay.
- Offer to be a part of your partner's projects or hobbies—don't fake enthrallment, but offering to hold the flashlight or find the flat-blade screwdriver is something any friend would do.
- Avoid unrealistic expectations—if you ask your partner to help you find a new pair of jeans, be willing to help your partner find a new remote for the DVR or a new wiper blade for the car or new pair of jeans themselves.
- If your partner just can't listen to 45 minutes of "why I hate my job," then simply give them the synopsis. Not all friends like opera.

- If your partner feels safe enough to open up and reveal his or her inner feelings to you, don't, please don't, beat them down, laugh at their feelings, or tell them to "man up and move on."
- Review the qualities listed on the Friendship Readiness Assessment—think about how you can show your partner each of these, even the ones that you don't think you are as good at yet as the others.
- If you've got a complaint, share it with your partner just as you would a friend.

FRIENDLY ACTIVITIES FOR LOVING COUPLES

Here are a few ideas to encourage you and your partner to find new ways to engage in shared activities. If none of them seem like a good fit, hopefully they can at least inspire you to develop some ideas on your own.

- Some couples call it "date night," but it could just as easily be "friend night." Each month, take turns choosing a favorite activity that you typically don't engage in together and make a commitment to try and enjoy your partner's choice. One woman said that her partner chose Sunday/Monday night football, and though she was reluctant early on, it became a family tradition for her to prepare themed meals based on the opposing team's hometown. She said that she enjoys the excitement of the game and has fun trying out new recipes, and her partner loves that there's another armchair ump and Monday-morning quarterback in the house.
- Check out volunteer opportunities in your community and choose something that has special meaning to you or your partner and offer your time. One couple got involved in a greyhound rescue operation and enjoyed the growth of their own friendship as well as developing friendships with other like-minded people. They added new "best friends" to their household in the form of rescued dogs, but also built up a much stronger friendship in a marriage that had gotten somewhat rocky. The volunteer responsibilities required road trips to racetracks in several different states to pick up the animals. The hours spent together in the car gave them a chance to relearn the art of one-on-one conversation with one another; to take turns choosing the ride's soundtrack; and to begin listening to books on tape. As Sandy shared, "Listening to the books gave us great topics for conversation on the rides. And nothing beats talking about a good book with a good friend." As noted earlier in the chapter, the greyhound rescue couple is now looking at becoming a "weekend warrior" couple as they make plans for motorcycle traveling.

- Double dating helps a couple strengthen their own friendship while establishing new friendships with others. Partners can take turns choosing a friend or acquaintance of their own that they would like to get to know better and they can invite the new friend and their partner to go out together on a double date. Sometimes listening to your partner making small talk and getting to know someone else can help you see a new side of them. Whether you end the evening making plans for another get-together or plan to spend the ride home critiquing the evening, keep the focus on your friendship with your partner and don't spend the ride home critiquing each other.

- When you were little, did you and your friends have a club or secret society with a list of membership rules? Did you plan to start a rock band? Start a business selling something homemade or "found"? Ask your partner the same questions and see if the two of you shared any childhood passions. Maybe you will want to resurrect one of the ideas and see where the two of you might take it today. One interviewee, Nancy, 29, shared that when she and her friends were young, they loved the idea of pirate ships and buried treasure. They would create intricate hand-drawn maps and go so far as to hide trinkets and coins where the "X marked the spot." Her parents began a tradition of using clues and maps to hide birthday gifts for the birthday child to find. Nancy and her partner had taken the reins and inaugurated treasure maps for their own kids' birthdays. Nancy still dreamed about the excitement of a real treasure hunt, and when she heard about geocaching, she approached her partner to see if it might be a shared interest. Indeed it was, and they now enjoy the excitement of seeking out the hidden "treasures" as well as revel in the fun of leaving something behind for the next lucky "pirate."

Research indicates that having a *variety* of people in your social network is the most beneficial to your well-being. Including your partner as a friend is one way to add to the diversity of your social support system. Keep in mind, however, that having a strong and healthy relationship with your spouse is even more effective in promoting well-being if you can add to this relationship with two or more additional close relationships. Depending on your partner to meet all of your relationship needs is placing too great a burden on anyone. Reestablish and deepen the friendship with your partner, but be sure to use the same skill set to widen your friendscape with a variety of close supportive others.

20

༄ ༆

Coming Full Circle
with a Circle of Friends

We hope that the earlier chapters have clearly illustrated the essential role that friends play in our lives. Biology, genetics, sociology,
psychology, and a variety of other disciplines have provided a lens to
explore the social connections between females throughout the lifespan.
Our need for social contact begins early and grows in sophistication and
specificity as we mature. Throughout the book, we've shared success stories and time-tested techniques for successful friendship building to assist
women who have experienced difficulty in approaching, developing, or
maintaining friendships. No matter how young or how old we are, it is
clear that creating a satisfying friendscape is essential to satisfying our
need for connection.

We've passed along words of wisdom from hundreds of females, rep-
resenting life stages from toddlerhood to older adulthood, who clearly
value the pleasures and perils inherent in friendship and social connectedness. Yet the most important friendship we can develop is one with
ourselves. If we are unable to unabashedly embrace both our own virtues and vices, love ourselves unconditionally, and treat ourselves with
patience and compassion, we will continually struggle to truly offer an
honest and satisfying friendship to others.

A woman in her forties, who is counted among the close friends of
many others, shared her experiences with learning this lesson: "My
friendship with myself is the most important consideration. I must maintain my personal relationship with myself. I cannot allow my love for my
friends to outweigh the love of self and who I am. If I compromise my
values, my conscience and self-worth suffer. Otherwise, I am not being

much of a friend to myself and I will resent my friend and myself for making a decision that is not congruent with who I am. Therefore, sometimes I must make personal boundaries to protect myself from harm." Her commitment to self-preservation does not preclude her willingness to commit wholeheartedly to a friendship, as she went on to affirm that she has "never regretted being vulnerable to friendships at the expense of loss. If I had backed away from so many opportunities, I would have lost an abundance of love." She is, indeed, coming full circle at her half-century mark with a circle of friends who know who she is, where her commitments lay, and how supportive she will be of you if you are lucky enough to be included within her circle of friends.

Each of us can learn how to be the type of friend in which others delight by attending to the suggestions of women who have decades of successful friendship experience to share. Following are two sets of lessons friendship-savvy women have learned about keeping their friendships alive and vibrant throughout the years. First we offer a list of behaviors generally considered toxic to friendships followed by a list of behaviors and attitudes that, if practiced, promise to encourage the creation of a thriving and flourishing friendscape that best meets your expectations of growth and splendor.

BEHAVIORS TO ROOT OUT BEFORE THEY TAKE HOLD

1. Being dishonest or disloyal with friends. This includes breaking their confidences or your promises.
   It is important to have a meaningful relationship based on trust. I enjoy people who are "real" (authentic). A relationship cannot evolve into the deeper, more meaningful love found in friendship unless both parties are accepting of one another and who they are.
   Don't blow off a friend just because "something better" came along.
   Avoid disclosing secrets . . . trust is a must in friendship.
2. Telling friends what to do or providing *unsolicited* advice.
   Sometimes you may think your friend is looking for your opinion or critique, but they may just need somebody to talk to.
   It's okay to listen and not comment. You can never take back words, so be careful how you use them.
   Don't tell me what I need to make my life better! Instead, offer me encouragement with my struggles.
3. Focusing only on yourself and your needs. This includes making unreasonable demands and taking things personally.
   Avoid being clingy or insecure. Incessant calling and continuing to talk when a friend has made it clear she has to go are not acceptable

behaviors. Avoid being wrapped up in yourself—the "It's all about me!" attitude must go if a friendship is to survive.

Always give your friends some space. A good friend understands that friends have a life outside of them. Don't force yourself on other people.

4. Meddling in their family business. This includes criticizing their partners or telling friends how to raise their kids.

Do not criticize your friends' partners—even if they are going through a tough time or separation with that person. Don't say things that would come back to haunt you if the couple were to make up and stay together.

Never tell a friend what you would do with her kids if they were yours. Just don't.

5. Gossiping—anywhere or anytime.

Avoid speaking it, listening to it, or even allowing others to engage in it in your presence.

6. Loaning or borrowing money among friends.

Give money to friends only if you are able to consider it a gift— with no strings or expectations attached. Better yet, never bring money into a friendship.

Letting these behaviors take hold in a relationship can be an easy way to see a healthy relationship wither and fade away. The following suggestions and caveats allow you to cultivate deep and enduring friendships.

LAYING A HEALTHY FOUNDATION

1. Love and honor yourself. Meet the needs of your friends, but do not make choices that compromise your own well-being.

Friends need boundaries in their relationships and should avoid overstepping those boundaries so that each person's personal space is sacred and protected.

2. Always offer the following golden quintet: Honesty. Openness. Confidentiality. Unconditional Positive Regard. Nonjudgmental Spirit.

As much as I love all of my friends, I am slowly learning that they are like everyone else and they are going to make decisions that I won't always agree with. That isn't quite a big deal in itself; it's just a fact that I have to not take things so personally. I care about them so much and sometimes I can be the "mother hen," so I need to learn that just because they make a choice that I don't think is right for them or something, I can't let their decision affect me if it's not hurting them.

3. Expect to reap from a friendship only what you have invested. Friendships require commitment and nurture from both sides and will not flourish without shared tending. Yet be sure to give without an expectation of what you want to receive in return.

   If friends are worth it, there isn't anything too great or too small you can do for them. I've had my share of friends that walk all over me and take advantage of my willingness to drop anything in my life for them when they have needed me. These types of friends make you appreciate the ones that not only do you want to be there for, but that you know wholeheartedly that they will be there for you when you need them.

4. Be there for friends when they face difficult times. Recognize that even if your presence and a warm hug are all that you can offer, these gestures speak volumes to a friend in need.

   I was pretty young when I lost my parents and each loss was like a crushing blow to my heart. Some of my childhood friends who'd known my family really well seemed to not know what to say or do to offer comfort. I'll never forget how much it meant to me when an old friend stopped by and said, "I can't imagine how much this loss hurts you, I don't have a clue what to say to help you feel better, but I am here to let you know how much I care for you and want to be there for you." That really said it all.

5. Laugh with your friends at least as much as you cry with your friends. It's important that you look to friends to share your joy, not just comfort you when you're down. Laughter heals the wounds we suffer in this world. Let your friends be a part of the healing.

   Life has thrown me a few curve balls over the years and having friends who are there to share my sorrow has been a gift. But the friends who also help me find the humor in life and who can share in my own joys are the very best friends I have.

6. Don't neglect a friendship that you believe is worth keeping.

   Make the friendship a priority. If it's not valued as a priority, it will die and it is hard to revive the friendships we lose through our own lack of nurturing.

   In the same way that most plants need water to stay alive, friendships need attention in some form. This can be a call, an email, or a note with a picture tucked inside, an invitation to a special event, a trip to an interesting destination, or even a trip to the mall for lunch. Anything that allows you to express interest concerning what's going on in a friend's life and share what is going on in yours will work.

7. Communicate. Communicate. Communicate.

   It is so important to keep in contact with those that mean the most to you; you must stay in touch. And if a lot of time has passed, reconnecting is often very rewarding and, in many instances, can pick up right where you left off. Shared experiences from the past are the stepping off point for reflection and current communications allows observations on where we have arrived in our life's journey. Friends can be the source of great mirroring and collective memory for us. Communicate!

8. Accept that friends and relationships shift over the years. If they're worth keeping, gently shift in response.

   Even though we may grow into different people, we can still respect the foundation of trust that has been built. Learning to appreciate our differences is an important aspect of keeping a friendship alive.

The metaphor of a garden of friends, regularly weeded and carefully tended, hopefully evokes an image of vibrant and fertile growth. Each image will be unique for each reader—some of us may imagine a friendscape that brings to mind formal gardens and careful plantings. Others may prefer a Zen-influenced landscape in which each friend is a carefully selected element chosen for what she brings as a unique part of the whole. Some women have imagined redwood forests composed of friends who offer shelter, stability, and an enduring presence. Whether you prefer a small garden of bright and cheerful friends or a place where wild and tangled vines grow amid the years of your life, you have the power to create the friendscape that would be most satisfying. As we have shared, there are many ways to find new friends, plant new friendships, and maintain these relationships. Each of these steps may take effort and patience, as the women we interviewed openly attested. And as we journey through life, our needs and desires for friends will shift. Just as we toil in the garden, growing a friendship takes time and energy, too. And as more than one woman reminded us, if you find one true friend, you have found a treasure for life.

Notes

INTRODUCTION

1. Sias, P. M., and Bartoo, H. (2009). Friendship, Social Support and Health. In L. L'Abate, D. D. Embrey, and M. S. Baggett (Eds.), *Handbook of low-cost interventions to promote physical and mental health: Theory, research, and practice* (455–472). Mahwah, NJ: Lawrence Erlbaum Publishers.

2. Rutter, M., and Garmezy, N. (1983). Developmental psychopathology. In P. H. Mussen (Series Ed.) and E. M. Hetherington (Vol. Ed.), *Handbook of child psychology, Vol. 4: Socialization, personality, and social development* (775–911). New York: Wiley.

3. Fehr, B. (1996). *Friendship Processes.* London: Sage.

4. Hays, R. B. (1998). Friendship. In S. Duck (Ed.), *Handbook of personal relationships: Theory, research, and interventions* (391–408). New York: Wiley.

5. Altman, I., and Taylor, D. A. (1973). *Social penetration: The development of interpersonal relationships.* New York: Holt, Rinehart and Winston.

6. Kelley, H. H., and Thibaut, J. W. (1978). *Interpersonal relationships.* New York: John Wiley and Sons.

CHAPTER 1

1. Gilligan, C. (1982). *In a different voice.* Cambridge, MA: Harvard University Press.

2. Eliot, L. (1999). *What's going on in there? How the brain and mind develop in the first five years of life.* New York: Bantam Books.

3. Insel, T. R., and Fernald, R. D. (2004). *Annual Review of Neuroscience, 27,* 697–722.

4. Goodson, J. L., and Bass, A. H. (2000). Forebrain peptides modulate sexually polymorphic vocal circuitry. *Nature, 6771,* 769–772.

5. Hiller, J. (2004). Speculations on the links between feelings, emotions and sexual behavior: Are vasopressin and oxytocin involved? *Sexual and Relationship Therapy, 19,* 393–412.

6. Heinrichs, M., and Domes, G. (2008). Neuropeptides and social behavior: Effects of oxytocin and vasopressin in humans. *Progress in Brain Research, 170,* 337–350.

7. Nissen, E., Gustavsson, P., Wildstom, A. M., and Uvnars-Moberg, K. (1998). Oxytocin, prolactin and cortisol levels in response to nursing in women after Sectio Caesarea and vaginal delivery—Relationship with changes in personality patterns post partum. *Journal of Psychosomatic Obstetrics and Gynaecology, 19,* 49–58.

8. Rimmele, U., Hediger, K., Heinrichs, M., and Klaver, P. (2008). Oxytocin makes a face in memory familiar. *The Journal of Neuroscience, 29*(1), 38–42.

9. Heinrichs and Domes (2008).

10. Eliot (1999).

11. Hines, M. (2006). Prenatal testosterone and gender-related behavior. *European Journal of Endocrinology, 155 Supplement,* S115–S121.

12. Hall, J. A. (1984). *Nonverbal sex-differences: Communication accuracy and expressive style.* Baltimore, MD: The Johns Hopkins University Press.

13. Rosenthal, R., Hall, J. A., DiMatteo, M. R., Rogers, P. L., Archer, D. (1979). *Sensitivity to nonverbal communication: The PONS Test.* Baltimore, MD: The Johns Hopkins University Press.

14. Sanchez-Andrade, G., and Kendrick, K. M. (2009). The main olfactory system and social learning in mammals. *Behavioural Brain Research, 200,* 323–335.

15. Eliot (1999).

16. Thuerauf, N., Reulbach, U., Lunkenheimer, J., Lunkenheimer, B., Spannenberger, R., Gossler, A., Malhofner, C., Bleich, S., Kornhuber, J., and Markovic, K. (2009). Emotional reactivity to odors: Olfactory sensitivity and the span of emotional evaluation separate the genders. *Neuroscience Letters, 456*(2), 74–79.

17. Eliot (1999).

18. Geary, D. C. (1998). Chapter 2: Sexual selection and sex differences in social cognition. In McGillicuddy-De Lisis, A., De Lisi, R. (Eds.), *Biology, Society, and Behavior: The Development of Sex Differences in Cognition* (23–53). Westport, CT: Ablex Publishing.

19. Malatesta, C. Z., and Haviland, J. M. (1982). Learning display rules: The socialization of emotion expression in infancy. *Child Development, 53,* 991–1003.

20. Leeb, R. T., and Rejskind, F. G. (2004). Here's looking at you, kid! A longitudinal study of perceived gender differences in mutual gaze behavior in young infants. *Sex Roles, 1/2,* 1–14.

21. Swaab, R. I., and Swaab, D. F. (2009). Sex differences in the effects of visual contact and eye contact in negotiations. *Journal of Experimental Social Psychology, 45,* 129–136.

22. Kimura, D. (2000). *Sex and cognition.* Cambridge, MA: A Bradford Book/The MIT Press.

23. Berninger, V. W., Nielsen, K. H., Abbott, R. D., Wijsman, E., and Raskind, W. (2008). Gender differences in severity of writing and reading disabilities. *Journal of School Psychology, 46*, 151–172.

24. Kimura (2000).

25. Phillips, M., Lowe, M., Lurito, J. T., Dzemidzic, M., and Matthews, V. (2001). Temporal lobe activation demonstrates sex-based differences during passive listening. *Radiology, 220*, 202–207.

26. Eliot (2001).

27. Rueckert, L., and Naybar, N. (2008). Gender differences in empathy: The role of the right hemisphere. *Brain and Cognition, 67*, 162–167.

28. Mestre, M. V., Samper, P., Frias, M. D., and Tur, A. M. Are women more empathetic than men? A longitudinal study in adolescence. *Spanish Journal of Psychology, 1*(12), 76–83.

29. Canli, T., Desmond, J. E., Zhao, Z., and Gabrieli, J. D. (2002). Sex differences in the neural basis of emotional memories. *Proceedings of the National Academy of Sciences of the United States of America, 99*, 10789–10794.

30. Killgore, S., Oki, M., and Yurgelun-Todd, D. (2001). Sex-specific developmental changes in amygdala responses to affective faces. *NeuroReport, 12*, 427–433.

31. Van Honk, J., Aarts, H., Josephs, R. A., and Schutter, J. L. G. (2009). Sex differences in social and mathematical cognition: An endocrine perspective. *Netherlands Journal of Psychology, 64*, 177–183.

32. Crombie, G., and Desjardins, M. J. (1993, March). *Predictors of gender: The relative importance of children's play, games and personality characteristics.* Paper presented at the biennial meeting of the Society for Research in Child Development, New Orleans.

33. Josephs, R. A., Markus, H. R., and Tafarodi, R. W. (1992). Gender and self-esteem. *Journal of Personality and Social Psychology, 663*, 391–402.

34. Josephs et al. (1992).

35. Van Honk et al. (2009).

36. Taylor, S. E., Klein, L. C., Lewis, B. P., Gruenewald, T. L., Gurung, R. A., and Updegraff, J. A. (2000). Behavioral responses to stress in females: Tend-and-befriend, not fight-or-flight. *Psychological Review, 107*, 411–429.

37. Grewen, K. M., Girdler, S. S., Amico, J., and Light, K. C. (2005). Effects of partner support on resting oxytocin, cortisol, norepinephrine, and blood pressure before and after warm partner contact. *Psychosomatic Medicine, 67*, 531–538.

CHAPTER 2

1. Hearn, F. (2007). *Moral order and social disorder: The American search for civil society.* New York: Walter de Gruyter, Inc.

2. Putnam, R. (2000). *Bowling alone: The collapse and revival of American community.* New York: Simon and Schuster.

3. United States Department of Labor. (2009). *Women in the labor force: A databook* (BLS, Report No. 1018).

4. Edwards, T. (2007). Renters four times more likely to move than homeowners (U.S. Census Bureau News No. CB07–146). Washington, DC.

5. Langer, G. (2005, February 13). Poll: Traffic in the United States: A Look Under the Hood of a Nation on Wheels. [Electronic Version]. ABC News Poll, Retrieved March 17, 2010, from http://abcnews.go.com/Technology/Traffic/story?id=485098andpage=1

6. Braun, M., Lewin-Epstein, N., Stier, H., and Baumgartner, M. (2008). Perceived equity in the gendered division of household labor. *Journal of Marriage and Family, 70,* 1145–1156.

7. Langer, G. (2005).

8. Vanderkam, L. (2009, May 29). Overestimating our overworking. *The Wall Street Journal,* p. W13.

9. Putnam, R. (2000).

10. Putnam, R. (2000).

11. Hu, F. B., Li, T. Y., Colditz, G. A. Willett, W. C., and Manson, J. E. (2003). Television watching and other sedentary behaviors in relation to risk of obesity and type 2 diabetes mellitus in women. *Journal of the American Medical Association, 289,* 1785–1791.

12. Hancox, R., Milne, B., and Poulton, R. (2004). Association between child and adolescent television viewing and adult health: A longitudinal birth cohort study. *The Lancet, 364,* 257–262.

13. Campbell, A. (2004). Female competition: Causes, constraints, content, and context. *The Journal of Sex Research, 41,* 16–26.

14. Campbell, A. (2004).

15. Hayek, T. S. (2006, December 18). Buoyed by bigger breasts. *USA Today.* Retrieved March 11, 2010, from http://www.usatoday.com

16. Saremi, J. (2007). The truth about implants and breast cancer. *American Fitness, 25,* 46–49.

17. Campbell, A. (2004).

18. Resnick, S. and Wolff, R. (2003). Exploitation, consumption, and the uniqueness of U.S. capitalism. *Historical Materialism, 11,* 209–226.

19. Putnam, R. (2000).

20. Lorenzi, P. (2008). Affluence, consumption, and the American lifestyle. *Society, 45,* 107–111.

21. Lorenzi, P. (2008).

22. Resnick, S. and Wolff, R. (2003).

23. Putnam, R. (2000).

24. Putnam, R. (2000).

CHAPTER 3

1. Fehr, B. (1996). *Friendship processes.* London: Sage.

2. Bleiszner, R., and Adams, R. G. (1992). *Adult friendship.* Newbury Park, CA: Sage.

3. Sias, P. M., and Cahill, D. J. (1998). From coworkers to friends: The development of peer friendships in the workplace. *Western Journal of Communication, 62,* 273–299.

4. Byrne, D. (1971). *The attraction paradigm.* New York: Academic Press.

5. Aboud, F. E., and Mendelson, M. J. (1996). Determinants of friendship selection and quality: Developmental perspectives. In W. M. Bukowski, A. F. Newcomb, and W. W. Hartup (Eds.), *The company they keep: Friendship in childhood and adolescence* (87–112). Cambridge: Cambridge University Press.

6. Benoit, M. (2003). The warm glow heuristic: When liking leads to familiarity. *Journal of Personality and Social Psychology, 85,* 1035–1048.

7. Cash, T. F., and Derlega, V. J. (1978). The matching hypothesis: Physical attractiveness among same-sexed friends. *Personality and Social Psychology Bulletin, 4,* 240–243.

8. Benoit, M. (2003).

9. Archer, R. L., and Berg, J. H. (1978). Disclosure reciprocity and its limits: A reactance analysis. *Journal of Experimental Social Psychology, 14,* 527–540.

10. Archer, R. L., and Burleson, J. A. (1980). The effects of timing of self-disclosure on attraction and reciprocity. *Journal of Personality and Social Psychology, 38,* 120–130.

11. Collins, N. L., and Miller, L. C. (1994). Self-disclosure and liking: A meta-analytic review. *Psychological Bulletin, 116,* 457–475.

12. Aron, A. P., Melinat, E., Aron, E. N., Vallone, R. D., and Bator, R. J. (1997). The experimental generation of interpersonal closeness: A procedure and some preliminary findings. *Personality and Social Psychology Bulletin, 23,* 363–377.

13. Vittengl, J. R., and Holt, C. S. (2000). Getting acquainted: The relationship of self-disclosure and social attraction to positive affect. *Journal of Social and Personal Relationships, 17,* 53–66.

14. Altman, I., and Taylor, D. A. (1973). *Social penetration: The development of interpersonal relationships.* New York: Holt, Rinehart and Winston.

15. Collins and Miller (1994).

16. Rodin, M. J. (1978). Liking and disliking. *Personality and Social Psychology Bulletin, 4,* 473–478.

17. Byrne, D. (1971). *The attraction paradigm.* New York: Academic Press.

18. Werner, C., and Parmelee, P. (1979). Similarity of activity preferences among friends: Those who play together stay together. *Social Psychology Quarterly, 42,* 62–66.

19. Fehr, B. (2008). Friendship formation. In S. Sprecher, A. Wenzel, and J. Harvey (Eds.), *The handbook of relationship initiation* (29–54). Hillsdale, N.J.: Erlbaum.

20. Fehr (2008).

21. Byrne (1971).

22. Pinel, E. C., Long, A. E., Landau, M. J., Alexander, K., and Pyszczynksi, T. (2006). Seeing I to I: A pathway to interpersonal connectedness. *Journal of Personality and Social Psychology, 90,* 243–257.

23. Rushton, J. P., and Bons, T. A. (2005). Mate choice and friendship in twins: Evidence for genetic similarity. *Psychological Science, 16,* 555–559.

24. Roberto, K. A. (2001). Older women's relationships: Weaving lives together. In J. D. Garner and S. O. Mercer (Eds.), *Women as they age* (2nd ed., 115–129). New York: Haworth.

25. Hall, R., and Rose, S. (1996). Friendships between African-American and White lesbians. In J. S. Weinstock and E. D. Rothblum (Eds.), *Lesbian friendships: For ourselves and each other* (165–191). New York: New York University Press.

26. Roberto, (2001).

27. Rawlins, W. K. (1992). *Friendship matters.* New York: Aldine de Gruyter.

28. Youniss, J. (1980). *Parents and peers in social development.* Chicago: The University of Chicago Press.

29. Hartup, W. W., and Stevens, N. (1997). Friendships and adaptation in the life course. *Psychological Bulletin, 121,* 355–370.

30. Clark, M. S., and Mills, J. (1993). The difference between communal and exchange relationships: What it is and is not. *Personality and Social Psychology Bulletin, 19,* 684–691.

31. Raymond, N. (1999, November). Hug drug: Friendship heals. *Psychology Today,* p. 1.

32. Festinger, L., Schachter, S., and Back, K. (1950). *Social Pressure in Informal Groups.* New York: Harper.

33. Newcomb, T. (1961). *The acquaintance process.* New York: Holt, Rinehart and Winston.

34. Moreland, R. L., and Beach, S. (1992). Exposure effects in the classroom: The development of affinity among students. *Journal of Experimental Social Psychology, 28,* 255–276.

35. Burger, J. M., and Soroka, S. (2001). The effect of fleeting attraction on compliance to requests. *Personality and Social Psychology Bulletin, 27,* 1578–1586.

36. Sias, P. M., and Cahill, D. J. (1998). From coworkers to friends: The development of peer friendships in the workplace. *Western Journal of Communication, 62,* 273–300.

37. Sias and Cahill (1998).

38. Sias, P. M., Krone, K. J., and Jablin, F. M. (2001). An ecological systems perspective on workplace relationships. In M. L. Knapp and J. Daly (Eds.), *Handbook of interpersonal communication* (3rd ed., 615–642). Newbury Park, CA: Sage.

39. Sias, P. M., and Bartoo, H. (2009). Friendship, social support and health. In L. L'Abate, D. D. Embrey, and M. S. Baggett (Eds.). *Handbook of low-cost interventions to promote physical and mental health: Theory, research, and practice* (455–472). Mahwah, NJ: Lawrence Erlbaum Publishers.

40. Goodenow, C., and Gaier, E. L. (1990). Best friends: The close reciprocal friendships of married and unmarried women. Unpublished paper.

41. Argyle, M., and Henderson, M. (1984). The rules of friendships. *Journal of Social and Personal Relationships, 1,* 211–237.

42. Argyle and Henderson, as cited in Samter, W., and Cupach, W. R. (1998). Friendly fire: Topical variations in conflict among same- and cross-sex friends. *Communication Studies, 49,* 121–138.

43. Allen, J., and Haccoun, D. (1976). Sex differences in emotionality: A multidimensional approach. *Human Relations, 29,* 711–722.

44. Davidson, J., and Duberman, L. (1982). Same-sex friendships: A gender comparison of dyads. *Sex Roles, 8,* 809–822.

45. Rubin, L. (1983). *Intimate strangers.* San Francisco: Harper and Rowe.

46. Agrawal, A., Jacobson, K. C., Prescott, C. A., and Kendler, K. S. (2002). A twin study of sex differences in social support. *Psychological Medicine, 32,* 1155–1164.

47. Baron-Cohen, S., and Wheelwright, S. (2004). The empathy quotient: An investigation of adults with Asperger syndrome or high functioning autism, and normal sex differences. *Journal of Autism and Developmental Disorders, 34,* 163–175.

48. Barbee. A. P., Cunningham, M. R., Winstead, B. A., Derlega, V. J., Gulley, M. R., Yankeelov, P. A., Druen, P. B. (1993). Effects of gender role expectations in the social support process. *Journal of Social Issues, 49,* 175–190.

49. Eisler, R. M. (1995). The relationship between masculine gender role stress and men's health risk. In R. F. Levant and W. S. Pollack (Eds.), *A new psychology of men* (207–225). New York: Basic Books.

50. Vigil, J. M. (2007). Asymmetries in the friendship preferences and social styles of men and women. *Human Nature, 18,* 143–161.

51. Burda, P. C., Jr., Vaux, A., and Schill, T. (1984). Social support resources: Variation across sex and sex role. *Personality and Social Psychology Bulletin, 10,* 119–126.

52. Barth, R. J., and Kinder, B. N. (1988). A theoretical analysis of sex differences in same-sex friendships. *Sex Roles, 19,* 349–363.

53. Block, J. D. (1980). *Friendship: How to give it, how to get it.* New York: Collier Books.

54. Greif, G. (2009). *Buddy system: Understanding male friendships.* New York: Oxford University Press.

55. McGill, M. E. (1985). *The McGill report on male intimacy.* New York: Holt, Rinehart and Winston.

56. Miller, S. (1983). *Men and friendship.* Boston: Houghton Mifflin Company.

57. Carbery, J., and Buhrmester, D. (1998). The changing significance of friendship across three phases of young adulthood. *Journal of Social and Personal Relationships, 15,* 393–409.

CHAPTER 4

1. Niffenegger, J., and Willer, L. (1998). Friendship behaviors during early childhood and beyond. *Early Childhood Education Journal, 26,* 95–99.

2. Lindsey, E. W. (2002). Preschool children's friendships and peer acceptance: Links to social competence. *Child Study Journal, 32,* 145–155.

3. Da Silva, E., and Winnykamen, F. (1998). Degree of sociability and interactive behaviors in dyadic situations of problem solving. *European Journal of Psychology of Education, 13,* 253–270.

4. Thompson, M., O'Neill Grace, C., and Cohen, L. (2001). *Best friends, worst enemies, understanding the social lives of children.* New York: Ballantine Books, Inc.

5. Snyder, J., West, L., Stockemer, V., Gibbons, S., and Almquist-Parks, L. (1996). A social learning model of peer choice in the natural environment. *Journal of Applied Developmental Psychology, 17,* 215–237.

6. Barbara Long (personal communication, September 22, 2009).

7. Newcomb and Bagwell study, as cited in Hartup, W., and Stevens, N. (1997). Friendship and adaptation in the life course. *Psychological Bulletin, 121,* 355–370.

8. Hartup, W. W., and Stevens, N. (1997). Friendships and adaptation in the life course. *Psychological Bulletin, 121,* 355–370.

9. Hallman study (as cited in Hartup and Stevens, 1997).

10. Castelli, L., Amicis, L., and Sherman, S. (2007). The loyal member effect: On the preference for ingroup members who engage in exclusive relations with the ingroup. *Developmental Psychology, 43,* 1347–1359.

11. Hartup, W., and van Lieshout, C. (1995). Personality development in social context. *Annual Review of Psychology, 46,* 655–687.

12. Lindsey (2002).

13. Putallaz, M., and Gottman, J. M. (1981). An interactional model of children's entry into peer groups. *Child Development, 52,* 986–994.

14. Scharf, M., and Mayseless, O. (2009). Socioemotional characteristics of elementary school children identified as exhibiting social leadership qualities. *The Journal of Genetic Psychology, 170*(1), 73–94.

15. Scharf and Mayseless (2009).

16. Niffenegger, J., and Willer, L. (1998). Friendship behaviors during early childhood and beyond. *Early Childhood Education Journal, 26,* 95–99.

17. Dodge, K., Pettit, G., McClaskey, C., and Brown, M. (1986). Social competence in children. *Monographs of the Society for Research in Child Development, 51*(2, Serial No. 213).

18. Putallaz, M., and Gottman, J. M. (1981). An interactional model of children's entry into peer groups. *Child Development, 52,* 986–994.

19. Benenson, J., and Heath, A. (2006). Boys withdraw more in one-on-one interactions, whereas girls withdraw more in groups. *Developmental Psychology, 42,* 272–282.

20. Bowlby, J. (1988). *A secure base: Parent-child attachment and healthy human development.* New York: Basic Books, Inc.

21. Scharf and Mayseless, (2009).

22. Sroufe, L. A. (1996). *Emotional development: The organinization of emotional life in the early years.* New York: Cambridge University Press.

23. Foot, H. C., Chapman, A., and Smith, J. (Eds.) (1995). *Friendship and social relations in children.* New Brunswick, NJ: Transaction Publishers, Inc.

24. Park, K. A., and Waters, E. (1989). Security of attachment and preschool friendships. *Child Development, 60,* 1076–1081.

25. Riggio, H. (1999). Personality and social skill differences between adults with and without siblings. *Journal of Psychology, 133,* 514–522.

26. Downey, D., and Condron, D. (2004). Playing well with others in kindergarten: The benefit of siblings at home. *Journal of Marriage and Family, 66,* 333–350.

27. Kernsmith, P. (2006). Gender differences in the impact of family of origin violence on perpetrators of domestic violence. *Journal of Family Violence, 21,* 163–171.

28. Louv, R. (2005). *Last child in the woods: Saving our children from nature-deficit disorder.* Chapel Hill, NC: Algonquin Books of Chapel Hill.

29. Hartup and Stevens (1997).

CHAPTER 5

1. Ge., X., Conger, R. D., and Elder, G. H. (1996). Coming of age too early: Pubertal influences on girls' vulnerability psychological distress. *Child Development, 67,* 3386–3400.

2. Smith, A. E., and Powers, S. I. (2009). Off-time pubertal timing predicts physiological reactivity to postpuberty interpersonal stress. *Journal of Research on Adolescence, 19,* 441–458.

3. Graber, J. A., Seely, J. R., Brooks-Gunn, J., and Lewinsohn, J. (2004). Is pubertal timing associated with psychopathology in young adulthood? *Journal of the American Academy of Child and Adolescent Psychiatry, 43,* 718–726.

4. South Carolina Department of Mental Health. (2006). "Eating disorder statistics." Retrieved January 22, 2010, from http://www.state.sc.us/dmh/anorexia/statistics.htm

5. Kinney, D. A. (1993). From nerds to normals: The recovery of identity among adolescents from middle school to high school. *Sociology of Education, 66,* 21–40.

6. Kinney (1993).

7. Kinney (1993).

8. Dijkstra, J., Verhulst, F., Ormel, J., and Veenstra, R. (2009). The relation between popularity and aggressive, destructive, and norm-breaking behaviors: Moderating effects of athletic abilities, physical attractiveness, and prosociality. *Journal of Research on Adolescence, 19,* 401–413.

9. Wiseman, R. (2009). *Queen bees and wannabes: Helping your daughter survive cliques, gossip, boyfriends, and the new realities of girl world* (2nd ed.). New York: Three Rivers Press.

10. Dijkstra et al. (2009).

11. Dijkstra et al. (2009).

12. Witkow, M. R. (2009). Academic achievement and adolescents' daily time use in the social and academic domains. *Journal of Research on Adolescence, 19,* 151–172.

13. Witkow (2009).

14. McElhaney, K., Antonishak, J., and Allen, J. (2008). "They like me, they like me not": Popularity and adolescents' perceptions of acceptance predicting social functioning over time. *Child Development, 79,* 720–731.

15. Bešić, N, and Kerr, M. (2009). Punks, goths, and other eye-catching peer crowds: Do they fulfill a function for shy youths? *Journal of Research on Adolescence, 19,* 113–121.

16. Kinney (1993).

17. Bešić and Kerr (2009).

18. McElhaney, Antonishak, and Allen (2008).

19. Botting and Conti-Ramsden (2008).

20. Kinney (1993).

21. Kinney (1993).

22. Kinney (1993), p. 34.

23. McElhaney, Antonishak, and Allen (2008).

24. McElhaney, Antonishak, and Allen (2008).

25. Kan, M. L., and McHale, S. M. (2007). Clusters and correlates of experiences with parents and peers during early adolescence. *Journal of Research on Adolescence, 17*, 565–586.

26. Mounts, N. (2007). Adolescents and their mothers' perceptions of parental management of peer relationships. *Journal of Research on Adolescence, 17*, 169–178.

27. Bohnert, A., Martin, N., and Garber, J. (2007). Predicting adolescents' organized activity involvement: The role of maternal depression history, family relationship quality and adolescent cognitions. *Journal of Research on Adolescence, 17*, 221–244.

28. Kan and McHale (2007).

29. Siyez, D. (2008). Adolescent self-esteem, problem behaviors, and perceived social support in Turkey. *Social Behavior and Personality: An International Journal, 36*, 973–985.

30. Falci, C., and McNeely, C. (2009). Social integration, network cohesion, and adolescent depressive symptoms. *Social Forces, 87*, 2031–2062.

CHAPTER 6

1. Oswald, D., and Clark, E. (2003). Best friends forever: High school best friendships and the transition to college. *Personal Relationships, 10*, 187–196.

2. Oswald and Clark (2003).

3. Oswald and Clark (2003).

4. Cutrona, C. (1982). Transition to college: Loneliness and the process of social adjustment. In L. A. Peplau and D. Perlman (Eds.), *Loneliness: A sourcebook of current theory, research, and therapy.* New York: Wiley-Interscience.

5. Arnett, J. J. (2000). Emerging adulthood. *American Psychologist, 55*, 469–480.

6. Bauer, C. (2005, December 12). The Daily Collegian Online. Retrieved from http://www.collegian.psu.edu/archive/2005/12/12–12–05CM/12–12-–05dnews-05.asp

7. United States Census Bureau. (2007, October). Renters four times more likely to move than homeowners. Retrieved May 26, 2010, from http://www.census.gov/newsroom/releases/archives/mobility_of_the_population/cb07–146.html

8. Marcia, J. E. (1976). Identity six years after: A follow-up study. *Journal of Youth and Adolescence, 5*, 145–160.

9. Waterman, A. (1982). Identity development from adolescence to adulthood: An extension of theory and a review of research. *Developmental Psychology, 18*, 341–358.

10. Erikson, E. (1980). *Identity and the life cycle.* New York: Norton.

11. Gilligan, C. (1983). *In a different voice.* Boston: Harvard University Press.

12. Johnson, D., Brady, E., McNair, R., Congdon, D., Niznik, J., and Anderson, S. (2007). Identity as moderator of gender differences in the emotional closeness of emerging adult's same and cross-sex friendships. *Adolescence, 42*, 1–23.

13. Johnson et. al. (2007).

14. Demir, M. (2009). Close relationships and happiness among emerging adults. *Journal of Happiness Studies, 11*, 293–313.

15. Gainey, C. B., Kennedy, A., McCabe, B., and Degges-White, S. (2009). Life satisfaction, self-esteem, and subjective age in women across the lifespan. *Adultspan, 8*, 29–42.

16. Arnett (2000).

17. Kadison, R., and Digeronimo, T. (2004). *College of the overwhelmed: The campus mental health crisis and what to do about it.* San Francisco: Jossey-Bass.

18. Rhoades, B., and Maggs, J. (2006). Do academic and social goals predict planned alcohol use among college-bound high school graduates? *Journal of Youth and Adolescence, 35*, 913–923.

19. Ravert, R. D. (2009). "You're only young once": Things college students report doing now before it is too late. *Journal of Adolescent Research, 24*, 376–396.

20. Wechsler, H., and Kuo, M. (2000). College students define binge drinking and estimate its prevalence: Results of a national survey. *College Health, 49*, 57–64.

21. Arnett (2000).

CHAPTER 7

1. Sheehy, S. (2000). *Connecting: The enduring power of female friendships.* New York: William Morrow.

2. Fischer, C. S., and Oliker, S. (1980, August). *Friendship, gender, and the lifecycle.* Paper presented at the American Sociological Association. New York.

3. Bryan, L., Fitzpatrick, J., Crawford, D., and Fischer, J. (2001). The role of network support and interference in women's perception of romantic, friend, and parental relationships. *Sex Roles, 45*, 481–499.

4. Doxey, C., and Holman, T. B. (2002). Social contexts influencing marital quality. In T. B. Holman (Ed.), *Premarital prediction of marital quality or breakup: Research, theory, and practice* (119–139). New York: Kluwer Academic/Plenum Publishers.

5. Huston, T., and Burgess, R. (1979). Social exchange in developing relationships: An overview. In R. Burgess and T. Huston (Eds.), *Social exchange in developing relationships* (3–28). New York: Academic Press.

6. Carbery, J., and Buhrmester, D. (1988). Friendships and need fulfillment during three phases of young adulthood. *Journal of Social and Personal Relationships, 15*, 393–409.

7. Milardo, R. M., and Allan, G. (1997). Social networks and marital relationships. In S. Duck (Ed.), *Handbook of personal relationships: Theory, research, and interventions* (2nd ed., 505–522). Chichester, England: Wiley.

8. Laursen, B., and Collins, W. A. (1994). Interpersonal conflict during adolescence. *Psychological Bulletin, 115*, 197–209.

9. Barbee, A., Gulley, M., and Cunningham, M. (1990). Support seeking in personal relationships. *Journal of Social and Personal Relationships, 7*, 531–540.

10. Fischer, C. S. (1982). *To dwell among friends: Personal networks in town and city.* Chicago: University of Chicago Press.

11. Rose, S. (1984). How friendships end: Patterns among young adults. *Journal of Social and Personal Relationships, 3*, 267–277.

12. Gullestad, M. (1984). *Kitchen table society.* Oslo: Universities Forlaget.

13. Rose, S. M. (2007). Enjoying the returns: Women's friendships after 50. In V. Muhlbauer and J. Chrisler (Eds.), *Women over 50: Psychological perspectives* (112–130). New York: Springer.

14. Burditt, K. S., and Antonucci, T. C. (2007). Relationship quality profiles and well-being among married adults. *Journal of Family Psychology, 21,* 595–604.

CHAPTER 8

1. O'Hara, M., and Swain, A. (1996). Rates and risk of postpartum depression—A meta-analysis. *International Review of Psychiatry, 8,* 37–55.

2. The MommiesNetwork.org. (2009). Retrieved April 21, 2010, from http://www.themommiesnetwork.org/index.shtml

3. Buzzanell, P., Meisenbach, R., Remke, R., Liu, M., Bowers, V., and Conn, C. (2005). The good working mother: Managerial women's sensemaking and feelings about work-family issues. *Communication Studies, 56,* 261–285.

4. Austin, H., and Carpenter, L. (2008). Troubled, troublesome, troubling mothers: The dilemma of difference in women's personal motherhood narratives. *Narrative Inquiry, 18,* 378–392.

5. Cowan, G., and Ullman, J. (2006). Ingroup rejection among women: The role of personal inadequacy. *Psychology of Women Quarterly, 30,* 399–409.

6. Gainey, C. B., Kennedy, A., McCabe, B., and Degges-White, S. (2009). Life satisfaction, self-esteem, and subjective age in women across the lifespan. *Adultspan, 8,* 29–42.

CHAPTER 9

1. Neugarten, B. L., Moore, J. W., and Lowe, J. C. (1965). Age norms, age constraints, and adult socialization. *American Journal of Sociology, 70,* 229–236.

2. Shulman, N. (1975). Life cycle variations in patterns of friendship. *Journal of Marriage and the Family, 37,* 813–821.

3. Degges-White, S., and Myers, J. E. (2006). Transitions, wellness, and life satisfaction: Implications for counseling midlife women. *Journal of Mental Health Counseling, 28*(2), 133–150.

4. Rose, S. M. (2007). Enjoying the returns: Women's friendships after 50. In V. Muhlbauer and J. Chrisler (Eds.), *Women over 50: Psychological perspectives* (112–130). New York: Springer.

5. Carstensen, L. L. (1995). Evidence for a life-span theory of socioemotional selectivity. *Current Directions in Psychological Science, 4*(5), 151–156.

6. Rawlins, W. K. (1992). *Friendship matters: Communication, dialects, and the life course.* Hawthorne, NY: Aldine de Gruyter.

7. Rawlins (1994), as cited in Canary, D. J., and Dainton, M. (Eds.). (2003). *Maintaining relationships through communication: Relational, contextual, and cultural variations.* Hillsdale, NJ: Erlbaum.

8. Tesch, S. A. (1983). Review of friendship development across the lifespan. *Human Development, 26,* 266–276.

9. Hartup, W. W., and Stevens, N. (1997). Friendships and adaptation in the life course. *Psychological Bulletin, 121,* 355–370.

10. Argyle, M., and Furnham, A. (1983). Sources of satisfaction and conflict in long-term relationships. *Journal of Marriage and Family, 45,* 481–493.

11. Howell, L. C. (2001). Implications of personal values in women's midlife development. *Counseling and Values, 46,* 54–65.

12. Newcomb, T. (1961). *The acquaintance process.* New York: Holt, Rinehart and Winston.

13. Sias, P. M., and Cahill, D. J. (1998). From coworkers to friends: The development of peer friendships in the workplace. *Western Journal of Communication, 62,* 273–300.

14. Sias, P. M., Krone, K. J., and Jablin, F. M. (2001). An ecological systems perspective on workplace relationships. In M. L. Knapp and J. Daly (Eds.), *Handbook of interpersonal communication* (3rd ed., 615–642). Newbury Park, CA: Sage.

15. Degges-White and Myers (2006).

16. Vaillant, G. E. (1977). *Adaptation to life.* Boston: Little, Brown.

17. Joseph, J. (2001). *Warning: When I am an old woman, I shall wear purple.* London: Souvenir Press Ltd.

18. Hartup, W. W., and Stevens, N. (1997). Friendships and adaptation in the life course. *Psychological Bulletin, 121,* 355–370.

19. Lefkowitz, E., and Fingerman, K. (2003). Positive and negative emotional feelings and behaviors in mother-daughter ties in late life. *Journal of Family Psychology, 17,* 607–617.

20. United States Bureau of the Census. (2008). Percent Never Married. *Statistical Abstract of the United States.* Washington, DC: U.S. Bureau of the Census.

21. Rose, S. M. (1985). Same and cross-sex friendships and the psychology of homosociality. *Sex Roles, 12,* 63–74. As cited in Canary and Dainton (2003), *Maintaining relationships through communication: Relational, contextual, and cultural variations.* Hillsdale, NJ: Erlbaum. Rose, S. M. (1985). Same and cross-sex friendships and the psychology of homosociality. *Sex Roles, 12,* 63–74.

22. U.S. Bureau of the Census (2008).

23. Canary and Dainton (Eds.). (2003).

CHAPTER 10

1. Chen, N. (2001). The meaning of aging. *Journal of Extension, 39.*

2. Aiken, L. R. (1998). *Human development in adulthood.* New York: Kluwer Academic/Plenum Publishers.

3. James, W. B., Witte, J. E., and Galbraith, M. W. (2006). Havighurst's social roles revisited. *Journal of Adult Development, 13,* 52–60.

4. Patterson, B. R., Bettini, L., and Nussbaum, J. F. (1993). The meaning of friendship across the lifespan: Two studies. *Communication Quarterly, 41,* 145–160.

5. Gurung, R. A. R., Taylor, S. E., and Seeman, T. E. (2003). Accounting for changes in social support among married older adults: Insights from the MacArthur Studies of Successful Aging. *Psychology and Aging, 18*, 487–496.

6. Arling, G. (1976). The elderly widow and her family, neighbors and friends. *Journal of Marriage and the Family, 38*, 757–768.

7. Matthews, S. (1986). *Friendships through the life course.* Beverly Hills, CA: Sage.

8. Rook, K. S. (1991). Facilitating friendship formation in late life: Puzzles and challenges. *American Journal of Community Psychology, 19*, 103–110.

9. Aiken (1998).

10. Antonucci, T. C., Lansford, J. E., and Akiyama, H. (2001). Impact of positive and negative aspects of marital relationships and friendships on well-being of older adults. *Applied Developmental Science, 5*, 68–75.

11. Carstensen, L. L., Isaacowitz, D. M., and Charles, S. T. (1999). Taking time seriously: A theory of socioemotional selectivity. *American Psychologist, 54*, 165–181.

12. Hess, B. (1971). *Amicability.* Unpublished doctoral dissertation. Rutgers University, New Brunswick, NJ.

13. Aiken (1998).

14. Adams, R. G., and Torr, R. (1998), as cited in Felmlee, D. H. (2003). Interaction in social networks. In J. Delamater (Ed.), *Handbook of social psychology* (389–409). New York: Kluwer Academic/Plenum Publishers.

15. Hartup, W. W., and Stevens, N. (1997). Friendships and adaptation in the life course. *Psychological Bulletin, 121*, 355–370.

16. Moremen, R. D. (2008). The role of confidantes in older women's health. *Journal of Women and Aging, 20*, 149–167.

17. Gurung, R. A. R., Taylor, S. E., and Seeman, T. E. (2003). Accounting for changes in social support among married older adults: Insights from the MacArthur Studies of Successful Aging. *Psychology and Aging, 18*, 487–496.

18. Stroebe, W., Stroebe, M., Abakoumkin, G., and Schut, H. (1996). The role of loneliness and social support in adjustment to loss: A test of attachment versus stress theory. *Journal of Personality and Social Psychology, 70*, 1241–1249.

19. Morgan, D., Carder, P., and Neal, M. (1992), as cited in Felmlee, D. H. (2003). Interaction in social networks. In J. Delamater (Ed.), *Handbook of social psychology* (389–409). New York: Kluwer Academic/Plenum Publishers.

20. Kitson, G. C., Lopata, H. Z., Holmes, W. M., and Meyering, S. M. (1980). Divorcees and widows: Similarities and differences. *American Journal of Orthopsychiatry, 50*, 291–301.

21. Roberto, K. A., and Scott, J. P. (1986). Friendships of older men and women: Exchange patterns and satisfaction. *Psychology and Aging, 1*, 103–109.

22. Roberto, K. A., and Scott, J. P. (1986). Friendships of older men and women: Exchange patterns and satisfaction. *Psychology and Aging, 1*, 103–109.

23. Jones, D. C., and Vaughan, K. (1990). Close friendships among senior adults. *Psychology and Aging, 5*, 451–457.

24. Ratcliff, K. S., and Bogdan, J. (1988). Unemployed women: When "social support" is not supportive. *Social Problems, 35*, 54–63.

25. Antonucci, T. C., Lansford, J. E., and Akiyama, H. (2001). Impact of positive and negative aspects of marital relationships and friendships on well-being of older adults. *Applied Developmental Science, 5,* 68–75.

26. Frank, J. S., Avery, S. M., and Laman, B. C. (1988), as cited in Aiken (1998).

27. Garstecki, D. C., and Erler, S. F. (1999). Older adult performance on the Communication Profile for the Hearing Impaired: Gender difference. *Journal of Speech, Language, and Hearing Research, 42,* 785–796.

28. Aikens (1998).

29. Oh, J. (2003). Assessing the social bonds of elderly neighbors: The roles of length of residence, crime victimization, and perceived disorder. *Sociological Inquiry, 73,* 490–510.

30. Aebischer, J. (2008). Loneliness among homebound older adults: Implications for home healthcare clinicians. *Home Healthcare Nurse, 26,* 521–522.

31. Steverink, N., Lindenberg, S., and Slaets, J. P. J. (2005). How to understand and improve older people's self-management of wellbeing. *European Journal of Ageing, 2,* 235–244.

32. Rook, K. S. (2009). Gaps in social support resources in later life: An adaptation challenge in need of further research. *Journal of Social and Personal Relationships, 26,* 103–112.

CHAPTER 11

1. Degges-White, S., and Borzumato-Gainey, C. (2009, March). Circle of friends: Helping women craft connections. Program presented at the American Counseling Association Conference, Charlotte, NC.

2. Anderson, N. H. (1968). Likableness ratings of 555 personality-trait words. *Journal of Personality and Social Psychology, 9,* 272–279, cited in Cottrell, C. A., Neuberg, S. L., and Li, N. P. (2007). What do people desire in others? A sociofunctional perspective on the importance of different valued characteristics. *Journal of Personality and Social Psychology, 92,* 208–231.

3. Cottrell et al. (2007).

4. Cottrell et al. (2007).

5. Cottrell et al. (2007).

6. Berndt, T. J. (1989). Exploring the effects of friendship quality on social development. In W. M. Bukowski, A. F. Newcomb, and W. W. Hartup (Eds.), *The company they keep: Friendships in childhood and adolescence* (346–365). New York: Cambridge University Press.

7. Degges-White and Borzumato-Gainey (2009).

8. Eliot (1999).

9. Jeffries, V. (1999). The integral paradigm: The truth of faith and the social sciences. *American Sociologist, 30*(4), 36–55.

10. Lyubomirsky, S., King, L., and Diener, E. (2005). The benefits of frequent positive affect: Does happiness lead to success? *Psychological Bulletin, 131,* 803–855.

11. Lyubomirsky et al. (2005).

12. Myers, D. G. (2000). The funds, friends, and faith of happy people. *American Psychologist, 55,* 56–67.

13. Gotlib, I. H. (1992). Interpersonal and cognitive aspects of depression. *Current Directions in Psychological Science, 1,* 149–154.

14. Segrin, C., and Dillard, J. P. (1992). The interactional theory of depression: A meta-analysis of the research literature. *Journal of Social and Clinical Psychology, 11,* 43–70.

15. Grotberg, E. H. (2000). International Resilience Research Project. In A. L. Comunian and U. Gielen (Eds.), *International Perspectives on Human Development* (379–399). Vienna: Pabst Science Publishers.

CHAPTER 12

1. Gazelle, H., and Druhen, M. J. (2009). Anxious solitude and peer exclusion predict social helplessness, upset affect, and vagal regulation in response to behavioral rejection by a friend. *Developmental Psychology, 45,* 1077–1096.

2. Willis, J., and Todorov, A. (2006). First impressions: Making up your mind after a 100-ms exposure to a face. *Psychological Science, 17,* 592–598.

CHAPTER 13

1. Kahn, R. L., and Antonucci, T. C. (1980). Convoys over the life course: Attachment, roles, and social support. In P. B. Baltes and O. G. Brim, Jr. (Eds.), *Life span development and behavior,* Vol. 3 (253–286). New York: Academic Press.

2. Moren-Cross, J. L., and Lin, N. (2006). Social networks and health. In R. H. Binstock and L. K. George (Eds.), *Handbook of aging and the social sciences* (6th ed., 111–126). Amsterdam: Elsevier.

CHAPTER 17

1. Dindia, K., and Canary, D. J. (1993). Definitions and theoretical perspectives on meaning in relationships. *Journal of Social and Personal Relationships, 10,* 163–173.

2. Canary, D. J., and Dainton, M. (Eds.) (2003). *Maintaining relationships through communication: Relational, contextual, and cultural variations.* Mahwah, NJ: Lawrence Erlbaum Associates.

3. Canary, D. J., Stafford, L., Hause, K. S., and Wallace, L. A. (1993). An inductive analysis of relational maintenance strategies: Comparisons among lovers, relatives, friends, and others. *Communication Research Reports, 1746–4099, 10,* 3–14.

4. Fehr, B. (2000). The life cycle of friendship. In C. Hendrick and S. S. Hendrick (Eds.), *Close relationships: A sourcebook* (71–82). Thousand Oaks, CA: Sage.

5. Johnson, A. J. (2000, July). A role theory approach to examining the maintenance of geographically close and long-distance friendships. Paper presented at the International Network on Personal Relationships Conference, Prescott, AZ.

6. Messman, S. J., Canary, D. J., and Hause, K. S. (2000). Motives to remain platonic, equity, and the use of maintenance strategies in opposite-sex friendships. *Journal of Social and Personal Relationships, 17,* 67–94.

7. Rawlins, W. K. (1994). Being there and growing apart: Sustaining friendships during adulthood. In D. J. Canary and L. Stafford (Eds.), *Communication and relational maintenance* (275–294). San Diego: Academic Press.

8. Barbee, A. P., Gulley, M. R., and Cunningham, M. R. (1990). Support seeking in close relationships. *Journal of Social and Personal Relationships, 7,* 531–540.

9. Burleson, B. R., and Samter, W. (1994). A social skills approach to relationship maintenance: How individual differences in communication skills affect the achievement of relationship functions. In D. J. Canary and L. S. Stafford (Eds.), *Communication and relational maintenance* (62–90). San Diego, CA: Academic Press.

10. Canary et al. (1993).

11. Fehr (2000).

12. Hays, R. B. (1984). The development and maintenance of friendship. *Journal of Social and Personal Relationships, 1,* 75–98.

13. Messman et al. (2000).

14. Nardi, P. M., and Sherrod, D. (1994). Friendships in the lives of gay men and lesbians. *Journal of Social and Personal Relationships, 11,* 185–200.

CHAPTER 18

1. Lenhart, A. (2009). The democratization of online social networks, October 8, 2009. Retreived January 7, 2010, from Pew Internet & American Life Project. http://pewinternet.org/Presentations/2009/41--The-Democratization-of-Online-Social-Networks.aspx.

2. Sheldon, P. (2008). The relationship between unwillingness-to-communicate and students' Facebook use. *Journal of Media Psychology, 20(2),* 67–75.

3. Valkenburg, P. M., and Peter, J. (2007). Preadolescents' and adolescents' online communication and their closeness to friends. *Developmental Psychology, 43,* 267-277.

CHAPTER 19

1. Birditt, K. S., and Antonucci, T. C. (2007). Relationship quality profiles and well-being among married adults. *Journal of Family Psychology, 21,* 595–604.

2. Bachand, L. L., and Caron, S. L. (2001). Ties that bind: A qualitative study of happy long-term marriages. *Contemporary Family Therapy, 23,* 105–121.

3. Marshall, A. G. (2007). *I love you, but I'm not in love with you: Seven steps to saving your relationship.* Deerfield Beach, FL: HCi.

Bibliography

Aboud, F. E., and Mendelson, M. J. (1996). Determinants of friendship selection and quality: Developmental perspectives. In W. M. Bukowski, A. F. Newcomb, and W. W. Hartup (Eds.), *The company they keep: Friendship in childhood and adolescence* (87–112). Cambridge: Cambridge University Press.

Adams, R. G., and Torr, R. (1998), as cited in Felmlee, D. H. (2003). Interaction in social networks. (pp. 389–409). In J. Delamater (Ed.), *Handbook of social psychology*. New York: Kluwer Academic/Plenum Publishers.

Aebischer, J. (2008). Loneliness among homebound older adults: Implications for home healthcare clinicians. *Home Healthcare Nurse, 26*, 521–522.

Agrawal, A., Jacobson, K. C., Prescott, C. A., and Kendler, K. S. (2002). A twin study of sex differences in social support. *Psychological Medicine, 32*, 1155–1164.

Aiken, L. R. (1998). *Human development in adulthood.* New York: Kluwer Academic/Plenum Publishers.

Allen, J., and Haccoun, D. (1976). Sex differences in emotionality: A multidimensional approach. *Human Relations, 29*, 711–722.

Altman, I., and Taylor, D. A. (1973). *Social penetration: The development of interpersonal relationships.* New York: Holt, Rinehart and Winston.

Anderson, N. H. (1968). Likableness ratings of 555 personality-trait words. *Journal of Personality and Social Psychology, 9*, 272–279 in Cottrell, Neuberg, and Li (2007).

Antonucci, T. C., Lansford, J. E., and Akiyama, H. (2001). Impact of positive and negative aspects of marital relationships and friendships on well-being of older adults. *Applied Developmental Science, 5*, 68–75.

Archer, R. L., and Berg, J. H. (1978). Disclosure reciprocity and its limits: A reactance analysis. *Journal of Experimental Social Psychology, 14*, 527–540.

Archer, R. L., and Burleson, J. A. (1980). The effects of timing of self-disclosure on attraction and reciprocity. *Journal of Personality and Social Psychology, 38*, 120–130.

Argyle, M., and Furnham, A. (1983). Sources of satisfaction and conflict in long-term relationships. *Journal of Marriage and Family, 45,* 481–493.

Argyle, M., and Henderson, M., as cited in Samter, W., and Cupach, W. R. (1998). Friendly fire: Topical variations in conflict among same- and cross-sex friends. *Communication Studies, 49,* 121–138.

Argyle, M., and Henderson, M. (1984). The rules of friendships. *Journal of Social and Personal Relationships, 1,* 211–237.

Arling, G. (1976). The elderly widow and her family, neighbors and friends. *Journal of Marriage and the Family, 38,* 757–768.

Arnett, J. J. (2000). Emerging adulthood. *American Psychologist, 55,* 469–480.

Aron, A. P., Melinat, E., Aron, E. N., Vallone, R. D., and Bator, R. J. (1997). The experimental generation of interpersonal closeness: A procedure and some preliminary findings. *Personality and Social Psychology Bulletin, 23,* 363–377.

Austin, H., and Carpenter, L. (2008). Troubled, troublesome, troubling mothers: The dilemma of difference in women's personal motherhood narratives. *Narrative Inquiry, 18,* 378–392.

Bachand, L. L., and Caron, S. L. (2001). Ties that bind: A qualitative study of happy long-term marriages. *Contemporary Family Therapy, 23,* 105–121.

Barbee, A. P., Gulley, M. R., and Cunningham, M. R. (1990). Support seeking in close relationships. *Journal of Social and Personal Relationships, 7,* 531–540.

Barbee. A. P., Cunningham, M. R., Winstead, B. A., Derlega, V. J., Gulley, M. R., Yankeelov, P. A., and Druen, P. B. (1993). Effects of gender role expectations in the social support process. *Journal of Social Issues, 49,* 175–190.

Baron-Cohen, S., and Wheelwright, S. (2004). The empathy quotient: An investigation of adults with Asperger syndrome or high functioning autism, and normal sex differences. *Journal of Autism and Developmental Disorders, 34,* 163–175.

Barth, R. J., and Kinder, B. N. (1988). A theoretical analysis of sex differences in same-sex friendships. *Sex Roles, 19,* 349–363.

Bauer, C. (2005, December 12). *The Daily Collegian Online.* Retrieved from http://www.collegian.psu.edu/archive/2005/12/12-12-05CM/12-12-05dnews-05.asp

Benenson, J., and Heath, A. (2006). Boys withdraw more in one-on-one interactions, whereas girls withdraw more in groups. *Developmental Psychology, 42,* 272–282.

Benoit, M. (2003). The warm glow heuristic: When liking leads to familiarity. *Journal of Personality and Social Psychology, 85,* 1035–1048.

Berndt, T. J. (1989). Exploring the effects of friendship quality on social development. In W. M. Bukowski, A. F. Newcomb, and W. W. Hartup (Eds.), *The Company They Keep: Friendships in Childhood and Adolescence* (346–365). New York: Cambridge University Press.

Berninger, V. W., Nielsen, K. H., Abbott, R. D., Wijsman, E., and Raskind, W. (2008). Gender differences in severity of writing and reading disabilities. *Journal of School Psychology, 46,* 151–172.

Bešić, N., and Kerr M. (2009). Punks, goths, and other eye-catching peer crowds: Do they fulfill a function for shy youths? *Journal of Research on Adolescence, 19,* 113–121.

Birditt, K. S., and Antonucci, T. C. (2007). Relationship quality profiles and well-being among married adults. *Journal of Family Psychology, 21,* 595–604.

Bleiszner, R., and Adams, R. G. (1992). *Adult friendship.* Newbury Park, CA: Sage.

Block, J. D. (1980). *Friendship: How to give it, how to get it.* New York: Collier Books.

Bohnert, A., Martin, N., and Garber, J. (2007). Predicting adolescents' organized activity involvement: The role of maternal depression history, family relationship quality and adolescent cognitions. *Journal of Research on Adolescence, 17,* 221–244.

Botting, N., and Conti-Ramsden, G. (2008). Social cognition, social behaviour and language in late adolescents with a history of SLI. *British Journal of Developmental Psychology, 26,* 281–300.

Bowlby, J. (1988). *A Secure Base: Parent-Child Attachment and Healthy Human Development.* New York: Basic Books, Inc.

Braun, M., Lewin-Epstein, N., Stier, H., and Baumgartner, M. (2008). Perceived equity in the gendered division of household labor. *Journal of Marriage and Family, 70,* 1145–1156.

Bryan, L., Fitzpatrick, J., Crawford, D., and Fischer, J. (2001). The role of network support and interference in women's perception of romantic, friend, and parental relationships. *Sex Roles, 45,* 481–499.

Burda, P. C., Jr., Vaux, A., and Schill, T. (1984). Social support resources: Variation across sex and sex role. *Personality and Social Psychology Bulletin, 10,* 119–126.

Burditt, K. S., and Antonucci, T. C. (2007). Relationship quality profiles and well-being among married adults. *Journal of Family Psychology, 21,* 595–604.

Burger, J. M., and Soroka, S. (2001). The effect of fleeting attraction on compliance to requests. *Personality and Social Psychology Bulletin, 27,* 1578–1586.

Burleson, B. R., and Samter, W. (1994). A social skills approach to relationship maintenance: How individual differences in communication skills affect the achievement of relationship functions. In D. J. Canary and L. S. Stafford (Eds.), *Communication and relational maintenance* (62–90). San Diego: Academic Press.

Buzzanell, P., Meisenbach, R., Remke, R., Liu, M., Bowers, V., and Conn, C. (2005). The good working mother: Managerial women's sensemaking and feelings about work-family issues. *Communication Studies, 56,* 261–285.

Byrne, D. (1971). *The attraction paradigm.* New York: Academic Press.

Campbell, A. (2004). Female competition: Causes, constraints, content, and context. *The Journal of Sex Research, 41,* 16–26.

Canary, D. J., and Dainton, M. (Eds.) (2003). *Maintaining relationships through communication: Relational, contextual, and cultural variations.* Mahwah, NJ: Lawrence Erlbaum Associates.

Canary, D. J., Stafford, L., Hause, K. S., and Wallace, L. A. (1993). An inductive analysis of relational maintenance strategies: Comparisons among lovers, relatives, friends, and others. *Communication Research Reports, 1746–4099, 10,* 3–14.

Canli, T., Desmond, J. E., Zhao, Z., and Gabrieli, J. D. (2002). Sex differences in the neural basis of emotional memories. *Proceedings of the National Academy of Sciences of the United States of America, 99,* 10789–10794.

Carbery, J., and Buhrmester, D. (1988). Friendships and need fulfillment during three phases of young adulthood. *Journal of Social and Personal Relationships, 15,* 393–409.

Carbery, J., and Buhrmester, D. (1998). The changing significance of friendship across three phases of young adulthood. *Journal of Social and Personal Relationships, 15,* 393–409.

Carstensen, L. L., Isaacowitz, D. M., and Charles, S. T. (1999). Taking time seriously: A theory of socioemotional selectivity. *American Psychologist, 54,* 165–181.

Carstensen, L. L. (1995). Evidence for a life-span theory of socioemotional selectivity. *Current Directions in Psychological Science,* 4(5), 151–156.

Cash, T. F., and Derlega, V. J. (1978). The matching hypothesis: physical attractiveness among same-sexed friends. *Personality and Social Psychology Bulletin, 4,* 240–243.

Castelli, L., Amicis, L., and Sherman, S. (2007). The loyal member effect: On the preference for ingroup members who engage in exclusive relations with the ingroup. *Developmental Psychology, 43,* 1347–1359.

Chen, N. (2001). The meaning of aging. *Journal of Extension, 39.*

Clark, M. S., and Mills, J. (1993). The difference between communal and exchange relationships: What it is and is not. *Personality and Social Psychology Bulletin, 19,* 684–691.

Collins, N. L., and Miller, L. C. (1994). Self-disclosure and liking: A meta-analytic review. *Psychological Bulletin, 116,* 457–475.

Cottrell, C. A., Neuberg, S. L., and Li, N. P. (2007). What do people desire in others? A sociofunctional perspective on the importance of different valued characteristics. *Journal of Personality and Social Psychology, 92,* 208–231.

Cowan, G., and Ullman, J. (2006). Ingroup rejection among women: The role of personal inadequacy. *Psychology of Women Quarterly, 30,* 399–409.

Crombie, G., and Desjardins, M. J. (1993, March). *Predictors of gender: The relative importance of children's play, games and personality characteristics.* Paper presented at the biennial meeting of the Society for Research in Child Development, New Orleans.

Cutrona, C. (1982). Transition to college: Loneliness and the process of social adjustment. In L. A. Peplau and D. Perlman (Eds.), *Loneliness: A sourcebook of current theory, research, and therapy.* New York: Wiley-Interscience.

Da Silva, E., and Winnykamen, F. (1998). Degree of sociability and interactive behaviors in dyadic situations of problem solving. *European Journal of Psychology of Education, 13,* 253–270.

Davidson, J., and Duberman, L. (1982). Same-sex friendships: A gender comparison of dyads. *Sex Roles, 8,* 809–822.

Degges-White, S., and Borzumato-Gainey, C. (2009, March). Circle of Friends: Helping Women Craft Connections. Program presented at the American Counseling Association Conference, Charlotte, NC.

Degges-White, S., and Myers, J. E. (2006). Transitions, wellness, and life satisfaction: Implications for counseling midlife women. *Journal of Mental Health Counseling,* 28(2), 133–150.

Demir, M. (2009). Close relationships and happiness among emerging adults. *Journal of Happiness Studies, 11,* 293–313.

Dijkstra, J., Verhulst, F., Ormel, J., and Veenstra, R. (2009). The relation between popularity and aggressive, destructive, and norm-breaking behaviors: Moderating effects of athletic abilities, physical attractiveness, and prosociality. *Journal of Research on Adolescence, 19,* 401–413.

Dindia, K., and Canary, D. J. (1993). Definitions and theoretical perspectives on meaning in relationships. *Journal of Social and Personal Relationships, 10,* 163–173.

Dodge, K. Pettit, G., McClaskey, C., and Brown, M. (1986). Social competence in children. *Monographs of the Society for Research in Child Development, 51*(2, Serial No. 213).

Downey, D., and Condron, D. (2004). Playing well with others in kindergarten: The benefit of siblings at home. *Journal of Marriage and Family, 66*, 333–350.

Doxey, C., and Holman, T. B. (2002). *Premarital prediction of marital quality or breakup: Research, theory, and practice* (119–139). New York: Kluwer Academic/Plenum Publishers.

Edwards, T. (2007). Renters four times more likely to move than homeowners (U.S. Census Bureau News No. CB07–146). Washington, DC.

Eisler, R. M. (1995). The relationship between masculine gender role stress and men's health risk. In R. F. Levant and W. S. Pollack (Eds.), *A new psychology of men* (207–225). New York: Basic Books.

Eliot, L. (1999). *What's going on in there? How the brain and mind develop in the first five years of life*. New York: Bantam Books.

Erikson, E. (1980). Identity and the life cycle. New York: Norton.

Falci, C., and McNeely, C. (2009). Social integration, network cohesion, and adolescent depressive symptoms. *Social Forces, 87*, 2031–2062.

Fehr, B. (1996). *Friendship processes*. London: Sage.

Fehr, B. (2000). The life cycle of friendship. In C. Hendrick and S. S. Hendrick (Eds.), *Close relationships: A sourcebook* (71–82). Thousand Oaks, CA: Sage.

Fehr, B. (2008). Friendship formation. In S. Sprecher, A. Wenzel, and J. Harvey (Eds.), *The Handbook of Relationship Initiation* (29–54). Hillsdale, NJ: Erlbaum.

Festinger, L., Schachter, S., and Back, K. (1950). *Social pressure in informal groups*. New York: Harper.

Fischer, C. S. (1982). *To dwell among friends: Personal networks in town and city*. Chicago: University of Chicago Press.

Fischer, C. S., and Oliker, S. (1980, August). Friendship, gender, and the lifecycle. Paper presented at the American Sociological Association. New York.

Foot, H. C., Chapman, A., and Smith, J. (Eds.). (1995). *Friendship and Social Relations in Children*. New Brunswick, NJ: Transaction Publishers, Inc.

Frank, J. S., Avery, S. M., and Laman, B. C. (1988), as cited in Aiken (1998).

Gainey, C. B., Kennedy, A., McCabe, B., and Degges-White, S. (2009). Life satisfaction, self-esteem, and subjective age in women across the lifespan. *Adultspan, 8*, 29–42.

Garstecki, D. C., and Erler, S. F. (1999). Older adult performance on the Communication Profile for the Hearing Impaired: Gender difference. *Journal of Speech, Language, and Hearing Research, 42*, 785–796.

Gazelle, H., and Druhen, M. J. (2009). Anxious solitude and peer exclusion predict social helplessness, upset affect, and vagal regulation in response to behavioral rejection by a friend. *Developmental Psychology, 45*, 1077–1096.

Ge, X., Conger, R. D., and Elder, G. H. (1996). Coming of age too early: Pubertal influences on girls' vulnerability psychological distress. *Child Development, 67*, 3386–3400.

Geary, D. C. (1998). Chapter 2: Sexual selection and sex differences in social cognition. In A. McGillicuddy-De Lisis and R. De Lisi (Eds.), *Biology, society, and behavior: The development of sex differences in cognition* (23–53). Westport, CT: Ablex Publishing.

Gilligan, C. (1982). *In a different voice.* Cambridge, MA: Harvard University Press.

Goodenow, C., and Gaier, E. L. (1990). Best friends: The close reciprocal friendships of married and unmarried women. Unpublished paper.

Goodson, J. L., and Bass, A. H. (2000). Forebrain peptides modulate sexually polymorphic vocal circuitry. *Nature, 6771,* 769–772.

Gotlib, I. H. (1992). Interpersonal and cognitive aspects of depression. *Current Directions in Psychological Science, 1,* 149–154.

Graber, J. A., Seely, J. R., Brooks-Gunn, J., and Lewinsohn, J. (2004). Is pubertal timing associated with psychopathology in young adulthood? *Journal of the American Academy of Child and Adolescent Psychiatry, 43,* 718–726.

Greif, G. (2009). *Buddy system: Understanding male friendships.* New York: Oxford University Press.

Grewen, K. M., Girdler, S. S., Amico, J., and Light, K. C. (2005). Effects of partner support on resting oxytocin, cortisol, norepinephrine, and blood pressure before and after warm partner contact. *Psychosomatic Medicine, 67,* 531–538.

Grotberg, E. H. (2000). International Resilience Research Project. In A. L. Comunian and U. Gielen (Eds.), *International Perspectives on Human Development* (379–399). Vienna: Pabst Science Publishers.

Gullestad, M. (1984). *Kitchen table society.* Oslo: Universities Forlaget.

Gurung, R. A. R., Taylor, S. E., and Seeman, T. E. (2003). Accounting for changes in social support among married older adults: Insights from the MacArthur Studies of Successful Aging. *Psychology and Aging, 18,* 487–496.

Hall, J. A. (1984). *Nonverbal sex-differences: Communication accuracy and expressive style.* Baltimore: The Johns Hopkins University Press.

Hall, R., and Rose, S. (1996). Friendships between African-American and White lesbians. In J. S. Weinstock and E. D. Rothblum (Eds.), *Lesbian friendships: For ourselves and each other* (165–191). New York: New York University Press.

Hancox, R., Milne, B., and Poulton, R. (2004). Association between child and adolescent television viewing and adult health: A longitudinal birth cohort study. *The Lancet, 364,* 257–262.

Hartup, W., and van Lieshout, C. (1995). Personality development in social context. *Annual Review of Psychology, 46,* 655–687.

Hartup, W. W., and Stevens, N. (1997). Friendships and adaptation in the life course. *Psychological Bulletin, 121,* 355–370.

Hayek, T. S. (2006, December 18). Buoyed by bigger breasts. *USA Today.* Retrieved March 11, 2010, from http://www.usatoday.com

Hays, R. B. (1984). The development and maintenance of friendship. *Journal of Social and Personal Relationships, 1,* 75–98.

Hays, R. B. (1998). Friendship. In S. Duck (Ed.), *Handbook of personal relationships: Theory, research, and interventions* (391–408). New York: Wiley.

Hearn, F. (2007). *Moral order and social disorder: The American search for civil society.* New York: Walter de Gruyter, Inc.

Heinrichs, M., and Domes, G. (2008). Neuropeptides and social behavior: Effects of oxytocin and vasopressin in humans. *Progress in Brain Research, 170,* 337–350.

Hess, B. (1971). *Amicability.* Unpublished doctoral dissertation. New Brunswick, NJ: Rutgers University.

Hiller, J. (2004). Speculations on the links between feelings, emotions and sexual behavior: Are vasopressin and oxytocin involved? *Sexual and Relationship Therapy, 19,* 393–412.

Hines, M. (2006). Prenatal testosterone and gender-related behavior. *European Journal of Endocrinology, 155 Supplement,* S115–S121.

Howell, L. C. (2001). Implications of personal values in women's midlife development. *Counseling and Values, 46,* 54–65.

Hu, F. B., Li, T. Y., Colditz, G. A., Willett, W. C., and Manson, J. E. (2003). Television watching and other sedentary behaviors in relation to risk of obesity and type 2 diabetes mellitus in women. *Journal of the American Medical Association, 289,* 1785–1791.

Huston, T., and Burgess, R. (1979). Social exchange in developing relationships: An overview. In R. Burgess and T. Huston (Eds.), *Social exchange in developing relationships* (3–28). New York: Academic Press.

Insel, T. R., and Fernald, R. D. (2004). *Annual Review of Neuroscience, 27,* 697–722.

James, W. B., Witte, J. E., and Galbraith, M. W. (2006). Havighurst's social roles revisited. *Journal of Adult Development, 13,* 52–60.

Jeffries, V. (1999). The integral paradigm: The truth of faith and the social sciences. *American Sociologist, 30*(4), 36–55.

Johnson, A. J. (2000, July). A role theory approach to examining the maintenance of geographically close and long-distance friendships. Paper presented at the International Network on Personal Relationships Conference, Prescott, AZ.

Johnson, D., Brady, E., McNair, R., Congdon, D., Niznik, J., and Anderson, S. (2007). Identity as moderator of gender differences in the emotional closeness of emerging adult's same and cross-sex friendships. *Adolescence, 42,* 1–23.

Jones, D. C., and Vaughan, K. (1990). Close friendships among senior adults. *Psychology and Aging, 5,* 451–457.

Joseph, J. (2001). *Warning: When I am an old woman, I shall wear purple.* London: Souvenir Press Ltd.

Josephs, R. A., Markus, H. R., and Tafarodi, R. W. (1992). Gender and self-esteem. *Journal of Personality and Social Psychology, 663,* 391–402.

Kadison, R., and Digeronimo, T. (2004). *College of the overwhelmed: The campus mental health crisis and what to do about it.* San Francisco: Jossey-Bass.

Kahn, R. L., and Antonucci, T. C. (1980). Convoys over the life course: Attachment, roles, and social support. In P. B. Baltes and O. G. Brim, Jr. (Eds.), *Life span development and behavior,* Vol. 3 (253–286). New York: Academic Press.

Kan, M. L., and McHale, S. M. (2007). Clusters and correlates of experiences with parents and peers during early adolescence. *Journal of Research on Adolescence, 17,* 565–586.

Kelley, H. H., and Thibaut, J. W. (1978). *Interpersonal relationships.* New York: John Wiley and Sons.

Kernsmith, P. (2006). Gender differences in the impact of family of origin violence on perpetrators of domestic violence. *Journal of Family Violence, 21,*163–171.

Killgore, S., Oki, M., and Yurgelun-Todd, D. (2001). Sex-specific developmental changes in amygdala responses to affective faces. *NeuroReport, 12,* 427–433.

Kimura, D. (2000). *Sex and cognition.* Cambridge, MA: A Bradford Book/The MIT Press.

Kinney, D. A. (1993). From nerds to normals: The recovery of identity among adolescents from middle school to high school. *Sociology of Education, 66,* 21–40.

Kitson, G. C., Lopata, H. Z., Holmes, W. M., and Meyering, S. M. (1980). Divorcees and widows: Similarities and differences. *American Journal of Orthopsychiatry, 50,* 291–301.

Langer, G. (2005, February 13). Poll: Traffic in the United States: A look under the hood of a nation on wheels. [Electronic version]. ABC News Poll, Retrieved March 17, 2010, from http://abcnews.go.com/Technology/Traffic/story?id=485098andpage=1

Laursen, B., and Collins, W. A. (1994). Interpersonal conflict during adolescence. *Psychological Bulletin, 115,* 197–209.

Leeb, R. T., and Rejskind, F. G. (2004). Here's looking at you, kid! A longitudinal study of perceived gender differences in mutual gaze behavior in young infants. *Sex Roles, 1/2,* 1–14.

Lefkowitz, E., and Fingerman, K. (2003). Positive and negative emotional feelings and behaviors in mother-daughter ties in late life. *Journal of Family Psychology, 17,* 607–617.

Lindsey, E. W. (2002). Preschool children's friendships and peer acceptance: Links to social competence. *Child Study Journal, 32,* 145–155.

Long, B., Personal Communication, September 22, 2009.

Lorenzi, P. (2008). Affluence, consumption, and the American lifestyle. *Society, 45,* 107–111.

Louv, R. (2005). *Last child in the woods: Saving our children from nature-deficit disorder.* Chapel Hill, NC: Algonquin Books of Chapel Hill.

Lyubomirsky, S., King, L., and Diener, E. (2005). The benefits of frequent positive affect: Does happiness lead to success? *Psychological Bulletin, 131,* 803–855.

Malatesta, C. Z., and Haviland, J. M. (1982). Learning display rules: The socialization of emotion expression in infancy. *Child Development, 53,* 991–1003.

Marcia, J. E. (1976). Identity six years after: A follow-up study. *Journal of Youth and Adolescence, 5,* 145–160.

Marshall, A. G. (2007). *I love you, but I'm not in love with you: Seven steps to saving your relationship.* Deerfield Beach, FL: HCi.

Matthews, S. (1986). *Friendships through the life course.* Beverly Hills, CA: Sage.

McElhaney, K., Antonishak, J., and Allen, J. (2008). "They like me, they like me not": Popularity and adolescents' perceptions of acceptance predicting social functioning over time. *Child Development, 79,* 720–731.

McGill, M. E. (1985). *The McGill report on male intimacy.* New York: Holt, Rinehart and Winston.

Messman, S. J., Canary, D. J., and Hause, K. S. (2000). Motives to remain platonic, equity, and the use of maintenance strategies in opposite-sex friendships. *Journal of Social and Personal Relationships, 17,* 67–94.

Mestre, M. V., Samper, P., Frias, M. D., and Tur, A. M. Are women more empathetic than men? A longitudinal study in adolescence. *Spanish Journal of Psychology, 1*(12), 76–83.

Milardo, R. M., and Allan, G. (1997). Social networks and marital relationships. In S. Duck (Ed.), *Handbook of personal relationships: Theory, research, and interventions* (2nd ed., 505–522). Chichester, England: Wiley.

Miller, S. (1983). *Men and friendship.* Boston: Houghton Mifflin Company.

Moreland, R. L., and Beach, S. (1992). Exposure effects in the classroom: The development of affinity among students. *Journal of Experimental Social Psychology, 28,* 255–276.

Moremen, R. D. (2008). The role of confidantes in older women's health. *Journal of Women and Aging, 20,* 149–167.

Moren-Cross, J. L., and Lin, N. (2006). Social networks and health. In R. H. Binstock and L. K. George (Eds.), *Handbook of aging and the social sciences* (6th ed., pp. 111–126). Amsterdam: Elsevier.

Morgan, D., Carder, P., and Neal, M. (1992), as cited in Felmlee, D. H. (2003). Interaction in social networks. In J. Delamater (Ed.), *Handbook of social psychology* (389–409). New York: Kluwer Academic/Plenum Publishers.

Mounts, N. (2007). Adolescents and their mothers' perceptions of parental management of peer relationships. *Journal of Research on Adolescence, 17,* 169–178.

Myers, D. G. (2000). The funds, friends, and faith of happy people. *American Psychologist, 55,* 56–67.

Nardi, P. M., and Sherrod, D. (1994). Friendships in the lives of gay men and lesbians. *Journal of Social and Personal Relationships, 11,* 185–200.

Neugarten, B. L., Moore, J. W., and Lowe, J. C. (1965). Age norms, age constraints, and adult socialization. *American Journal of Sociology, 70,* 229–236.

Newcomb T. (1961). *The acquaintance process.* New York: Holt, Rinehart and Winston.

Newcomb, A. F., and Bagwell, C. (1995). Children's friendship relations: A meta-analytic review. *Psychological Bulletin, 117,* 306–347.

Niffenegger, J., and Willer, L. (1998). Friendship behaviors during early childhood and beyond. *Early Childhood Education Journal, 26,* 95–99.

Nissen, E., Gustavsson, P., Wildstom, A. M., and Uvnars-Moberg, K. (1998) Oxytocin, prolactin and cortisol levels in response to nursing in women after Sectio Caesarea and vaginal delivery—Relationship with changes in personality patterns post partum. *Journal of Psychosomatic Obstetrics and Gynaecology, 19,* 49–58.

Oh, J. (2003). Assessing the social bonds of elderly neighbors: The roles of length of residence, crime victimization, and perceived disorder. *Sociological Inquiry, 73,* 490–510.

O'Hara, M., and Swain, A. (1996). Rates and risk of postpartum depression—A meta-analysis. *International Review of Psychiatry, 8,* 37–55.

Oswald, D., and Clark, E. (2003). Best friends forever: High school best friendships and the transition to college. *Personal Relationships, 10,* 187–196.

Park, K. A., and Waters, E. (1989). Security of attachment and preschool friendships. *Child Development, 60,* 1076–1081.

Patterson, B. R., Bettini, L., and Nussbaum, J. F. (1993). The meaning of friendship across the lifespan: Two studies. *Communication Quarterly, 41,* 145–160.

Phillips, M., Lowe, M., Lurito, J. T., Dzemidzic, M., and Matthews, V. (2001). Temporal lobe activation demonstrates sex-based differences during passive listening. *Radiology, 220,* 202–207.

Pinel, E. C., Long, A. E., Landau, M. J., Alexander, K., and Pyszczynksi, T. (2006). Seeing I to I: A pathway to interpersonal connectedness. *Journal of Personality and Social Psychology, 90,* 243–257.

Putallaz, M., and Gottman, J. M. (1981). An interactional model of children's entry into peer groups. *Child Development, 52,* 986–994.

Putnam, R. (2000). *Bowling alone: The collapse and revival of American community.* New York: Simon and Schuster.

Ratcliff, K. S., and Bogdan, J. (1988). Unemployed women: When "social support" is not supportive. *Social Problems, 35,* 54–63.

Ravert, R. D. (2009). "You're only young once": Things college students report doing now before it is too late. *Journal of Adolescent Research, 24,* 376–396.

Rawlins, W. K. (1994), as cited in Canary, D. J., and Dainton, M. (Eds.). (2003). *Maintaining relationships through communication: Relational, contextual, and cultural variations.* Hillsdale, NJ: Erlbaum.

Rawlins, W. K. (1992). *Friendship matters: Communication, dialects, and the life course.* Hawthorne, NY: Aldine de Gruyter.

Rawlins, W. K. (1994). Being there and growing apart: Sustaining friendships during adulthood. In D. J. Canary and L. Stafford (Eds.), *Communication and relational maintenance* (275–294). San Diego: Academic Press.

Raymond, N. (1999, November/December). Hug drug: Friendship heals. *Psychology Today, 1.*

Resnick, S., and Wolff, R. (2003). Exploitation, consumption, and the uniqueness of U.S. capitalism. *Historical Materialism, 11,* 209–226.

Rhoades, B., and Maggs, J. (2006). Do academic and social goals predict planned alcohol use among college-bound high school graduates? *Journal of Youth and Adolescence, 35,* 913–923.

Riggio, H. (1999). Personality and social skill differences between adults with and without siblings. *Journal of Psychology, 133,* 514–522.

Rimmele, U., Hediger, K., Heinrichs, M., and Klaver, P. (2008). Oxytocin makes a face in memory familiar. *Journal of Neuroscience, 29*(1), 38–42.

Roberto, K. A. (2001). Older women's relationships: Weaving lives together. In J. D. Garner and S. O. Mercer (Eds.), *Women as they age* (2nd ed., 115–129). New York: Haworth.

Roberto, K. A., and Scott, J. P. (1986). Friendships of older men and women: Exchange patterns and satisfaction. *Psychology and Aging, 1,* 103–109.

Roberto, K. A. (2001). Older women's relationships: Weaving lives together. In J. D. Garner and S. O. Mercer (Eds.), *Women as they age* (2nd ed., 115–129). New York: Haworth.

Rodin, M. J. (1978). Liking and disliking. *Personality and Social Psychology Bulletin, 4,* 473–478.

Rook, K. S. (1991). Facilitating friendship formation in late life: Puzzles and challenges. *American Journal of Community Psychology, 19,* 103–110.

Rook, K. S. (2009). Gaps in social support resources in later life: An adaptation challenge in need of further research. *Journal of Social and Personal Relationships, 26* 103–112.

Rose, S. M. (1985). Same and cross-sex friendships and the psychology of homosociality. *Sex Roles, 12,* 63–74.

Rose, S. (1984). How friendships end: Patterns among young adults. *Journal of Social and Personal Relationships, 3,* 267–277.

Rose, S. M. (2007). Enjoying the returns: Women's friendships after 50. In V. Muhlbauer and J. Chrisler (Eds.), *Women Over 50: Psychological Perspectives* (112–130). New York: Springer.

Rosenthal, R., Hall, J. A., DiMatteo, M. R., Rogers, P. L., and Archer, D. (1979). *Sensitivity to nonverbal communication: The PONS Test.* Baltimore: The Johns Hopkins University Press.

Rubin, L. (1983). *Intimate strangers.* San Francisco: Harper and Row.

Rueckert, L., and Naybar, N. (2008). Gender differences in empathy: The role of the right hemisphere. *Brain and Cognition, 67,* 162–167.

Rushton, J. P., and Bons, T. A. (2005). Mate choice and friendship in twins: Evidence for genetic similarity. *Psychological Science, 16,* 555–559.

Rutter, M., and Garmezy, N. (1983). Developmental psychopathology. In P. H. Mussen (Series Ed.) and E. M. Hetherington (Vol. Ed.), *Handbook of child psychology, Vol. 4: Socialization, personality, and social development* (775–911). New York: Wiley.

Sanchez-Andrade, G., and Kendrick, K. M. (2009). The main olfactory system and social learning in mammals. *Behavioural Brain Research, 200,* 323–335.

Saremi, J. (2007). The truth about implants and breast cancer. *American Fitness, 25,* 46–49.

Scharf, M., and Mayseless, O. (2009). Socioemotional characteristics of elementary school children identified as exhibiting social leadership qualities. *Journal of Genetic Psychology, 170*(1), 73–94.

Segrin, C., and Dillard, J. P. (1992). The interactional theory of depression: A meta-analysis of the research literature. *Journal of Social and Clinical Psychology, 11,* 43–70.

Sheehy, S. (2000). *Connecting: The enduring power of female friendships.* New York: William Morrow.

Shulman, N. (1975). Life cycle variations in patterns of friendship. *Journal of Marriage and the Family, 37,* 813–821.

Sias, P. M., and Cahill, D. J. (1998). From coworkers to friends: The development of peer friendships in the workplace. *Western Journal of Communication, 62,* 273–300.

Sias, P. M., Krone, K. J., and Jablin, F. M. (2001). An ecological systems perspective on workplace relationships. In M. L. Knapp and J. Daly (Eds.), *Handbook of interpersonal communication* (3rd ed.). Newbury Park, CA: Sage.

Sias, P. M., and Bartoo, H. (2009). Friendship, social support and health. In L. L'Abate, D. D. Embrey, and M. S. Baggett (Eds.), *Handbook of low-cost interventions to promote physical and mental health: Theory, research, and practice* (455–472). Mahwah, NJ: Lawrence Erlbaum Publishers.

Siyez, D. (2008). Adolescent self-esteem, problem behaviors, and perceived social support in Turkey. *Social Behavior and Personality: An International Journal, 36,* 973–985.

Smith, A. E., and Powers, S. I. (2009). Off-time pubertal timing predicts physiological reactivity to postpuberty interpersonal stress. *Journal of Research on Adolescence, 19,* 441–458.

Snyder, J., West, L., Stockemer, V., Gibbons, S., and Almquist-Parks, L. (1996). A social learning model of peer choice in the natural environment. *Journal of Applied Developmental Psychology, 17,* 215–237.

South Carolina Department of Mental Health. (2006). Eating disorder statistics. Retrieved January 22, 2010, from http://www.state.sc.us/dmh/anorexia/statistics.htm

Sroufe, L. A. (1996). *Emotional development: The organinization of emotional life in the early years.* New York: Cambridge University Press.

Steverink, N., Lindenberg, S., and Slaets, J. P. J. (2005). How to understand and improve older people's self-management of wellbeing. *European Journal of Ageing, 2,* 235–244.

Stroebe, W., Stroebe, M., Abakoumkin, G., and Schut, H. (1996). The role of loneliness and social support in adjustment to loss: A test of attachment versus stress theory. *Journal of Personality and Social Psychology, 70,* 1241–1249.

Swaab, R. I., and Swaab, D. F. (2009). Sex differences in the effects of visual contact and eye contact in negotiations. *Journal of Experimental Social Psychology, 45,* 129–136.

Taylor, S. E., Klein, L. C., Lewis, B. P., Gruenewald, T. L., Gurung, R. A., and Updegraff, J. A. (2000). Behavioral responses to stress in females: Tend-and-befriend, not fight-or-flight. *Psychological Review, 107,* 411–429.

Tesch, S. A. (1983). Review of friendship development across the lifespan. *Human Development, 26,* 266–276.

The MommiesNetwork.org. (2009). Retrieved April 21, 2010, from http://www.themommiesnetwork.org/index.shtml

Thompson, M., O'Neill Grace, C., and Cohen, L. (2001). *Best friends, worst enemies, understanding the social lives of children.* New York: Ballantine Books, Inc.

Thuerauf, N., Reulbach, U., Lunkenheimer, J., Lunkenheimer, B., Spannenberger, R., Gossler, A., Malhofner, C., Bleich, S., Kornhuber, J., and Markovic, K. (2009). Emotional reactivity to odors: Olfactory sensitivity and the span of emotional evaluation separate the genders. *Neuroscience Letters, 456*(2), 74–79.

United States Bureau of the Census. (2008). Percent never married. *Statistical Abstract of the United States.* Washington, DC: U.S. Bureau of the Census.

United States Bureau of the Census. (2007, October). Renters four times more likely to move than homeowners. Retrieved May 26, 2010, from http://www.census.gov/newsroom/releases/archives/mobility_of_the_population/cb07–146.html

United States Department of Labor. (2009). *Women in the labor force: A databook* (BLS, Report No. 1018).

Vaillant, G. E. (1977). *Adaptation to life.* Boston: Little, Brown.

Van Honk, J., Aarts, H., Josephs, R. A., and Schutter, J. L. G. (2009). Sex differences in social and mathematical cognition: An endocrine perspective. *Netherlands Journal of Psychology, 64,* 177–183.

Vanderkam, L. (2009, May 29). Overestimating our overworking. *The Wall Street Journal,* p. W13.

Vigil, J. M. (2007). Asymmetries in the friendship preferences and social styles of men and women. *Human Nature, 18,* 143–161.

Vittengl, J. R., and Holt, C. S. (2000). Getting acquainted: The relationship of self-disclosure and social attraction to positive affect. *Journal of Social and Personal Relationships, 17,* 53–66.

Waterman, A. (1982). Identity development from adolescence to adulthood: An extension of theory and a review of research. *Developmental Psychology, 18,* 341–358.

Wechsler, H., and Kuo, M. (2000). College students define binge drinking and estimate its prevalence: Results of a national survey. *College Health, 49,* 57–64.

Werner, C., and Parmelee, P. (1979). Similarity of activity preferences among friends: Those who play together stay together. *Social Psychology Quarterly, 42,* 62–66.

Willis, J., and Todorov, A. (2006). First impressions: Making up your mind after a 100-ms exposure to a face. *Psychological Science, 17,* 592–598.

Wiseman, R. (2009). *Queen bees and wannabes: Helping your daughter survive cliques, gossip, boyfriends, and the new realities of girl world* (2nd ed.). New York: Three Rivers Press.

Witkow, M. R. (2009). Academic achievement and adolescents' daily time use in the social and academic domains. *Journal of Research on Adolescence, 19,* 151–172.

Youniss, J. (1980). *Parents and peers in social development.* Chicago: The University of Chicago Press.

Index

About the Authors

Suzanne Degges-White, PhD, is an associate professor of counseling and development at Purdue University Calumet. She earned a doctorate in counseling and counselor education and a graduate certificate in women's studies from the University of North Carolina-Greensboro. She has authored numerous articles and book chapters addressing women's development over the lifespan. Also a licensed counselor in private practice, she specializes in working with adolescent and adult women dealing with life's transitions and relationship concerns. She and her family reside in Chesterton, Indiana, where warm friendships are essential to enduring the frigid Midwest winters.

Christine Borzumato-Gainey, PhD, is a counselor and adjunct professor at Elon University. She resides in Burlington, North Carolina, with her spouse, Howard, two very active children, Brooke and Drew, and their yellow lab, Safari. In her clinical work, she relishes working with a wide variety of people and problems but specializes in relationship issues, substance abuse, transitions, anxiety, and loss. In her little bit of spare time, she reads and tries to use what she learned from writing this book—share fun time with friends.